AMERICAN MARITAIN ASSOCIATION PUBLICATIONS
DISTRIBUTED BY
UNIVERSITY OF NOTRE DAME PRESS

General Editor: Anthony O. Simon

1988 *Jacques Maritain: The Man and His Metaphysics*
Edited by John F.X. Knasas
ISBN 0-268-01205-9

1989 *Freedom in the Modern World: Jacques Maritain,*
Yves R. Simon, Mortimer J. Adler
Edited by Michael D. Torre
ISBN 0-268-00978-3

1990 *From Twilight to Dawn: The Cultural Vision of*
Jacques Maritain
Edited by Peter A. Redpath
ISBN 0-268-00979-1

1991 Title to be Announced
Editors: Deal W. Hudson and Dennis W. Moran

From Twilight to Dawn: The Cultural Vision of Jacques Maritain

Edited by Peter A. Redpath

Introduction by James V. Schall

American Maritain Association

Distributed by University of Notre Dame Press

Cover by William Schickel

LC 90-50611
ISBN 0-268-00979-1
Printed in the United States of America

Distributed by University of Notre Dame Press
Notre Dame, Indiana 46556

American Maritain Association
Anthony O. Simon, General Editor
508 Travers Circle
Mishawaka, Indiana 46545

TABLE OF CONTENTS

Part IV Knowledge and Its Foundations

Part V Unnatural Humanisms and Post-Civilized Minds

Part VI Civilization at the Crossroads

Part VII A New Dawn: Transfiguring Integration

Acknowledgements

The publication of this work is the result of the cooperative effort of a number of individuals whose behind-the-scenes contributions deserve to be recognized. I am deeply indebted to Anthony O. Simon, Deal W. Hudson, and to Raymond Dennehy for their numerous suggestions and advice regarding the preparation of the volume as a whole, and also to John Ehmann, Administrative Director of the University of Notre Dame Press, for technical advice regarding the layout and design of the book. I owe thanks to my devoted wife, Lorraine, for the *creative intuition* by means of which she provided me with the marvelously appropriate title for this edition; and I am, likewise, indebted to William Schickel for so brilliantly capturing the cultural vision of Jacques Maritain in the portrait drawing which he has done for the cover of this book.

Beyond all the above, I owe a debt to all the authors whose contributions are included herein for the quality of the scholarly work which they have displayed. In particular, I would like to thank James V. Schall, S.J., both for consenting to write the "Introduction" to this work and for capturing so well in words the spirit of the included papers.

In addition, I would like to thank the Faculty Support Centers at St. John's University (Staten Island and Jamaica, New York)--in particular, James Edleman and Richard Lejeune--for numerous occasions of assistance in the preparation of the typescript for publication; I would like to thank Nicholas E. Purpura, president of Wings Publications Ltd. and publisher of *The Eagle* newspaper, for providing me with the use of office equipment which greatly facilitated my ability to edit this volume in a timely fashion; and I would, also, like to express my gratitude to Michael Aquilina for proofreading the final draft of the typescript of this work.

Finally, I would like to thank my sons, Paul and Peter, and my daughter, Korri--each of whom I am most proud--for their understanding and cooperation over the months which it took me to finish this edition. I hope some day they will have the opportunity to read and digest the contents of this work and that, just as so many others, they will benefit from the cultural vision of Jacques Maritain.

About the Cover

The cover of this book was prepared by American sculptor, painter, and designer, William Schickel. Schickel is a graduate of Notre Dame University with a graduate degree from New York State School of Design. He served apprenticeships with Hungarian sculptor Eugene Kormandi and stained glass designer Emil Frei. Schickel depicts Jacques Maritain as a "Man of the Cross and the Holy Spirit." He says his view of Maritain is inspired by the latter's "courage in standing intellectually at the intersection of good and evil without blinking"; it is in the light of this spirit that Schickel opened the Maritain Gallery in Loveland, Ohio--namely, for the purpose of nurturing a cultural and spiritual renaissance in America with art as its principal medium. The portrait of Maritain as a "Man of the Cross and the Holy Spirit" is available in a limited edition poster through the Maritain Gallery. The Maritain Gallery is located at 127 West Loveland Avenue, Loveland, Ohio 45140.

James V. Schall, S.J.

Introduction: Calvary
or the Slaughter-house

Somewhere in his *Notebooks*, Jacques Maritain brought up the question of the mission or activity of human souls after death. He wondered what function they might have with respect to those of us still in this world. Maritain suggested that after death human beings could be expected to remain interested in their loved ones and in the causes and purposes for which they devoted their lives while they were still on earth. If this theory is at all plausible, we can expect Maritain to be most interested in what those who read him still think of his *The Twilight of Civilization*, the Lecture to which these papers seek to address themselves.[1] No doubt, as many of the authors of this volume have remarked in one way or another, the major threats with which Maritain was immediately concerned in his Lecture of 1939--Nazism, Fascism, and now Marxism--have either disappeared or fallen on hard times. Maritain's thought would, at first sight, seem overcome by events. Events, however, have origins in the spirit, the attention to which is, at its highest, the vocation of the philosopher.

Yet the selection of this particular Parisian Lecture of Maritain for consideration in the final decade of the Twentieth Century was, on the part of the organizers of the University of San Francisco Maritain Conference, a shrewd one. The question immediately arises whether the thought that Maritain saw to be at the bottom of the most notoriously embodied ideologies of his time is, in any significant manner, undermined with the apparent demise of most of their representatives. It may

---

[1]Jacques Maritain, *The Twilight of Civilization*, trans. Lionel Landry (New York: Sheed and Ward, 1944).

well have shifted, as several authors suspect, to more dangerous and subtle grounds--ones, in fact, closer to home.

"Nietzsche did not grasp," Maritain observed in his Lecture, "that man has no choice except between two roads: the road to Calvary and the road to the slaughter-house."[2] This is, indeed, a memorable passage. The road to Calvary, while we live in the midst of suffering [Califano], is not the one that is being taken,though it could well, after all the other roads have been tried, appear to have been the most rational one after all; and our slaughter-houses--our abortion rates, our euthanasia temptations, our concentration camps, our drug consumption--we do not always admit them to be locales of human deaths or human deeds. We think this unclarity about what they are will enable us to live with them, to *choose* them. Our philosophies of pure choice have no objects of their choice except what they choose. Their merit is a ruthless consistency.

The essential sign of intellectual disorder is improperly to name what we are doing--*what is*. This can only happen on a massive scale if we permit a philosophy of subjective choice to replace a philosophy of being. The principle that Maritain most worried about was this: "*that man alone and by himself alone works out his salvation*."[3] Notice that Maritain said that this would be the *twilight* not of man, but of *civilization*, an order that prided itself on upholding, not destroying, human life and worth.

Essentially, modernity describes itself as *humanism* [McInerny]. "Humanism" is a word with ancient derivations, from the Roman word *humanitas*. *Humanitas* is an abstract word coming from the Latin word *homo*, human being. It emphasizes those elevated and unique aspects that belong to man alone; hence its affinity to civilization. This is not Greek in origin because for the Greeks man was not the highest being, nor was politics the highest science. In a real sense, for the Greeks, man was most man when he was giving himself to divine things to which all human affairs, at least indirectly, were ordered. This was the teaching of Plato in the *Republic* and of Aristotle at the end of the *Nichomachean Ethics*. This is why Christianity is more of a Greek than a Roman thing in its philosophical roots.

Among the Romans, however, there was a tendency to exalt the practical sciences at the expense of the theoretical sciences. A certain

---

[2]*Ibid.*, 9.
[3]*Ibid.*, 10.

autonomy began to appear in the post-Aristotelians, the Stoics and the Epicureans, that was taken up again in early modern times and developed further into a notion of *humanism* which claimed all independence from nature and nature's God. Humanism began to be conceived in opposition to the things of God. One had to choose between man and God, rather than to choose man through choosing God, which the revelational tradition had held. Humanism became secularized and atheist.

An understanding of humanism arose in which man was seen to be completely autonomous and malleable, grounded in nothing but himself. What man is, in this development, does not derive from an ordered nature itself dependent for its intelligibility on a source in a First Mind. For epistemological reasons, Hume's "the contrary of every matter of fact is possible," and Grotius's "the natural law would be the natural law even if God did not exist," were essential to justify autonomous humanism. According to the first, no knowledge of external order was possible since any fact could be otherwise. According to the second, the natural law depended on man himself if it were to have any intelligibility at all. The human mind was not subject to anything outside for any real knowledge. The classic idea of contemplation, of the possibility of receiving being and truth from what is other, was rejected. Man wanted to be his own cause. There are, no doubt, many ways in which this autonomy can manifest itself--through individualism, collectivism, liberalism, even conservatism. Modernity is essentially a working out in practice of these theoretical alternatives in the public order. They all produce their own worldly shape which we must inevitably confront with our minds to see what they are.

Maritain identified a number of different kinds of left and right humanisms. At its best, humanism was intended to manifest man's

> original greatness by enabling him to partake of everything in nature and in history capable of enriching him. It requires both that man develop the latent tendencies he possesses, his creative powers and the life of reason, and that he work to transform into instruments of his liberty the forces of the physical universe.[4]

---

[4]*Ibid.*, 3.

As it stands, this definition of humanism is compatible with Christianity if liberty is itself ordered to *what is*. Indeed, Maritain held that unless humanism is, in fact, open to all reality, including revelation, not merely its own constructs, it is not a true humanism. Maritain's intellectiual career in art, metaphysics, epistemology, politics, and history was an effort to show how this open humanism is not only possible but required by truth itself. To defend man's glory, more than man has to be praised.

Those humanisms which affirm "human nature as closed in upon itself or absolutely self-sufficient" leave man with no limit but what man wills;[5] and what man wills is not a theoretic limit, only another choice. Modernity, again, is the working out of these self-sufficient wills placed into reality by the philosopher-politician of this century. This disordered relation of art to politics, as Maritain saw it in his famous essay on Machiavelli, is what makes this sort of humanism most dangerous [Redpath]. When politics does not derive the ends of its human subjects from a what is that did not itself originate in man, it has no limits. The truth of politics becomes what the politician proposes for the good of the public order and his success in carrying it out. Freedom becomes simply the denial that there are limits, particularly limits deriving from *what is* or revelation.

Joseph Califano states modern humanism's problem very well in his essay:

> Once man sought to be civilized; now man seeks merely to be free.
> Man seeks to be free in a total sense, that is, indeterminate sense
> where freedom makes no sense and freedom has no meaning. Man
> seeks to be free from the reality of himself and the reality of the other
> whether the other is another human person or God.

Califano's suspicion that suffering somehow gets to the heart of the problem is not only basic to the religion of Calvary but something that Maritain understood, particularly through his relation with his wife, Raissa. The slaughter-houses of modernity are populated with people who, on the basis of a philosophy of compassion and will, are to be put

---

[5]*Ibid.*, 4.

out of their suffering. A mis-placed mercy, as Flannery O'Connor re-marked has the most terrible of human consequences. The Greek idea that man learns by suffering, or the Christian idea that salvation is from the Cross--wherein evil lies in choice not suffering--are specifically rejected. Maritain's concern about the dire consequences of an autonomous humanism is by no means out of date.

The essays in this book have asked the essential questions about the abidingness of Maritain's thought in our time. Are the good things produced in modern times rooted in that deeper humanism that came from *Genesis* and from the limits placed on this world when the City of God is properly located? Are the issues that lie at the heart of public disorder still products of that sort of modernity that produced the totalitarianisms of this century which we all now reject? The discussions on John Caputo [Boyle], Richard Rorty [Asselin], Allan Bloom [Hancock], Allen Tate [Dunaway], Jacques Derrida [Royal], and others take up the alternatives to the sort of solution that Maritain had proposed through the tradition of faith and reason. That this faith and reason dimension is the key intellectual issue--even if it must be undertaken in what are today obscure places over now almost forgotten thinkers like Maritain--should not be doubted.

Following Aristotle and St. Thomas, Maritain knew that civilizations rise and fall over the understanding of small errors in the beginning which lead to huge errors in the end. Maritain is sometimes accused of being perhaps too intellectual. No doubt he was, but great intelligence is not the fault. Maritain studied the great philosophers--Descartes, in particular--too long ever to doubt that disorders in the world begin in disorders in the mind, even in minds long before our era.

Maritain remains a guide to the heart of things for those who would suspect that the last word on modernity is not yet spoken in the public order. No doubt, Maritain expected after World War II that a return to sanity, to a consideration of the deepest spiritual roots of which we still do not adequately comprehend, might very well leave us open as much to a new form of modernity as to the traditional understanding of *what is*. The wars of the world remain the wars of the mind.

Deconstructionism, the latest academic candidate to invigorate modernity, is correctly seen to be not an admission that modernity was wrong but that it was not pushed far enough, that there is still hope that its principles will work [Royal]. Interestingly enough, the only thinker who seems to be in the same realist set of mind as Maritain was Leo Strauss [Asselin]. Even Alasdair MacIntyre is seen to be rather on the side of an intellectual subjectivism which is not rooted directly in being but in a tradition of argument that need not be directly metaphysical in the Thomist sense that Maritain used it [Asselin].

What was the most unique of these essays--the discussions of Bernanos and Maritain--touched on an issue, perhaps the remnants of the long relation of Augustinianism and Thomism--namely, the relation of faith to the world [Bush]. Maritain always must be read in light of *The Peasant of the Garonne*,[6] wherein, before he died, he saw some of the problems connected with religious enthusiasm over improving the world. Still, Maritain devoted his life to the proposition that faith made a difference in the world. Maritain's discussion of political authority reformulated the central thesis of Aristotle and St. Thomas about the need for authority [O'Donnell]. The answer to totalitarianism is not *no authority*, or even *limited authority*--but, rather, *legitimate authority*, which might, indeed, have to be strong and intelligent at the same time. Maritain's brief essay on ethics in a barbarian society in *Man and the State*[7] remains necessary and sober reading for those who would either be overly naive about the goodness in the actual human heart or about the kinds of problems with which even valid authority has to deal. Bernanos was, however, worried about Maritain's emphasis on democracy. His worry, in spite of first impressions that only a French reactionary would question democracy, is worth considering. Bernanos, though a few years younger than Maritain seemed to be critical of Maritain's effort to capture for the faith modern ideas of democracy, which, in France in particular, had distinctly ideological roots. Maritain belonged to those many of our era who want to claim that the faith *ought* also to transform the political and economic order. Maritain did not, to be sure, claim either that the faith is about politics or that the Gospels contain a formula for economic success.

The position of Maritain on democracy might not be impossible in theory. Faith and reason are not contradictory. Indeed, faith ought to correct even political reason; but, in Bernanos's eyes, Maritain's thesis contained the danger of forgetting that most of the human beings--

---

[6]Jacques Maritain, *The Peasant of the Garonne* (New York: Holt, Rinehart and Winston, Inc., 1968).

[7]Jacques Maritain, *Man and the State* (Chicago: University of Chicago Press, 1951).

including Christians--who ever lived did not live in democracies, and still do not--however *modern* states may be called. If the faith is about political order, then it is of little use for most men in most eras, including the France of history and of our own time. For the faith to concern itself so much with external, political forms, and to identify its success with their establishment, would leave most men without profound teaching about what it is for which they are ultimately to aim in this life. It is by no means clear that citizens of democracies save their souls at any faster rate than those of tyrannies. Bernanos and Solzhenitsyn, neither of whom praised tyrannies, would have had much in common in this regard. The essential question the Lord will ask at the Judgment will not be, "Did you work hard for democracy?"

Maritain, of course, was right to look for an alternative to what had, in fact, been produced by modern thought from Descartes, Machiavelli, and Bacon. Maritain was quite aware that the principal defensive strategy of Christianity was to establish that it was not intrinsically opposed to those aspects of modernity that had, in fact, improved the human lot. Maritain's American illusions, perhaps, were overly sanguine, but not because he did not see the American virtues correctly [Mancini]. Rather, he did not anticipate the direction of autonomous man in democratic societies themselves. The comparison of de Tocqueville with Maritain is always instructive in this regard. De Tocqueville worried about democratic tyrannies in a way Maritain, though aware of its possibilities through Rousseau, did not.

Why Maritain's *Reflections on America*[8] remains central, however, is its emphasis on the practical, productive economy which does not have the capacity of materially improving the lot of most people--something Maritain felt was a legitimate heritage from Aristotle, from the Catholic tradition, and from the American experience. The curious phenomenon of liberation theology does not, I think, have roots in *Reflections on America*, but represents its exact antithesis, an antithesis supported even more strongly by *Man and the State*, with its careful distinction between the spheres of politics and religion, without denying the range of each. The European left never forgave the the author of *Integral Humanism*[9] for

---

[8]Jacques Maritain, *Reflections on America* (New York: Charles Scribner's Sons, 1958).

[9]Jacques Maritain, *Integral Humanism: Temporal and Spiritual Problems*

writing *Reflections on America*. In a sense, even the social doctrine of the Church has not caught up with the basic issue which Maritain sensed in *Reflections on America*--namely, that the issue of poverty is not independent of the issue of productivity and its conditions. We have no option for the poor without understanding why people are not poor in the first place.

The relation of Strauss and Maritain is worthy of reflection. *Man and the State* and *Natural Right and History*[10] were given in subsequent years at the University of Chicago in the early 1950s. Strauss did not see any possibility of revelation directing itself to reason. He could not exclude the possibility of revelation whose possibility he defended; but for him the highest vocation was that of philosopher. For Maritain the philosopher's vocation was also his, but it was this very vocation that excluded a closed humanism. Both Strauss and Maritain returned to the Greeks, but only Maritain returned also through those medievals who were not Averroists. Both understood modernity in the same way, and both recognized that the modern era contained aberrations of the deepest sort.

Strauss was less willing than Maritain to come to terms with what seemed to be the good in modernity. Strauss was, in a way, closer to Bernanos or Augustine in expecting that we would not find any good actual cities. Maritain, however, expected that the post war era would produce a better social order. In many ways it did; but there is a gnawing realization from the themes of *The Twilight of Civilization*, the condition of our education and the condition of our moral life, that the forms of democracy by themselves do not hold a sophisticated barbarism back [Hudson, Hancock, Boyle].

Both Strauss and Maritain sought to think through the status of the social sciences [Nelson]. Strauss was more unwilling to grant that the modern social sciences have redeeming value. He thought they were, in fact, essentially the causes of the problems of modernity. Maritain sought to rethink the whole nature of the sciences, not merely in their modern sense but also in their medieval and classical understandings. Maritain's

---

of a New Christendom, trans. Joseph W. Evans (New York: Charles Scribner's Sons, 1958).

[10]Leo Strauss, *Natural Right and History* (Chicago: University of Chicago Press, 1953).

terminology was sometimes rather daunting, but he thought that it was possible to classify even Freud and make proper use of his efforts. Since science claimed to lie at the heart of modernity or an autonomous humanism, both Strauss and Maritain devoted long discussions to the intellectual validity of science, to its roots not in modernity but in the classics.

Just what Maritain would have made of Rifkin and environmentalism is a problem [Royal, Trapani]. I am inclined to think, with Royal, that environmentalism is the successor to socialism as the latest form of autonomous modernity. No doubt, the notion of harmony of work and nature was a heritage from the early Benedictines in Western civilization. Both Aristotle and *Genesis* had established the relation of man to nature. Civilization was, indeed, the addition of man and his work and art to nature. The belated fate of science and technology in modernity has been to pass from a sort of substitute for religion to a kind of cause of apocalypse.

The enemy of environmentalism is development. Already here we have a conflict between one side of modernity which wanted to make men happy through science and another side which saw man as only a function of nature, not its purpose and guide. The irrationalist side of humanism which Maritain saw in theories of race and nation have rather strong affinity with worrisome strands in environmentalism or ecology. The most recent candidate for the absolute state, for the *good* of man, of course, comes from this area, with the reabsorption into the species in order to keep on-going *nature* alive, as it is said.

Maritain concerned himself with the worldly condition. Bernanos, though he preferred classical French monarchy, was sure that we are called to save our souls in whatever society in which we find ourselves, good or bad. Maritain would not have denied this, of course; but Maritain was not a Platonist who thought that the city in speech was the best we could do. Maritain's grandfather was a Prime Minister in the Third Republic; so he was not likely to be a monarchist, even of the French kind. Maritain did think, however, that the city in speech, the best city possible, needed to be intellectually elaborated [Hellman]. He had the insight to propose its essential outlines, not just in speech, but in practice. Maritain's influence at UNESCO, and even at the Vatican, to which he was French Ambassador took his worldly duties seriously. Maritain's political writings, furthermore, are full of admonitions about human weakness, variety, and contrariety. He knew that practical things are tenuous, but he considered it necessary and worthwhile to act where he could.

What is still the most dangerous failure of clarification in modern political and, especially, ecclesiastical thought is the intellectual status of *human rights*. To his credit Maritain tried to save the notion of *rights* from their undoubted modernist origins. Strauss was much more blunt here. It could not be done, Strauss thought. Modern natural, or human, rights, the kind we hear and speak of, are anti-human. In modern theory, they mean nothing more or nothing less than that autonomous will stands at their origin producing their content. Maritain's treatments of natural rights can be defended as coming from a different tradition, the Thomist natural law position, though one stemming, as Strauss's, from Plato and Aristotle.

Maritain could metaphysically ground natural rights as he did in *Man and the State* and *The Rights of Man and the Natural Law*. He could propose that moderns *practically* accept these rights without necessarily having the same intellectual justifications found in the work of Hobbes or Locke. Though I would accept the originality of Maritain's solution, I have always been leery of this hope of Maritain. In Strauss's terms, when we hear the word "human rights," we almost invariably hear modern natural rights, which have no root but will. However judiciously it is used, I do not think that the term "natural rights" can be saved from its subjective origins in Hobbes, Locke, and Rousseau. We should do with it as Maritain himself did with the word "sovereignty"--that is, simply not use it since it can only cause confusion and harm.

Nothing is more confounding and nothing serves to introduce the next ideological stages of modernity into contemporary society, which these essays seek to trace, than *Human Rights* based in will alone. What Professor Raymond Dennehy rightly called "the ontological status of human rights"[11] remains impossible in a will theory of rights. With *rights* now being claimed for everything from trees to tree owls, from abortions to any conceivable sort of life-style, this concept of *human rights* serves to promote exactly what classic natural law was designed to limit or prevent in the end, such *rights* are no longer natural *rights*. They are only civil rights to be determined by the state's will presupposed to nothing but its

---

[11]Raymond Dennehy, "The Ontological Basis of Human Rights," *The Thomist* 42 (July, 1978): 434-63.

own will. Even constitutions are reinterpreted in this light.

The place of work, and its relation to civilization, was long a topic of interest to Maritain and his esteemed student Yves R. Simon [Doering]. In a yet unresolved comparison with Josef Pieper's study of leisure, the place of work in civilization is a controverted one. Pieper was most reluctant to call the activities of contemplation also *work,* as modern popes have tended to do. No doubt, under the influence of Christianity, the status of all work has been enhanced, if looked upon, particularly, from the standpoint of the worker. The Greeks distinguished rather on the basis of the object of activity and hierarchized their analysis accordingly. There were things done for their own sakes and things done simply for use. The Greeks did not think a man a slave because of his legal or political status, but because of the sort of work he did. The link between slavery and technology is already in Aristotle, who said that if machines could replace certain works of drudgery we would not need slaves. When this replacement came about through modern technology, in particular, there was a certain widespread confusion about the value of work.

In reading *Genesis* Christians have seen"working by the sweat of their brows" to be a sort of penance, something caused by The Fall. Aristotle had distinguished between artistic and slave work. The crafts did something very human. They made necessary tools and could make them and their products beautiful in their own ways. Christianity, in looking to the worker, with St. Joseph as the paradigm, has tended to pay less attention to the divisions within the world of work to which Pieper was attuned. Whether Maritain (and Weil and Simon) would have been so unhappy with America on the grounds of work conditions [Doering] might be questioned.

No revolution seems more in line with the sort of freeing tool to the mind and workplace as the personal computer which makes possible work in the home as the kind of entrepreneurship that makes such power available on a wide scale. Analyses of causes of economic growth in recent years have shown that small and medium sized companies are the main sources for the new products and methods in the economy. Moreover, the size of the economy is itself a product of the freeing on a more worldwide scale of individual sources of ideas and institutions. If the only real wealth in the world is the human brain, there are many positive things that would, I think, have pleased Maritain and Simon about the conditions and nature of work.

Maritain's capacity for friendship has been often noted. We have several discussions of the power of his personal interest and character [Suther, Dunaway]. I have remarked that the wars of the world take place first in wars in the mind, but wars in the mind can be genteel and friendly. Professor Suther's reflection is worth emphasis in this regard:

> So if the example has any validity, perhaps the spirit of pluralism can survive in the most contentious of climates. Perhaps the clamor of -isms that raged in France beween the two world wars is not the only echo that will be heard in another fifty years. The polarizing language of dogmatism and belief that became a fashionable vernacular of those times may not constitute the sole surviving script as the record is read and reread and revised. Without ascribing a false heroism to Jacques Maritain, I do think he contributed some indelible lines to an alternative script of his times.

Maritain's relationships with a Cocteau, with a Bernanos, with a Gide, and others was friendly and intelligent. The point is not so much that it is good for *pluralisms* to continue to exist, for this is itself merely a modernist ideology, but for truth to be engaged in a fashion that does not destroy the city while, at the same time, really coming to grips with serious issues of human being and the nature of *what is*. The very purpose of the human mind is to make *dogmas*, as Chesterton said. Maritain knew that truth was found in the judgment, and the purpose of our powers of judgment was exactly to judge, to conclude to what is true. Near the end of *The Twilight of Civilization*, Maritain remarked:

> If it is correct to say that there will always be rightist temperaments and leftist temperaments, it is nonetheless also correct to say that political philosophy is neither rightist nor leftist; it must simply be true.[12]

Civilization does not exist for the sake of pluralism. Pluralism exists because there are many ways to do practical things and to arrange civil orders. Pluralism also exists because it takes time and effort to come judgment about what is right and wrong. Pluralism, however, does not exist for its own sake, as if there were no judgments to be made. Ultimately, pluralism exists for the truth. At some basic level, philosphers must engage in the sober and difficult enterprise of seeking the

---

[12]Jacques Maritain, *The Twilight of Civilization*, 57.

truth itself, not merely *seeking* it, but finding it. Maritain would be the first to admit that this cannot be done without humility, but he would also recognize that the skeptical thesis, that pluralism exists because no truth is possible, is itself the primary cause of the moral failure of modern society.

"The Christian religion is annexed to no temporal regime: it is compatible with all forms of legitimate government."[13] If the Christian religion is annexed to no temporal regime, it must mean that the sources of what it is to be a temporal regime are derived not from religion but from philosophy and the experience of living; but Maritain's whole essay was written in a period when it was clear that some temporal regimes claimed more than temporal authority. Why they did this was itself the philosophical problem addressed in *The Twilight of Civilization*. Some forms of government, in other words, were not legitimate. The spelling out of why this was so was one of Maritain's abiding contributions. Maritain was quite aware of what he once called them, of "the things that were not Caesar's." In these papers the writers have reflected both the Maritain dealing with political modernity and with the Maritain dealing with those things which transcend politics. Maritain remains one of the few philosophers of this century in whom justice is done to both of these aspects of reality--to the world and to what transcends the world.

If we are to sum up the essential problem that Maritain had with an atheist humanism, or with modernity that might continue even after the apparent demise of socialism, we can do no better than to cite Professor Redpath's accurate observation:

Modern philosophy...is not an age in which practical science dominates over theoretical science. Rather, it is an age in which unbridled artistic creativity (creativity based upon uprooted, realistically blind, and subjective inspiration) is the measure of all truths--those of practical and theoretical science included.

It is no accident that artistic creativity, itself a subject of so much insightful analysis in Maritain, assumes the central role. If man is already a certain kind of natural reality, with his own being and intelligibility, as

---

[13]*Ibid.*, 60.

Aristotle maintained, then the relation of civilization to him is not to be based on *artistic creativity*--which is, at bottom, the claim of modern natural rights--but of prudence itself rooted in a metaphysics open to revelation.

Speaking of the German philosopher Carl Schmitt, Maritain wrote that Schmitt's famous distinction about friend and foe being the essence of politics was not the essence of politics itself, but it was the essence of *pagan* politics; and the study of pagan politics revealed to us "...what a terrible reality is the political divorced from the eternal law and from the vivifying energies of Christ, the political as the spirit of the world puts it into practice--and with what delight, what ferocity!"[14] Political philosophy is to be *true*, as Maritain maintained--true not just to itself, to what it is open to, but also to its record and its causes.

The intellectual concerns that Maritain articulated in *The Twilight of Civilization* bear much affinity with the historical development we have seen since he spoke in Paris in 1939. What is surprising, however, in following the evolution of autonomous humanism, is how often Maritain's concern remains at the heart of civilization in whose twilight he brooded [Gallagher]. It is not the dawn until the intellectual core of modern thought is based not on will but on *what is*, a what is that is by its own nature open also to receive what it could not have anticipated. Why the work of Jacques Maritain remains worth deep study, as these essays show, is because he is one of the few guides to take both the order of the world and the City of God seriously enough to discover their mutual affinity with each other.

---

[14]*Ibid.*, 37.

Part I
Philosopher in the City

Judith D. Suther

Dogmatism & Belief in French Cultural Life in the 1930s

What follows is a cautionary tale about belief and certainty and insularity. With fifty years' perspective--in some instances, more--it requires no great insight to trace patterns of conflict in French artistic and intellectual life in the 1930s; and the origins and extensions of the patterns in earlier and later decades. What may not be so easy, for advocates of one or another persuasion, is to entertain the idea that there was no mainstream in the highly pluralistic climate of France in the decade before World War II. This cautionary tale entertains such an idea, and in the end proposes Jacques Maritain as a moderating voice in a contentious arena.

To reduce the argument to manageable proportions, I will single out only four competing currents: Catholicism, Modernism, Surrealism, and Existentialism. Certainly, the phenomenon called the Catholic Renaissance in the between-war years cannot be contained within the decade of the 1930s. Modernism and Surrealism also have their origins earlier in the century. Existentialism only began to gather momentum in the thirties and then flourished in the decade following. Nonetheless, in the years immediately preceding World War II, all four coexisted as conflicting systems of belief—as the French would put it, they cohabited, in a *cohabitation difficile;* and here is where the cautionary tale begins: adherents to each of the four were inclined to see themselves as the core or center of the intellectual and artistic life of their time. They all tended to regard their persuasion as the mainstream which would save France from darkness, wrongheadedness, or mediocrity.

With no polemical intent, I wish to observe that each of these groups defended its principles with something very akin to religious fervor. I, therefore, frame the cautionary tale in the language of belief--sometimes used ironically, sometimes not. That is the language frequently used by the Catholics, Modernists, Surrealists, and Existentialists I discuss, and by their critics. It is also the language best suited to the conventions of this particular cautionary tale; for there is an edge of self-righteousness, of implied rightness and wrongness, to the polemical writings of all four of the groups. Only the Catholics explicitly acknowledged that they believed truth was in their camp, and that art and discourse should reflect the truth; but the others behaved and wrote as if they believed it. All of them regularly censured members of other faiths; they also censured members of their own for straying from a perceived orthodoxy. When that happened, the language of belief became that of dogmatism.

Some preliminary examples may clarify these observations. It is no accident that André Breton was dubbed the Pope of the Surrealists for his zeal at setting dogma and excommunicating the lapsed. It is no accident that Sartre was dubbed the Pope of the Existentialists, for the same reason, and his disciple Francis Jameson, the Cardinal; or that Simone de Beauvoir wrote a 500+-page book, *The Mandarins* (1954), in which she exhaustively and belatedly excommunicated Camus, disguised as Henri, for contumacy and moral turpitude. The French Modernists didn't have a pope, probably because there were two acknowledged giants of Modernist prose in France--Proust and Gide; and each made up an exclusive congregation of one. Proust has been described by Henri Peyre as having concelebrated daily mass with himself in his cork-lined sanctuary.[1] So what if Peyre made the remark with a twinkle in his eye? Not so much given to twinkles as to dodges, Gide once explained his flirtation with the Communist party as a way of deflecting those who insisted on anointing him as the papal arbiter of Modernism.[2]

What I am proposing in this tale of camps and congregations and believers is that all four of the groups to which I am alluding—Catholics, Modernists, Surrealists, and Existentialists—tended to attract convertible personalities, many of whom did undergo some kind of conversion experience and then felt marked with the colors of a cause. In their new lives, they usually saw themselves as standard bearers or guardians of

---

[1] Henri Peyre in discussion at a session on the modern French novel at the Modern Language Association national meeting in New York City (December 1985).

[2] Judith D. Suther in conversation with Gabriel Marcel (Paris, June 1980).

lofty and exclusive principles. Not only can the Catholic artists and intellectuals be characterized in this way, as is traditional; the Modernists, Surrealists, and Existentialists were fired with equal conviction.

For the Modernists, Gide's journey from a comfortable middle class background to a credo of questioning everything is an apt model of the Modernist conversion. His novel *The Counterfeiters* (1926) is a paradigm of an old order in dissolution and a new one always just out of reach. Gide, and the Modernists in general, rejected not only high culture and inherited values; they rejected the possibility of stable meaning itself. Once they had invested themselves in the inquiry, inquiry itself became the new god--again the language of belief shades toward dogmatism. True to the model of Gide, other Modernist conversions, such as Valery's, were gradual and deliberate, akin to Bunyan's account of his own in *Grace Abounding*. Valery's early essay *"An Evening with Monsieur Teste "*(1896) is a long intellectual preparation for his most famous Modernist statement, the statement that appears above the *Musée de l'Homme* in Paris: *"Nous autres civilisations, nous savons maintenant que nous sommes mortels"* ("Now we know that our civilizations too are mortal").

For the French Surrealists, there is a wide field of candidates to serve as conversion models. Breton is not a voice crying in the wilderness. One of his earliest disciples is an almost caricatural Surrealist conversion figure: Yves Tanguy was riding on a bus in Paris in 1925 when he saw one of Giorgio de Chirico's *metaphysical* paintings displayed in a gallery window. He jumped off the bus, in a state of high excitement examined the painting, and, by his own account, became a Surrealist on the spot.[3] In the closed economy of this cautionary tale, the nature of Tanguy's work and his loyalties after that encounter make it fair to compare his experience with the experience of Paul on the road to Damascus. Tanguy underwent a sudden metamorphosis, as opposed to the slow transformation experienced by Gide and Valery. Knowing full well that I can never prove it, I will hazard the opinion that these contrasting patterns of conversion are generally valid for other Modernist and Surrealist figures. Certainly, strength of conviction and reform of manners following the conversion experience *are* typical of all of them.

---

[3]Recounted by Patrick Waldberg in *Yves Tanguy* (Brussels: André de Rache, 1977), 90-91. Tanguy himself also recounted the incident numerous times to critics and interviewers.

For the Existentialists, again the best-known exemplar, Sartre--the Alsatian burgher turned Parisian iconoclast--is not the only candidate for conversion model. Camus presents a better paradigm, at least a more dramatic and attractive one, in his youthful battle with the demon of mortality, which for him took the form of tuberculosis. He emerged momentarily the victor, in 1930; and as long as he lived, espoused some variation of Humanism, for lack of a more precise word. I say Humanism, rather than Existentialism, because Camus himself objected to the label *Existentialist*, although it is the term most often applied to his work. As the editor of the wartime underground newspaper, *Combat*, and the writer of a strangely lean and sensual prose, he was a great agent of secular conversion for those who had lost every faith. The fact that he did not accept this role only increased his effectiveness.

To return to the thread of the cautionary tale, the beliefs of each of the coexisting groups tended to take on the characteristics of a holy mission. From there to the conviction that one's own mission represented the mainstream of the historical moment is a very small step. Most of the converts to each of the groups I have named took the step. What makes the proposition doubly interesting is that there was very little crossing of lines, of professing more than one allegiance. The Modernists tended not to be Catholic, and vice versa. The Surrealists tended to be unsympathetic to the Existentialists, and vice versa; and so on and so forth, in all directions. The tendency toward exclusiveness applied to all the groups. It is as if each of them professed a religion, and as if the religions were mutually exclusive. Members of each group used religious terms disparagingly to characterize members of another group. Raïssa Maritain wrote for all to read in her autobiography that Modernism was the *heresy* of the between-war years.[4] She also wrote, but this time in her journal for no one to read, that Paul Sabon "felt the devil in the surrealists" and got away just in time.[5] In "Sense and Non-Sense in Poetry," she asserts that the Surrealists "burdened [poetry] with the duties of sanctity, without the means of sanctity."[6] In "Poetry as Spiritual Experience," a talk

[4]Raïssa Maritain, *Les Grandes Amitiés* (Paris: Desclée de Brouwer, 1944), 392.

[5]Raïssa Maritain, *Journal de Raissa.*, ed. Jacques Maritain (Paris: Desclée de Brouwer, 1963), 177-78.

[6]Raïssa Maritain, *Poèmes et Essais.*, ed. Jacques Maritain (Paris: Desclée de Brouwer, 1968), 219.

later revised into an essay, she states that Paul Eluard is a poet who achieves spiritual heights *despite* his Surrealist affiliation [her emphasis].[7]

Other converts—converts as defined in this cautionary tale—express themselves in terms similar to those used by Raïssa. Gide wrote in his journal that Jacques Maritain was priestly and proselytizing, which was not a compliment. "The stooped, bent carriage of his head and his whole person displeased me," said Gide, as did "a certain clerical unction in his gesture and voice."[8] Peggy Guggenheim, a kind of surrogate Surrealist, wrote in her memoirs that Yves Tanguy "seemed to think his whole life depended on his being a Surrealist. It was worse than having a religion," she declared, "and it governed all his actions."[9] There is a whole body of critical writing by Christians, mainly Catholics, postulating that if Camus had lived beyond the age of forty-six, he would have converted from the *illusory* religion which he espoused, Existentialism, to their religion. They liked the poor boy from Algiers who wrote such seductive prose. They wanted him in their camp. Both Sartre and de Beauvoir, for their parts, expended many pages explaining that if you were Catholic, you were intellectually bankrupt and, therefore, morally stunted. Pierre Mabille, a tireless zealot of the Surrealist persuasion, added a clinical dimension to the lexicon of disdain. He wrote an entire book on Thérèse of Lisieux, explaining how she was the victim of a parasitic faith because her parents, indeed her grandparents, had already been *infected* with the *deadly virus* of Catholicism. Mabille, a physician, manages to equate the Catholic faith with disease, while propagating his own faith, Surrealism *cum* Marxism.[10] In this welter of self-righteous accusations, a common denominator links accusers and accused: survivors of a war and heirs to more than one failed panacea for the ailments of their society (positivism, materialism, militarism; somewhat later, Communism and populism), they all suffered from a sense of loss, and they all sought something in which to believe. When they settled on what it would be, they formalized their beliefs into systems (for the Catholics,

---

[7]*Ibid.*, 280.

[8]André Gide, *Journal d'André Gide, 1889-1939* (Paris: Gallimard, 1951), I, 772.

[9]Peggy Guggenheim, *Out of this Century: Confessions of an Art Addict* (New York: Universe Books, 1987), 182.

[10]Pierre Mabille, *Thérèse de Lisieux* (Paris: Corti, 1936).

the institution of the Church was already in place).

Each group then conceptualized its own system as the main current, the cleansing agent that alone represented the artistic and intellectual future of France. This attitude automatically marginalized all currents except one's own; it also led quite naturally to the dogmatic vocabulary appropriated by members of the conflicting factions. In the massive demoralization of France after World War I, it may have been impossible to conceive of a successfully pluralistic society; the dominant position which each group claimed for its own beliefs, once they had been constructed from beyond despair, may have been inevitable.

I wish to shift out of the linguistic register of dogmatism and belief now, and propose Jacques Maritain as the modest hero of this cautionary tale. Despite a quick temper and a prolific output of position papers and manifestoes, he has left a record more leavened by understanding than marred by intolerance. No stranger to polemics, even bitter polemics, he seems, nonetheless, to have been more receptive to artistic and intellectual pluralism than most of his contemporaries. This is not to question his unwavering commitment to what he called "philosophizing in the faith." On the contrary, to an observer who knows more about Modernists, Surrealists, and Existentialists than about Catholic philosophers, Jacques Maritain appears to have been that rare presence among them all: that is, the convert who could look, listen, learn, and change, win some, lose some, lash out on occasion, but ultimately remain open to great art, surprising ideas, or intellectual honesty from any quarter. He seems to me to have branded only faintly by the insularity so often seen in his Modernist, Surrealist, and Existentialist contemporaries—indeed, his Catholic contemporaries.

To illustrate, with a final set of examples: from early in his career, Jacques Maritain engaged in combat, usually courteous on his part, with various members of the Modernist, Surrealist, and Existentialist groups. His most extended contact with any of them was with the Modernists and Modernist critics at Princeton. To judge by the evolution of his taste from the youthful manifesto *Antimoderne* (1922) to *Creative Intuition in Art and Poetry* (1953), this longest association was probably also the most satisfying to him. During and after World War II, in the United States, he continued to be the target of ironic anti-Catholic barbs aimed at him by Modernist spokesmen, framed in the familiar dogmatic language. A long article in a 1942 issue of the *Partisan Review* attacking his anti-Modernist views on esthetics is called, with curled lip, "The Profession of Poetry or, Trials Through the Night for M. Maritain."[11] In most instances Maritain did not rise to the bait, and he continued to evince a genuine and admiring interest in Modernist works, particularly those of English-language writers such as Hart Crane, Eliot, John Crowe Ransom, Wallace Stevens, and Allen Tate (Tate and his wife Caroline Gordon, Modernists and Catholic converts, are notable exceptions to the pattern of exclusiveness which I have put forward). When Maritain criticized the work of American Modernists, he generally did so in measured terms of courtesy and respect, free of charged language. For example, of Eliot's essay, "Tradition and the Individual Talent," he writes discreetly, "I am afraid that T. S. Eliot...missed the distinction between creative Self and self-centered ego....That is probably why...he uses the word 'personality' where *individuality* is the proper term."[12] In a recent article in *The American Scholar*, entitled "Remembering Jacques Maritain," Wallace Fowlie reports that Maritain was fascinated with Eliot's poetry, despite reservations about his critical writing. According to Fowlie, Maritain liked to hear the last lines of "Ash-Wednesday" read aloud by a native English-speaking voice:

> Blessed sister, holy mother, spirit of the fountain,
>   spirit of the garden,
> Suffer us not to mock ourselves with falsehood
> Teach us to care and not to care
> Teach us to sit still
> Even among these rocks,
> Our peace in His will
> And even among these rocks
> Sister, mother
> And spirit of the river, spirit of the sea,
> Suffer me not to be separated
>
> And let my cry come unto Thee.

---

[11] Harold Rosenberg, "The Profession of Poetry or, Trials Through the Night for M. Maritain," *Partisan Review* 9 (Sept.-Oct. 1942): 392-413.

[12] Jacques Maritain, *Creative Intuition in Art and Poetry* (New York: Bollingen Foundation by PantheonBooks, 1953), 313, n. 18.

Fowlie says that Maritain listened enthralled to these lines and asked if Eliot were a religious man. When told yes, he did not pose sectarian questions.[13]

With the Surrealists and Existentialists, Maritain's relations were of lesser duration, but on his side at least, no less marked by decorum and an attempt to understand views different from his own. His admiration for Reverdy's work and his friendship with him did not diminish after Reverdy's loss of faith and his period of frequenting the Surrealist commune on the *rue du Chateau*—in fact, living there for awhile. The same can be said of Maritain's relations with Cocteau. Years after the standoff following their exchange of letters in the 1920s, eventually published in English as *Art and Faith* (1948), Maritain would name Cocteau as one of the truly inventive and versatile artists of this century.[14] He did not censure Cocteau for what to some looked like a staged conversion to Catholicism and a betrayal of a friend's good will. As for his efforts at keeping the dialogue open with the Existentialists, Maritain's brief book *Existence and the Existent* (1948) is probably the best summary he left. Written under pressure, when his political engagements were approaching fever pitch, this "short treatise on existence and the existent," as the French title reads, is remarkably balanced and, on the whole, coolly argued. Even after a burst of typical Maritainian invective at the Sartrian doctrine of freedom, Maritain backs off and reflects. "M. Sartre is right in declaring himself firmly optimistic and in leaving the tragic sense to Christians," he writes, a bit pompously. Then he ends the passage with an admission of what really bothers him in the existentialist atheology: it is the "astounding renunciation of any measure of grandeur" for the human person in the absence of God. This is hardly a statement of intolerance or disdain. It reads more like a sorrowful recognition of human incompleteness than like an antagonist's sally.[15]

---

[13]Wallace Fowlie, "Remembering Jacques Maritain," *The American Scholar* (Summer 1987), 355-66.

[14]Judith D. Suther in conversation with Gabriel Marcel, Paris, June 1980).

[15]Jacques Maritain, *Existence and the Existent*, trans. Lewis Galantiere and Gerald B. Phelan (Westport, CT: Greenwood Press, Publishers, 1975), 9.

So, if the example of Maritain has any validity, perhaps the spirit of pluralism can survive in the most contentious of climates. Perhaps the clamor of -isms that raged in France between the two world wars is not the only echo that will be heard in another fifty years. The polarizing language of dogmatism and belief that became a fashionable vernacular of those times may not constitute the sole surviving script, as the record is read and reread and revised. Without ascribing a false heroism to Jacques Maritain, I think he contributed some indelible lines to an alternative script of his time.

The cautionary tale ends with a few lines written by Maritain in a footnote to *Creative Intuition*. They have nothing to do with the -isms and other antagonisms discussed here; they carry no polemical freight. By their very vulnerability, they suggest that if dogmatism occasionally blurred Maritain's vision, he had an instinct for correcting the distortion. The lines from *Creative Intuition* read: "In *Man and Superman*, Bernard Shaw condemned Shakespeare on the ground that his philosophy was 'only his wounded humanity.' Well, I do not complain of being taught by the *wounded humanity of a Shakespeare* about man and human existence, and many things which matter to me in the reality of this world."[16]

---

[16] Jacques Maritain, *Creative Intuition in Art and Poetry*, 131, n. 19.

John M. Dunaway

Exiles and Fugitives: The Maritain-Tate-Gordon Letters

When I was writing a book on Maritain[1] in the mid-seventies, I wrote letters to a whole list of American writers who I thought might have been influenced by Maritain. The responses were quite interesting, but none so generous and enthusiastic as that of Caroline Gordon. Miss Gordon wrote several pages, in which she spoke in glowing terms of what Maritain had meant to her personally, spiritually, and in her writing career. She enclosed a copy of a wonderful letter that Maritain had sent to her after reading one of her novels, *The Malefactors*,[2] and encouraged me to keep in touch, saying she had in her possession other "material which I think will be helpful to you. It has not hitherto been accessible to the public." I quoted from this letter—as well as a short one from Allen Tate—in my book, but as I continued to find interesting examples of Maritain's influence among American writers, a seed was planted somewhere in my mind. It was the germ of a project that I finally began to pursue in 1988 when I was in France and visited Mme. Grunelius at the Maritain center in Kolbsheim—namely, to compile and publish the letters between the two Catholic literary couples.

During the years of Jacques Maritain's American residence he made some rather significant and lasting friendships, relationships that ended up exerting a decisive influence on the history of thought and letters in this country. Among the more enduring of such "*grandes amitiés*," if we may anachronistically appropriate Raïssa's phrase from her 1941 mem-

---

[1] John M. Dunaway, *Jacques Maritain* (Boston: G.K. Hall, 1978).
[2] Caroline Gordon, *The Malefactors* (New York: Harcourt Brace, 1956).

27

oir, was one the Maritains enjoyed with the poet Allen Tate and his first wife, novelist Caroline Gordon.

It is often remarked that one of the greatest gifts with which Jacques Maritain was blessed was his genius for friendship. The fact that his contacts ranged much farther than the world of philosophy or theology is an indication of the special nature of his calling as a *philosophe dans la cité*. Knowing statesmen, poets, painters, priests, labor leaders, novelists, and musicians, Maritain made it his business to communicate with them in their own idiom in order to bring to bear on their diverse problems the fruitful perspectives of Thomistic wisdom.

Such a vision as the Maritains had of making their home a *centre de rayonnement* (a center for a kind of sphere of spiritual influence) in the modern world for the timeless truths of St. Thomas's work was a guiding force in the forming of their friendships, especially at Meudon in the years between the wars, but also at Princeton, Notre Dame, Chicago, and the other American cities where they lived during their long exile from their beloved France. One of the things that they held in common with the Tates was precisely the radiant hospitality that brought so many creative people to their homes. *Benfolly*, the farm overlooking the Cumberland River, was home not only to the Tates, but, for varying periods of time, Ford Madox Ford (and his wife, secretary, and sister-in-law), Robert Lowell (who showed up uninvited and pitched a tent in the lawn),and Katherine Anne Porter. Throughout their marriage, writers and artists, especially those associated with the Fugitive Agrarian movement, enjoyed the hospitality of the Tates: the Robert Penn Warrens, the Malcolm Cowleys, the Mark Van Dorens, the Andrew Lytles, and so on.

Both of these Catholic literary couples began their careers in literary renaissances: movements that favored the wisdom of the ancients over the prophets of modern secularism. Indeed, the *Renouveau catholique* in France had certain sources in common with the Southern Renaissance in the U. S., which began with the Fugitive Agrarians in Tate's undergraduate days at Vanderbilt.

The richest flowering of Southern literature probably owed as great a debt to Allen Tate as to any other single writer. His poetry and literary theory and criticism remain significant entries in the canon, and his *The Fathers*[3] is one of the most remarkable first novels in American literature. While Caroline Gordon does not rank among the best known fiction

---

[3]Allen Tate, *The Fathers* (Baton Rouge: Louisiana State University

writers, she had an admirable gift for rendering detail and was a peculiarly insightful student and teacher of the craft of fiction, and readers of *The Southern Mandarins*[4] will hardly be surprised to hear her called a gifted epistolary stylist.

The letters exchanged between the Maritains and the Tates during their lifetimes reveal a rich tapestry of mutual respect, of intellectual fervor, and of constructive criticism. There is a lively flow of ideas and advice, as well as the kind of support and counsel that can only spring from deeply shared experience.

The Tates' letters are fewer and farther between but testify to a genuine devotion to the French philosopher. Gordon's are more numerous, much longer and more directly focused on Maritain's writings, as they impinge on her own thought and fiction.

Allen Tate has stated that "Jacques Maritain's influence on me was pervasive from the time I first knew him in 1940 until his death." Yet although the Maritains eventually became the godparents of Tate and Gordon, I think it unlikely that Maritain had any decisive role in Tate's conversion, shortly after that of his wife, to Roman Catholicism in the late '40s. It is certainly clear that the Southern writer—in the absence of religious training—had arrived at the point of decision through a similar intellectual route, having long been an Aristotelian with a strong classical formation and preferring, among modern poets, such figures as T. S. Eliot and Baudelaire. Walter Sullivan observes that Tate was indeed predisposed toward the Neo-Scholastic worldview. So it is probably more likely to surmise a meeting of like minds than an influence.

The earliest reference to a face-to-face meeting between the two couples is in 1949 in New York. The first exchange of letters—these in 1944 between Jacques and Allen—concerns the latter's request for an article for the *Sewanee Review*, which Tate was directing in the mid-forties.

Press, 1977 (revised from original edition, New York: G. P. Putnam's Sons, 1938)).

[4]Caroline Gordon, *The Southern Mandarins, Letters of Caroline Gordon to Sally Wood, 1924-37*, ed. Sally Wood (Baton Rouge: Louisiana State University Press, 1984).

The upshot was a translation of Maritain's *Réponse à Jean Cocteau*,[5] published as "The Double Heart" in the *Sewanee Review* that year.

As the relationship matures, we read of Maritain asking Tate to critique an essay, especially in regard to his English usage, about which he was quite self-conscious. Caroline offers to take Raïssa for an automobile ride during one of her extended recuperations. There is mention of a bill in the Congress that is proposed in order to obtain a permanent visa for Vera. The bill is introduced by Congressman John F. Kennedy, and Tate enlists the support of Senator Taft. In 1951 there is an exchange that includes Raïssa because of her involvement with Jacques in translating Tate's "Ode to the Confederate Dead" into French. The French version was published in this country in the *Sewanee Review* and in France in the *Figaro litteraire*.

One of the more interesting discussions in the correspondence concerns Tate's role, with Frederick Morgan, the editor of the *Hudson Review*, and Father William Lynch in the creation of an organization of Catholic men of letters. It seems that they became involved in a controversy in 1951-52 over a motion picture being shown in New York called *The Miracle*. Part of a Roberto Rosselini trilogy entitled *Ways of Love*, it was the story of an imbecilic peasant woman (Anna Magnani) who is seduced by a man she believes to be a saint. Cardinal Francis Spellman publicly condemned the film as blasphemous and insulting to Italian womanhood and called for a boycott among Roman Catholics. Pickets, counterpickets, lawsuits—in short, a full-blown *cause célèbre*—ensued, and the stream of articles in the *New York Times* during those months included a letter from Allen Tate.

Apparently, Fred Morgan and others in the laymen's group wished to take legal action against Cardinal Spellman in the affair, but Tate was instrumental in heading off this potentially divisive tactic. Maritain wrote to him—as well as Morgan—that the group would be more effective if it were "concerned with creative and constructive work, not with ecclesiastical politics." Tate wrote back that he fully agreed with Maritain. "My opinion from the beginning...was that we should form a Catholic literary academy, not a group for political action....I agree with you that the only way to make works of imagination and sensibility a part of Catholic life is to produce enough of them, of sufficient power and

[5]Jacques Maritain, *Réponse à Jean Cocteau* (Paris: Stock, 1926).

distinction, [to] affect the education of the Catholic community as a whole, clergy as well as laity."

Thus we find Maritain and Tate in perfect accord on the ideal strategy for Catholic writers collectively to exert an effective influence on society; and Maritain supported Tate's individual public expression of opinion via the letter to the editor: "There is nothing in common between expressing one's mind on the matter, as you did, and starting a collective action which would raise the flag of a theologico-political crusade."

This much can be learned from the correspondence. However, if we read Tate's letter to the *New York Times*, we discover another important issue of this whole controversy in which the two are in apparent disagreement. In the letter to the editor, Tate argues that because of the separation of church and state there is no institution in this country with a "legitimate authority to suppress books and motion pictures, however disagreeable they may be to certain persons on theological grounds." He closes the letter by charging, "In the long run what Cardinal Spellman will have succeeded in doing is insulting the intelligence and faith of American Catholics with the assumption that a second-rate motion picture could in any way undermine their morals or shake their faith."

The clear implication in this text is that Allen Tate opposed censorship on any grounds, whether theological or moral; but his beloved friend Jacques Maritain would never have taken such a position, judging from what he wrote in *The Responsibility of the Artist*. "When it comes to the moral or immoral value of a literary work, the community may have to guard its standards against it to the extent that it is an incitation to action....We cannot deny that people who are not specialists in literature have a right to be warned against reading authors whose artistic talent is but a means to unburden their vices and obsessions on us."[6]

Such reasoning, I submit, would indeed be salubrious today to counter the strident voices heard everywhere around us, lamenting so-called unfair government censorship in cases where it is not even a question of censorship or freedom of speech but of governmental subsidies for art that is offensive and degrading.

---

[6] Jacques Maritain, *The Responsibility of the Artist* (New York: Gordian, 1972) (reprint of the original edition, Charles Scribner's Sons, 1960), 79-80.

In 1954 there is a letter from Maritain praising Miss Gordon's story "Emmanuele! Emmanuele!" The story, which appeared that year in the *Sewanee Review*, is a thinly veiled fiction whose principal character is easily recognizable to students of French literature as André Gide. Gide's stormy relationships with his wife Madeleine Rondeaux and with Paul Claudel are recreated here with what Maritain terms "such power of emotion, human compassion and generosity." The stroke of genius in Gordon's treatment, however, is to entrust the narrative perspective to an otherwise relatively minor character, an impressionable young professor and would-be poet who is hired as Gide's amanuensis. His adoring, awe struck attitude toward the great writer is replete with bitter irony, somewhat reminiscent of the Curé de Luzarne's toward Antoine Saint-Marin, Bernanos's fictionalized version of Anatole France in *Sous le Soleil de Satan*.[7] Indeed, the French Catholic novelist would have been well pleased with Miss Gordon's satirical treatment of the legendary Gide.

Perhaps the richest literary exchange is the one occasioned by the publication of *The Malefactors*, Gordon's 1956 novel, which carried as dedicatory epigraph a quote from Maritain's *The Frontiers of Poetry*:."Few books [have] moved me so deeply," writes Maritain, "perhaps because I felt everywhere the vivid presence of your heart. This book is full of poetry,—implacable and loving, and with an admirably assured design. ...But the great thing is the sense of the loving kindness of Our Lord which permeates the entire book." Miss Gordon was particularly gratified that Maritain was one of the relatively few readers to understand that whereas real people like Hart Crane, Dorothy Day, and Peter Maurin were recognizable in the characters of her story, it had nothing to do with a *roman à clef*, "Maritain was the only critic who realized," as she wrote to me in 1976, "that I had achieved what Ezra Pound years ago labelled 'an invention.' He also recognized the technique I used: adding an extra dimension to the 'literal level' (to borrow Dante's phrase)." Several years later (December 24, 1961) she enthusiastically mentions to Maritain an essay that takes these ideas as a point of departure. Ashley Brown's "The Novel As Christian Comedy"[8] is one of the most creative interpretations that has been written on *The Malefactors*. In addition to Maritain, it

---

[7]Georges Bernanos, *Sous le soleil de Satan* (Paris: Plon, 1926).

[8]Ashley Brown, "The Novel as Christian Comedy," in *Reality and Myth: Essays in American Literature in Honor of Richard Croom Beatty*, ed.

borrows liberally from Francis Fergusson's work on the *Purgatorio, Dante's Dream of the Mind*. So we find in a text like Brown's a remarkable confluence of Maritain's friends and students.

The deep and enduring friendship between Flannery O'Connor and Caroline Gordon has been documented in *The Habit of Being*[9] and in the critical commentaries published on the two writers. It is now widely acknowledged that for many years Miss Gordon was the principal mentor in Miss O'Connor's career. There are several mentions of Flannery's fiction in these letters, and we may infer that Maritain owed much of his familiarity with the author of *Wise Blood* to Gordon. In one letter she encloses some peacock feathers from Flannery's Georgia farm, Andalusia. Then she speaks of sending a photograph of Maritain to a Father Charles at the Trappist Monastery in Conyers, Georgia. "Father Charles—originally one of the most dissolute young men who ever came Dorothy Day's way, she says—is a great admirer of yours and of Raïssa's and will be very happy to have it. These monks have sort of adopted Flannery O'Connor and me as pipe-lines to the outer world."

In a subsequent letter, Gordon writes, "I have just finished a piece in which I tried to compare the last story in Flannery O'Connor's posthumous volume, *Everything That Rises Must Converge*, with the several versions of Flaubert's *Temptations de Saint Antoine* [sic]. It seems to me that Flannery succeeded where the great Flaubert failed, chiefly, because she confined herself to a portrayal of the operations of one heresy whereas Flaubert had nineteen or twenty parade past Saint Anthony."

There are two letters in 1968 and '69 in which Miss Gordon speaks of Eugene McCarthy's presidential campaign. "We knew McCarthy and his wife in Minnesota. They are wonderful people. Gene is, doubtless, the best educated man in American politics. He is a devout Catholic—has taken St. Thomas More as his patron. Everybody says he can't possibly win...but a good many people are beginning to realize that he is attempting something that hasn't been attempted before [You might almost say that he is creating a new political climate]." She even compares McCarthy's significance in America to that of the Little Brothers of

William E. Walher and Robert L. Weller (Nashville: Vanderbilt University Press, 1964).

[9]Flannery O'Connor, *The Habit of Being: The Letters of Flannery O'Connor*, ed. Sally Fitzgerald (New York: Farrar, Strauss, and Giroux, 1979).

Charles de Foucauld in France. At this time Miss Gordon was beginning her third reading of *The Peasant of the Garonne*,[10] about which she was extremely enthusiastic. She told anyone who would listen that "if they want to understand their own times they had better read this book." The example she gives is a very lengthy account of her daughter Nancy's dealings with McCarthy. Nancy Tate Wood had worked quite hard in the campaign and in the fall of '69 was trying to help build the foundation for another McCarthy run at the Presidency. "Their conversation, which lasted three hours, was mostly about angels—angelism, she said. (At this point I was reminded of something you said in print years ago, that our chief danger was not from the atom bomb but from 'angelism,' man's effort to use his own intellect as if it were an angel's intellect.)" She reports that McCarthy attributed Bobby Kennedy's opportunism in the campaign to his "succumbing to the guidance of his dark angel." There are, of course, more personal notes in these letters from time to time, concerning Tate's and Gordon's marital difficulties. However, the details are sketchy enough that there is practically no material for literary muckrakers. Maritain plays the role of peacemaker on occasion, but he has the wisdom to keep his interventions at a minimum. In March of 1957 Tate writes to thank him for his faithful support during the definitive breakup of the marriage. "Your letter has been like a beacon in the night—the compassion and charity which do not judge. I am deeply grateful, and send you all my love." Maritain's reply a few days later: "I was touched to the heart by your letter,—as I was also by my talk with Caroline. So deep a mutual love, and such suffering at the core of it!"

At the beginning of this essay I mentioned Maritain's vision of his home's becoming a *centre de rayonnement*, where writers and artists would encounter the reality of divine grace and its energizing possibilities for them. That vision reappeared in a more generalized form near the end of his life in the concept of the "little flocks of the laity," which he hoped would exert such a profound influence on modern culture. While the Tates were unable to continue to operate together along these lines after the 1950s, up until that point they had indeed fulfilled many of Maritain's cherished goals. That they continued to work toward them individually after their divorce is perhaps best evidenced in Caroline

---

[10]Jacques Maritain, *Le Paysan de la Garonne* (Paris: Desclée de Brouwer, 1966).

Gordon's plan to bequeath a portion of her papers to the Raïssa Maritain Library, run by the Sisters of the Sacred Heart. "One reason for leaving my stuff to the library at Stuart Hall is the chance that some earnest young writer may meet Mother Kirby or some of the other Sisters of the Sacred Heart and, consequently, have a little light thrown on his pathway....I hope the deposits will serve the purpose we both have at heart to lead people not of the faith to Raïssa who will, as you say, lead them to Christ."

To a whole generation of American Catholics, Jacques Maritain was *the* authoritative thinker and theologian (even though he persistently refused the latter role himself). The Maritains were even godparents to a considerable number of converts—American as well as French. His importance to both Allen Tate and Caroline Gordon was illustrative of the position he commanded in American religious and intellectual circles in the two decades following the Second World War.

Allen Tate, Caroline Gordon, and the Maritains devoted much of their careers to the renewal of modern culture in the West. A succinct expression of the essential hope for such a renewal is found in the following passage of Miss Gordon's letter to Maritain of May 7, 1954: "Allen is representing the United States at Mayor La Pira's Christian Congress in Florence. His speech will be largely his comments on your new book: 'It will be just the right thing,'" she quotes Tate as saying, "'for Jacques' theory of art boils down to the doctrine that Culture cannot survive without Revelation.'"

Part II
Habits of the Heart

Matthew J. Mancini

Maritain's American Illusions

Jacques Maritain never permitted his well-known affection for the United States to go too far. It was always a wary sort of attachment, hedged about with all manner of uncertainties and a keen sense of the possibilities for disenchantment. He was never a mere apologist, even though he sometimes gave the impression during his long period of residence on the American strand that he could scarcely believe his good fortune in finding himself among such a great and caring people. A careful reading of his works in which he comments on the United States reveals a caution well-grounded in both a philosophy of critical realism and a lifetime rich in pondered experience.

Yet in one way, at least, he tended toward an undue sanguinity in his assessment of American culture; and he did so in an area crucial to his interpretation of this nation's great potential destiny as a seed-ground for an integrally humanist social order. He seems, I would maintain, to have underestimated the centrifugal forces in American civilization, those tendencies that drive men and women toward isolation from one another and from society. He was laboring under certain illusions here, I believe, and so I have called my article "Maritain's American Illusions." I hope that the title does not sound contentious; but I do want it to seem, as it were, disputatious. For what I propose to do here is to set up the terms of an imaginary disputation, in the sense in which that term was described in the beautiful seventh chapter of Josef Pieper's *Guide to Thomas Aquinas*. In that chapter Pieper portrayed a model of disciplined argument animated by a profound spirit of mutual respect between the parties and motivated by a humble desire to discover a truth. With careful precision disputants strove to articulate the argument of the opposing party, so that a refutation was not a mere victory in a contest between sportsmen but a means by which a truth could be clarified.

In the present case I wish not to present a detailed script, but simply to establish the scenario for such a disputaion and to suggest the general direction of the argument; and I propose, as interlocutor in the discussion, a man named Alexis de Tocqueville, a compatriot of Maritainwho himself had acquired something of a reputation for commenting on American beliefs and practices. The *articulus*, or question at issue which I am proposing, is as follows: "Whether the Americans are Cartesian."

Few topics could be more central to an understanding of Maritain's career. If we may look upon that career as a positive effort to infuse Thomism into the anemic bloodstream of modern thought, we might also view it as, negatively, a struggle against the proliferation of errors whose origins can be traced to the spirit of Cartesian philosophy. That is, Maritain was as much an anti-Cartesian as he was a Thomist; and though it is certainly true that the two labels describe different aspects of the same reality, they do represent different perspectives on it. In this view the truly pivotal book in the Maritain canon is *Three Reformers: Luther-- Descartes--Rousseau*, in which his quarrel with Descartes is raised to a high level of articulation.

Yet as important as *Three Reformers* is, the true index of its centrality is the frequency with which Maritain returned to the anti-Cartesian theme in the half-century after its publication in 1925. Descartes, after all, had committed "the original sin of modern philosophy," Maritain had said;[1] and that is an assertion rich with implications about the seriousness of Maritain's concerns.

Three Reformers was brilliant, eccentric, irascible. In it Descartes emerged as a wilful man, almost intoxicated with his beautiful errors. Even though the tone of Maritain's opposition would soon show a penchant for gentle, ironic humor (in 1931 he referred to "my dear enemy René Descartes"[2]), the firm and consistent opposition persisted. There was no subject in Maritain's work that did not begin as an attempt to counteract the Cartesian error.

Just what was Descartes's terrible deed? It was to tear apart the fabric of human nature, thus creating two domains--that of the intellect, and that of *extension*, or the properties of bodies. Descartes had reasoned that,

---

[1] Jacques Maritain, *Three Reformers* (New York: Charles Scribner's Sons, 1929), 77.

[2] Jacques Maritain, "Religion and Culture," *Essays in Order*, trans. J.F. Scanlon (London: Sheed and Ward, 1931), 24.

since it is derived from a realm radically unlike that inhabited by the body, the mind cannot grasp certain knowledge of things as they truly are. All that one's intellect can grasp are appearances; and, were it not for his faith that God could not deceive him, he would despair of there being any congruence between what he thinks he knows and the nature of the extended bodies outside of him. Just as Marx after him, Descartes took the orthodox philosophy of his day and stood it on its head. In Marx's case, the orthodox philosophy was Hegelianism; in Descartes's it was the Scholastic teaching about angels.

Maritain's opposition to what he saw as the Cartesian derailment of modern thought was full of meaning for his encounter with America; for the United States, he averred in a well-known passage of *Reflections on America*, was the potential home of a new Christendom.[3] By a new Christendom he meant an integral humanism--as is clear from the full title of his work *Integral Humanism:Temporal and Spiritual Problems of a New Christendom*; and an integral humanism, a humanism of the incarnation, entailed a renewal of the human personality, its reconstruction in the wake of the Cartesian split.

Maritain labeled the Cartesian doctrine *angelism*. Angelism is a subject on which I need not elaborate here; but I would like to note, nonetheless, something about the historic legacy left by this modern form of idealism. What Descartes managed to accomplish was to give a kind of philosophic permission to Jean Jacques Rousseau, with his confused notion of how to build a state out of a collection of self-sufficient individuals, and his famous and monstrous compensatory myth of the General Will.

At the base of the manifold failures of the modern democracies, then, lies the great bourgeois myth of the self-sufficient individual pursuing his narrow self-interest. The errors of the modern democracies "correspond to the advent of the bourgeois class and ideology," Maritain wrote, and are "deadly to democracy";[4] and the true progenitor of the myth was the twenty-three-year-old René Descartes who had once found himself

---

[3]Jacques Maritain, *Reflections on America* (New York: Scribner's, 1958), 188.

[4]Jacques Maritain, *Christianity and Democracy*, trans. Doris C. Anson (London: Geoffrey Bles, 1945), 48.

"all day alone in a warm room," with, significantly, neither a companion nor a book, where he experienced the great revelation that, as he had put it, "I am...residing in my body, as a pilot in his ship." I will be the judge of thought for and by myself alone, Descartes had said; and he thus became the first example of what Herman Melville would call "*isolato*." "Over Descartesian vortices you hover," Ishmael learns from his self-absorbed reveries on the mast-head. "Heed it well, ye Pantheists!"[5]

Thus Maritain's famous antipathy to bourgeois individualism was of a piece with his fierce opposition to the Cartesian legacy. That aversion to the bourgeois was, in turn, linked to Maritain's perception of the United States. "You have no bourgeois," he asserted to what I imagine to have been a roomful of raised eyebrows at Chicago in 1956. "That is one of the blessings of this country."[6] The explanation he put forward for this absence of a bourgeois was that, while social classes do exist in the New World, they are not bound up with a sense of fatalism. A person born into such a class in the United States does not feel as if he will never leave it; it is not taken as his unchanging lot in life; but actually Maritain's assertion can be seen to emerge from deeper levels of social analysis. If bourgeois are Cartesian, they must be idealist; and, indeed, in excoriating bourgeois man in *Integral Humanism* Maritain wrote of his characteristic malady, "A whole idealist and nominalist metaphysic underlies his comportment. Hence, in the world created by him, the primacy of the sign: of opinion in political life, of money in economic life."[7]

Now, for Maritain could such charges legitimately be brought against the Americans? By no means! In fact, Maritain insisted, allegations that Americans are egocentric materialists are just an *old tag*, a fable belied by the actual good nature, generosity, concern for moral values, and respect for intellectual freedom that this remarkable people evinces. Those charges involve bourgeois characteristics; and America has no bourgeois; so clearly Americans could not have those characteristics.

Here I must emphasize the point I mentioned at the outset, that

---

[5]Herman Melville, *Moby Dick* (New York: Airmont Books, 1964), 142.

[6]Jacques Maritain, *Reflections on America*, 87.

[7]Jacques Maritain, *Integral Humanism: Temporal and Spiritual Problems of a New Christendom*, trans. Joseph W. Evans (New York: Scribner's, 1968), 78-79.

Maritain was no apologist. For him the absence of a European class structure was exhilarating to contemplate. Such a lack led him to speak of the American future with great hope--but with a warning as well. Americans need an *explicit philosophy* of democracy in the modern world, he continually asserted--or else they will one day awaken to find themselves simply defending capitalism.[8]

This need to be explicit is a major theme of Maritain's writings on democracy, which constantly uphold the vital Thomistic distinction between the individual and the person. If this and other distinctions are not maintained, the result must be an empty search for individual fulfillment.

> A time will come when people will give up in practice those values about which they no longer have an intellectual conviction. Hence we realize how necessary the function of a sound moral philosophy is in human society....
>
> These remarks apply to democracy in a particularly cogent way, for the foundations of a society of free men are essentially moral. There are a certain number of moral tenets--about the dignity of the human person, human rights, human equality, freedom, law, mutual respect and tolerance, the unity of mankind and the ideal of peace among men--on which democracy presupposes a common consent; without a general, firm, and reasoned-out conviction concerning such tenets, democracy cannot survive.[9]

To summarize Maritain's thoughts, then, about the possible Cartesian nature of Americans: Descartes is the progenitor of bourgeois habits of thought; he gave rise to Rousseau, whose myth of Democratism perverted democracy at the moment of its modern formulation; Descartes tore human nature apart; and, as a consequence, a re-integration of the human personality has become the task of philosophy and must be the goal of a new kind of democracy--an integrally human democracy; Americans, however, are not bourgeois; moreover, though they too suffer from these Cartesian mistakes which have become the world's

---

[8]Jacques Maritain, *Reflections on America*, 29-42.
[9]Jacques Maritain, *On the Use of Philosophy* (Princeton: Princeton University Press, 1961), 12.

inheritance, the United States is the place most promising for the development of such an integrally humanist society.

The conclusion is there for anyone to draw: The Americans are not Cartesian.

Here I must stress that the premises, or steps, in the argument are Maritain's, but the conclusion is mine. It is an inference I drew from the foregoing evidence.

The question whether the Americans could develop an explicit philosophy is, if anything, more urgent today than it was a quarter of a century ago, when Maritain wrote the words just quoted above. It is also a more highly visible problem today than it was then. The recent book by Robert Bellah and his collaborators, *Habits of the Heart*, is just one of the contemporary examples of the concern. That book's little title comes from Tocqueville, a man who had his own opinion about the prospects for an explicit American philosophy.

In *Democracy in America* he wrote: "I think that in no country in the civilized world is less attention paid to philosophy than in the United States."

> The Americans have no philosophical school of their own; and they care but little for all the schools into which Europe is divided, the very names of which are scarcely known to them. Yet it is easy to perceive that almost all the inhabitants of the United States use their minds in the same manner, and direct them according to the same rules; that is to say, without ever having taken the trouble to define the rules, they have a philosophical method common to the whole people....But if I go further and seek among these characteristics the principal one, which includes almost all the rest, I discover that in most of the operations of the mind each American appeals only to the individual effort of his own under standing.
>
> America is therefore one of the countries where the precepts of Descartes are least studied and are best applied.[10]

So we find Tocqueville not only giving Maritain's urgings for an

---

[10]Alexis de Tocqueville, *Democracy in America*, ed. Phillips Bradley (New York: Vintage, 1945), Vol. 2, 3-4.

explicit philosophy for the Americans but also his dubbing Americans the world's leading Cartesians! What a dreary thought for anyone even remotely sympathetic to Maritain's concerns! How could Tocqueville be so at odds with Maritain on the question? Perhaps it is simply because the two were writing a century apart. To be sure, this imaginary disputation, this thought-experiment, is ahistorical. The burgeoning agricultural, tumultuously egalitarian society that Tocqueville visited in 1832 was enormously distant in social, economic, and even political terms from the nation Maritain surveyed in depression, war, and cold war in the twentieth century. Yet this point having been conceded, it remains that the American past forged the pressent, and this is as true of the Jacksonian years, during which Tocqueville had visited the United States, as of any other, with the possible exception of the Federalist era. Moreover, the uncanny relevance of Tocqueville's writings to our modern condition is a characteristic so striking that no commentator seems able to refrain from remarking about it. Nor would I.

The mystery deepens when it becomes clear that Tocqueville and Maritain were many times in agreement. For instance, both were astounded at the accommodation between religion and democracy that the Americans had effected. In the first quarter of the twentieth century, the French church was the enemy of republicanism, and both republicans and churchmen knew it. "What the ecclesiastical history of this century shows above all," writes Theodore Zeldin, "is a crisis of communication: churchmen and free-thinkers were so carried away by the bitterness of their disagreements that they became confused as to what their quarrels were about."[11] In short, no intellectual tradition linked French Catholics with the secular, rationalist roots of French democracy. It would be Maritain who, more than anyone, forged those links.

For Tocqueville, reared as he had been, in the aristocratic atmosphere of antagonism between religion and democracy, the discovery in America of harmony between the two was a revelation and, in fact, one of the most important sources of fascination for him. In Europe, he says, religion is "entangled with those institutions which democracy de-

---

[11]Theodore Zeldin, *Intellect, Taste and Anxiety*, Vol. 2 of *France 1848-1945* (Oxford: The Clarendon Press, 1977), 983.

stroys."[12] "What has always most struck me in my country, especially of late years," he wrote to Gobineau in 1836, "has been to see ranged on one side men who value morality, religion, and order, and on the other those who love liberty and legal equality. To me this is as extraordinary as it is deplorable....Men can only be great and happy when they are combined."[13] Such a conjunction, however, was precisely what he had perceived in America, where, as he said in *Democracy in America,* "the *spirit of religion* and the *spirit of liberty* are as one."[14] Those words are recognizably Maritainian in spirit.

Of course, when it comes to the point of our discussion, the Americans' characteristic approach to thought and feeling--their "habits of the heart"--one finds the path of close agreement between Maritain and Tocqueville diverging into different roads. "Who does not perceive," wrote Alexis de Tocqueville, "that Luther, Descartes, and [no--it is not Rousseau; that would be too fortunate a conjunction!] Voltaire employed the same method, and that they differed only in the greater or less use which they professed should be made of it?"[15] Yet this apparent agreement with Tocqueville was something which Maritain allowed to slip out of his grasp. For instance, he saw clearly enough the loneliness of Americans. "In the midst of general kindness and the busiest social life," Maritain observed, "it is not rare to find in individuals a feeling of loneliness"; but rather than follow up on the insight, he allowed it to fade. "This is a point I only submit. I don't know, but it seems to me that there is something there."[16]

There is, indeed, something there. Tocqueville saw it, and feared it, and expressed it in grim and famous words: "Thus not only does democracy make every man forget his ancestors, but it hides his descendants and separates his contemporaries from him; it throws him back

---

[12] Alexis de Tocqueville, *Democracy in America,* Vol. 1, 12.

[13] Quoted in Joachim Wach, "The Role of Religion in the Social Philosophy of Alexis de Tocqueville," *Journal of the History of Ideas* 7 (January 1947): 76.

[14] Alexis de Tocqueville, *Democracy in America,* Vol. 1, 45.

[15] *Ibid.,* Vol. 2, 5.

[16] Jacques Maritain, *Reflections on America,* 70.

forever upon himself alone and threatens in the end to confine him entirely within the solitude of his own heart."[17]

Upon close investigation, one can scarcely fail to notice that the characteristics which Tocqueville ascribes to Americans are almost exactly the same as those Maritain ascribes to Descartes in the searing pages of *Three Reformers*. It should be clear, from the title of this article, at least, that my own conclusion on the question is close to Tocqueville's; but the question remains, as it should, an open one; and it cannot be answered merely by citing Robert Bellah or Christopher Lasch, as probing and wise as their own analyses have been.

One further question remains. What explains Maritain's illusion, if, indeed, we are justified in calling it so? I can only suggest an approach to the question. During the Second World War, Maritain's political involvements reached a new level of intensity. Just as intellectuals everywhere among Allied nations, he was convinced that only a postwar society committed to social justice could begin to redeem the suffering of the world's peoples. At the same time, the war years were the time of Maritain's enforced exile in the United States. Here he was presented daily with acts of generosity, with kindnesses small and large. Moreover, he naturally contrasted Americans to his own people--a people who, he thought, were more individualistic than Americans. Perhaps these two factors--his enforced exile and the intensification of his call for integrally human democracy--worked synergistically. America became for him (though only potentially, and with many qualifications) the seedbed of an integrally human, rather than a bourgeois, form of democracy. Like European intellectuals since the Renaissance, then--like Montaigne, like Locke, like Tocqueville himself--Jacques Maritain could not keep from projecting his own best hopes onto the New World.

---

[17]Alexis de Tocqueville, *Democracy in America*, Vol. 2, 106.

Bernard Doering

The Philosophy of Work and the Future of Civilization: Maritain, Weil and Simon

In this paper devoted to Philosophy and the Future of Civilization, it may not be without some merit to reflect for a few moments on the philosophy of work and the future of civilization. Most people spend the great majority of the waking hours of their lives at work. The kind of work they do during these many hours and the attitudes they take toward that work impact profoundly on their development as persons, on the solidity of their sense of self and on the nature of the culture they produce in common. Not long ago Robert Bellah and a group of his colleagues, in a fascinating but deeply disturbing book called *Habits of the Heart: Individualism and Commitment in American Life,*[1] drew a very disquieting portrait of what Christopher Lasch, in a review, called that "beleaguered, empty and minimal self," produced by contemporary American culture, a self that "retains only a tenuous grip on its surroundings and on its own identity."[2] Is it possible that this beleaguered, empty, minimal self has some relation to a rather generalized attitude toward work in American society today?

Three contemporary philosophers--Jacques Maritain, Yves R. Simon and Simone Weil--who either knew one another and the work they produced, or who shared a very intimate friendship, recognized the impact of a philosophy of work on the development of the individual human personality and the culture or civilization produced by a commu-

---

[1] Robert Bellah, *Habits of the Heart: Individualism and Commitment in American Life* (Berkeley: University of California Press, 1985).

[2] For a more extensive critique of such a view of the self see Christopher Lasch's *The Culture of Narcissism* (New York: Norton), 1978.

nity of persons. I would like to reflect for a few moments on what seem to me to be fundamental ideas concerning work and civilization which Maritain expressed only indirectly and by implication in his essay "Exister avec le Peuple," in his book *Reflections on America*[3] and in his very last essay, which he finished the night before he died, "A Society without Money," ideas which Yves R. Simon developed fully and explicitly in essays which were collected and edited by Vucan Kuic in 1971 in the book *Work, Society and Culture*,[4] and which Simone Weil treated at length in her books *La Condition Ouvrière*[5] and *Réflections sur les Causes de la Liberté et de l'Oppression Sociale*.[6] In April 1937 Maritain published an article *"Con el Pueblo"* in the Spanish periodical *Sur*. He felt that the miserable and hopeless plight of the dispossessed proletariat was more evident at that time in Spain than in any other country of the West. In June the French periodical *Sept* published this article under the title *"Exister avec le peuple"* along with others by François Mauriac and Etienne Borne, in a special issue devoted to the working classes. All of the contributors to the issue were of bourgeois origin and none of them had any immediate experience of proletarian existence. Mauriac's article was filled with passionate indignation over the injustices imposed on the proletariat by the rapacious bourgeois and with an anguished sense of responsibility, incurred by his belonging to the *guilty class*. Borne's article was full of exultation that the day of retribution had arrived and that nothing could stop the march of the proletariat toward the vindication of their rights; but for all the expressions of sympathy, solidarity and enthusiasm, it is not difficult to detect what a reviewer in *Esprit* called

> a certain manner of speaking which certainly does not touch the
> profound realities involved but which, in a way that Catholics who

---

[3]Jacques Maritain, *Reflections on America* (Garden City, NY: Doubleday, 1958).

[4]Yves R. Simon, *Work, Society and Culture,* ed. Vukan Kuic (New York: Fordham University Press, 1989).

[5]Simone Weil, *La Condition Ouvrière* (Paris: Gallimard, 1951).

[6]Simone Weil, *Réflexions sur les Causes de la Liberté et de l'Oppression Sociale* (Paris: Gallimard, 1955).

live in a closed social milieu hardly realize, grates on the ears of those they wish and ought to win over.[7]

Maritain's "Exister avec le Peuple," however, was exceptional in that the author seemed to have been able vicariously to identify himself completely with a class to which he did not belong. It was perhaps his long and intimate association with Léon Bloy and Charles Péguy which made him capable of such an identification. He insisted that what was needed to win the working classes was not a *love of benevolence* but a *love of unity*, a love born of "co-naturality" (as he would put it), of communion and compassion, in the real sense of those words.

> If we love that living and human thing which we call the people, a difficult thing to define, I realize, as are all living and human things, but which is all the more real for that very reason, we will wish first and foremost to exist with them, to suffer and to remain in communion with them.
> Before 'doing good' to them, and working for their benefit, before practicing the politics of one group or another,... we must first choose to exist with them and to suffer with them, to make their pain and their destiny our own.[8]

Maritain looked on the people as "the great resevoir of vital spontaneity and nonphariseeism...the reservoir of a new civilization." I do not know whether or not Jacques Maritain ever met Simone Weil in person. They did exchange two letters, I believe. It is hard to imagine that he was ignorant of what she was doing and writing in the early thirties, that is, in the years preceding his publication of "Exister avec le Peuple." If Maritain, as a member of the bourgeois class, was able in a very special way to *exist* vicariously with the working classes, Simone Weil, another member of French bourgeois society, was able to exist with them in actuality and in fact. We all know how this fervent and fragile young woman, this eminently impractical intellectual, in order to understand the plight of the worker, actually became one, how she took a painful and

---

[7]*Esprit*, Mar. 1, 1937, 935f.

[8]Jacques Maritain, *Raison et Raisons* (Paris: Egloff, 1947), 239-240 passim.

difficult job in a factory working before a huge furnace that belched fire from five holes, how she insisted on associating with the other workers, joining them for lunch in their bistros, accompanying them to the cinema, participating in their *fêtes populaires*, asking them to invite her into their homes, and dressing more simply than their wives; how she resolved to live on the income of the poorest workers and eat only what they ate, limiting herself at one time to five francs a day because that was the allotment passed out to the workers on strike in Puy, a practice which contributed to her poor health and eventually to her untimely death.

In "Exister avec le Peuple," Maritain tried to define the nebulous and equivocal term "people." He was careful, first of all, to distinguish *people* from *class*. It is rather, he said,

> a community of the under-privileged...centered around manual work, characterized by a certain historical patrimony...of suffering, of effort and of hope...by a certain way of understanding and living out poverty, suffering and pain...by a certain way of being always the same ones who get themselves killed.[9]

The people, he maintained, cannot be equated with the *plebs* or *populus* of antiquity, particularly since Christianity added to it "the idea of the little people of God," "the poor to whom the beatitudes are promised." The nineteenth century had seen take place in the people, claimed Maritain, "a recognition...of the dignity of the human person in the worker as such," and the twentieth century had seen the people develop "the consciousness of a personality in a state of becoming, the condition necessary for the future flowering of a personalist democracy." He felt that Marx, in his obsession with the economic structure of society, was wrong to identify a class (the proletariat) with *the people*, having the former include the latter. Maritain considered this an unnatural inclusion, since for him only the broader concept of *the people*, not that of *class*, "is possessed of a primordial social value on a genuinely human level."[10] Maritain lists some of the characteristics of the group he calls *the people*. They have no inheritance other than their lowly status, they are con-

---

[9]Jacques Maritain, *Raison et Raisons*, 241-242 passim.
[10]*Ibid.*, 243.

demned to a condition of poverty (a condition, remarks Maritain, that was shared by many middle-class people of the thirties) and they subsist in a state of servitude and oppression.[11]

Simone Weil and Yves R. Simon both attributed the same characteristics to the working class, but they did not find it necessary to distinguish between the people and the proletariat. Weil wrote that a whole generation of workers throughout the world is trapped in a life that does no more than vegetate, a generation that has become acutely conscious of the fact that it has no future, that it has no place in the universe. "We live in a time," she said, "that has no future. The expectation of what is to come is filled, not with hope, but with anguish."[12] In an article entitled "Condition Prèmiere d'un Travail non Servile," she wrote:

> Every condition in which the worker finds himself of necessity on the last day of a period of a month, a year, or twenty years of effort as he found himself on the first day is a kind of slavery. And the reason for this is the impossibility for him of aspiring toward anything other than what he has or of orienting his efforts toward the acquisition of a good. His effort is directed solely toward staying alive.[13]

It is this slavery of condition, according to Yves R. Simon, which turns Maritain's *people* or the *working class* into the *proletariat*. Just as Simone Weil, he felt that if a wage-earner has no reasonable hope of escaping from his condition, even after twenty years of effort and even though he has the desire and capability of escaping, then, whether or not he is poor, he is a member of an enslaved proletariat. "This unique sociological entity appears," writes Simon, "only when the position of wage-erners becomes historically solidified in the economic system."[14] For Simon, poverty is not necessarily implied in the proletarian condition, as it seems to be for Maritain; however, subjection and exploitation are.

This subjection or enslavement, and the exploitation that accompa-

---

[11]*Ibid.*

[12]Simone Weil, *Reflexions sur les Causes de la Liberté et de l'Oppression Sociale* (Paris: Gallimard, 1955), 10f.

[13]*Ibid.*, 262.

[14]Yves R. Simon, *Work Society and Culture*, 100ff.

nies it, is not due solely for either Weil or Simon to the fact that the proletarian and his children have no hope of rising above their condition. It is due also to the very nature of the system in which he is trapped. Simon wrote:

> The proletarians as a social class are defined by their position in the system of exchange and distribution known as the free market. Because labor in this system is a commodity bought and sold in the market, the working man becomes a sort of unit of exchange, and the community of the working people, as if by an enormous accident, becomes a distinct social class which, deprived of a functional share in the common good, develops a strong tendency toward secession.[15]

Since the central institution of the *laissez-faire* system is the free market where labor is just another item of merchandise, the sale and the price of which are determined by the so-called law of supply and demand, it is not surprising that a fundamental operating principle of the system is to keep labor lean and hungry. Both Maritain and Simon spent a good number of their most productive years at the same time in America. Maritain came here for the first time in 1933, returned regularly for lecture tours, and, with the fall of France in 1940, came to live in the United States, where, with the exception of the few years he spent in Rome as French Ambassador to the Vatican, he remained until his wife Raïssa's death in 1960. Simon lived and worked in the United States from 1938 until his death in 1961. Both were astounded by and expressed their enthusiasm for what they found here. In 1958, in his *Reflections on America*, Maritain expressed his admiration for a society which was for the most part classless and in which he saw the beginnings, but only the beginnings, of the ideal society he envisaged in his *Humanisme Intégral*.[16] Simon shared Maritain's admiration. He wrote:

> My friend Jacques Maritain, who is not a social observer by vocation, has written in his books on the United States that, generally speaking, there is no bourgeoisie in this country. The tendency to ape

---

[15]*Ibid.*, 104.
[16]Jacques Maritain, *Reflections on America*, 51, 58-65.

the aristocracy in its capacity of leisure class appears here in the sort of person whom we call a *parvenu*, an upstart. In whatever may be called the real upper class in America, with the exception of an older and comparatively small section, there is no such tendency. The urge to conspicuous leisure is distinctly not American. Now, I think Maritain is right...The European middle-class attitudes, even today include a certain undervaluation of work, an inclination to dissociate work and culture and to set them in opposition to each other, and thus to consider freedom from work a praiseworthy evidence that the primary condition for culture has been realized....This is not a typical American outlook....The life of work and the life of culture are not so sharply separated. This means, all things considered, that there is no classical society in America, and perhaps there really never was one. Here, work has never been held in contempt or in irreconcilable opposition to culture. And that is also in part the reason why a distinct proletarian class has never come into being here.[17]

Simone Weil had no firsthand, intimate knowledge of life in America and perhaps shared some of the typical Old World prejudices which writers like Georges Duhamel and André Siegfried expressed concerning the brash, aggressive and shallow upstart civilization they found there. However, she felt it indispensable to try to describe, even in the vaguest of terms, the kind of civilization that might be considered desirable for the future, just as Maritain had tried to do in *Humanise Intégral* and in "A Society without Money." The center of this new civilization, she wrote, would be manual work:

> ...The most fully human civilization will be one which has manual work for its center, one in which manual work constitutes the supreme value. It has nothing to do with that religion of production which reigned in America during the period of prosperity, or which reigns in Russia since the start of the five year plan; for this religion has as its true object, not the worker, but the products of his work, that is, things not man. It is not because of its relationship with what is produced that manual work ought to become the highest value,

---

[17] Yves R. Simon, *Work Society and Culture*, 149ff.

but because of its relationship with the man who does the work; [manual work is] what each human being needs most essentially so that his life of itself may take on a meaning and a value in his own eyes....In our time what a marvelous fullness of life could we not expect of a civilization in which work would be so transformed as to exercise fully all human faculties and constitute the human act *par excellence*. It must, then, be found at the very center of culture.[18]

Though, in this particular text, Weil does not include intellectual activities in her concept of work, as Maritain and Simon are always careful to do, she does not exclude them. Elsewhere she bemoans "that degrading division of work into manual work and intellectual work which is the basis of our culture.[19] All three, however, describe, either indirectly and by implication, or directly and explicitly, the characteristics of that *work* which will be the foundation and center of the new culture. The first characteristic of work is that it is a blessing, not a curse. This "human act *par excellence*" ennobles man, civilizes him, liberates him, and at the same time, draws him into a community of persons. Weil expressly rejects that "ancient and hopeless curse of Genesis which painted the world as a hard labor camp and work as the mark of man's baseness and slavery." Instead she goes so far as to maintain that "the notion of work considered as a human value is without any doubt the sole spiritual conquest that human thought has made since the miracle of Greece."[20]

In Maritain's utopia, his "Society without Money," each qualifying individual would be required to work half the day, (four hours), either manually or intellectually, in the profession or trade of his choice in order to assure a free income at a common basic level consonant with his dignity as a person. This work Maritain called *requêtes de base* (basic requirements). The other half of the day people would still have to work, as it pleased them to do so, however, in what Maritain called *expansion de surcroît*, a term which I have translated as "life enhancement activities."[21]

---

[18]Simone Weil, *Réflexions sur les Causes de la Liberté et de l'Oppression Sociale*, 118ff.

[19]*Ibid.*, 16.

[20]*Ibid.*, 122.

[21]Jacques Maritain, "Une Société sans Argent," *Cahiers Jacques Mari-*

It is interesting that Scott Nearing, who died recently, made the same distinction in his book *Living the Good Life*. Anyone was welcome in the little community he founded, but in exchange for the necessities and comforts offered by the community, each member or visitor had to provide one half day of what Nearing called "bread labor."[22] What is important for our present consideration is that Maritain makes no distinction between the kinds of work done during the two halves of the work day, as if the activities done as *basic requirements* were the *dirty work*, the effects of the biblical curse, and the *life enhancement activities* were nothing but play and recreation. In his "Society without Money," Maritain says, an intellectual who spends his mornings in his books or in teaching may choose vegetable gardening or cabinetmaking for his *life enhancement activity*; a bricklayer may want to spend his afternoons reading, painting, or playing music. In fact someone may decide to spend the whole day in the same work. In other words, all work can be *life-enhancing*, and the very concept of work loses the connotation of punishment.

In 1947, the same year that Maritain published his *Reflections on America*, Yves R. Simon, as his contribution to a symposium on work, delivered an address entitled, "The Concept of Work,"[23] in which he made exactly the same distinction that Maritain made in 1973 in "A Society without Money." I would suggest that Maritain borrowed the distinction directly from his friend. Simon had made this distinction as early as 1940 in an article in the *Review of Politics* entitled "Work and Workman: A Philosophical and Sociological Inquiry"[24] where he gave specific examples of what he called "activities of legal fulfillment" and "activities of free development."

I cultivate my garden to produce vegetables for my family: legal fulfillment. I cultivate my garden because I find, in doing so, an interesting and agreeable exercise: free expansion. A young girl practices piano two hours a day, according to the program imposed

---

Vol. 4-5, November, 1982, 68 and 70 (an English version appeared in the *Review of Social Economy*, XLIII, April, 1985).

[22]Scott Nearing, *Living the Good Life* (New York: 1970), 42ff.

[23]Published in *The Works of the Mind* (Chicago: University of Chicago Press, 1966).

[24]Vol. 2, 1, 63-86.

on her by her mother: legal fulfillment. She sits down at the piano to play a tune she loves: free expansion.[25]

Here Simone Weil ran up against a problem. Certain types of work, by their very nature, involve a high degree of effort, stress, or even physical pain, for example, the work done in steel mills and coal mines. How can the constraint, the coercion, the irksomeness and above all the pain associated with many forms of work, especially the work of *basic requirements*, *bread labor*, or *legal fulfillment*, be reconciled with the free development and expansion of the human personality that is supposed to be the result of this "human act *par excellence* "?

Work [wrote Weil] can be painful (even very painful) in two ways. Pain can be felt as a part of the victorious conquest over matter and over oneself, or as part of a degrading slavery. (There are intermediate stages, of course.) Why the difference? A difference in salary is surely involved, it seems to me. But the essential factor is certainly the very nature of the pain. This is a question that merits serious study in order to arrive at some very clear distinctions, and, if possible, classification.[26]

Yves R. Simon tried to make such distinctions. He noted that work is by its essence a serious activity, not only because it is something that has to be done in order that man may live (producing food), or that he may live in a way consonant with his dignity (cleaning sewers and disposing of waste), but also because it has to be done in a way which is largely predetermined, that is, according to laws of its own (the laws of hydrodynamics, gravity, or mechanics). Work is done then, not only to fulfill personal needs and certain social obligations, but also in consonance with or in fulfillment of certain natural laws—that is, laws considered not as statutes, but laws considered in the broadest possible sense (hence his use of the term "legal"). Though he admits that work does not necessarily have to be irksome, nevertheless he is careful to insist that, since work is an activity invariably govemed to a large extent by laws which the worker has no power to change, it must be acknowledged "that

---

[25]Yves R. Simon, *Work, Society and Culture*, 25.
[26]SimonWeil, *La Condition Ouvrière* (Paris: Gallimard), 1951.

there exists in work a permanent foundation for irksomeness." Simon rejects the use of the words "compulsion" or "constraint" which some writers use to describe this irksome aspect of work; the term he prefers is the one he invented: activities of "legal fulfillment." He feels that this term refutes the millenial utopianism of Marx and Engels, who, together with Fourier, "seem actually to expect that under certain specified social circumstances the very irksomeness of work will completely wither away and that work will no longer be work."[27] In other words, for Marx and Engels, work is not an activity of legal fulfillment, compulsion or constraint, but rather an activity of free development. Maritain, Weil, and Simon all reject this illusion.

Simon affirms categorically that "work is not, and can never be, an activity of free development."[28] In this very categorical statement, I do not think Simon is saying that work done in "legal fulfillment" can never be satisfying or contribute to the "free development," the expansion or the enhancement of the worker as a person. Simon, as a philosopher, is making a purely formal distinction. Work is a human act, the human act *par excellence*, says Weil. Every human act to be truly human must be informed by an intention; and the same human act, materially considered, can be formally either good or bad according to the intention that motivates it, and this is a very real distinction which applies to the human act of work. Simon gives a specific example of what he means. He wrote:

> ...Scientists...spend a good deal of their time working—that is, in activities of legal fulfillment. Scientific research...is such an activity—it is definitely work. But should we say that the scientist doing pure research is being "constrained"? This sounds rather awkward. Yet, if he is thought to be free of any constraint, is he still working?

Simon answers *no* to his first question and *yes* to the second because he defines work not as any kind of *compulsion* but as an activity of "legal fulfillment," a terrn which he feels gets him off any semantic hooks.[29] He cites the famous rocket-builder Wernher von Braun who said: "Basic research is when I am doing what I don't know what I am doing." Von

---

[27] Yves R. Simon, *Work, Society and Culture*, 31.
[28] *Ibid.*
[29] *Ibid.*, 23-32 passim.

Braun was not under any compulsion to choose scientific research as his avocation, and he was perfectly free to follow the direction of his research wherever it led him; yet, because he was under contract to NASA and was paid for his research, and because he did his research in conformity to and in fulfillment of the natural laws that govern bodies in motion, his research cannot be considered as an activity of free development, according to Simon, even if he would have done exactly the same thing for his own enjoyment without any contract or remuneration.

This is, I suppose, a very necessary distinction. However, I find it difficult to see how a human activity must be considered one of legal fulfillment simply because, as Simon puts it, "things have to be done according to laws of their own...(it does not matter whether these laws are recognized in theory or just empirically). In all cases, man while working deals with things according to their own laws."[30] So the compulsion, coercion, irksomeness, or legal obligation comes not only from without (social obligation) but also from within (a natural law). Simon distinguishes between himself who toiled at philosophy in order to support his family and Pascal's *honnête homme,* a seventeenth century gentleman of leisure and culture, who, when he philosophized, did not have to toil at it, but did so with ease and grace purely for his own enjoyment; but if all actions that "have to be done according to laws of their own" are by that very fact excluded from activities of free development, then the leisurely philosophizing of Pascal's *honnête homme* must be an activity of legal fulfillment too because he was just as much bound by the laws of logic and the principles of identity and contradiction as was Simon himself. Antoine-Laurent de Lavoisier, the eighteenth century French gentleman of leisure, in his research on the combustion of air, was just as much bound by the laws of the composition of matter as von Braun was in his research by the laws governing bodies in motion. Simon's little girl who, as an activity of free development, sits down to play a song she loves is constrained to respect the laws of rhythm and harmony. I can readily see how any activity becomes one of *legal fulfillment* as soon as an obligation is imposed from without, either by society as a whole or by an individual, or is imposed from within by the purpose or end for the fulfillment of which the activity is undertaken ("I do something I have to do in order to..."); but I find it difficult to see how

---

[30]*Ibid.,* 31ff.

an obligation imposed by a natural law residing in the thing or the matter which is the focus of the activity necessarily excludes that activity from the classification of "free expansion."

It may be precious distinctions like this that lead laymen to look on professional philosophers (and amateur philosophers like me) with condescending smiles. All this mountainous labor of distinction then has produced, not a mental mole, I hope, but the important point that work in itself is a blessing, not a curse. One man's work is another man's leisure. Any activity of itself can be a *life-enhancing* activity of *free development* and whatever constraint, irksomeness, or pain is involved, if freely and lovingly accepted, can be the occasion, as Weil says, of a "victorious conquest over matter and over oneself."[31] The French poet Theophile Gautier tells the artist:

> *Lutte avec le carrare*
> *Avec le paros dur*
> *et rare*
> *Guardiens du contour pur*

(Struggle with the carrara, with the paros hard and rare, guardians of the pure line). "By the sweat of thy brow [it is written] thou shalt eat bread." Well, maybe so. But it was in sorrow and in pain that Flaubert brought forth his *Madame Bovary*, by the sweat of his brow Michelangelo carved his *David*, and by the sweat of my brow I grow flowers and vegetables. Who would wish it otherwise?

Another characteristic of work is that it is a social activity which draws man into a community of persons. Yves R. Simon calls this the primary and most salient feature of work.

> In regard to work, [he wrote] I myself insist, first of all, that it cannot be fully defined without reference to society; an intelligible definition of work must have a social component.[32]

Simone Weil waxes lyrical over this social component of work. The highest degree of happiness will be found, she wrote, in

---

[31]Simone Weil, *La Condition Ouvrière*, 122.
[32]Yves R. Simon, *Work, Society and Culture*, 31.

... a life passed freely in a community of free people and consecrated entirely to a painful and dangerous physical labor, but carried out in the midst of fraternal cooperation.[33]

For Simon this social component is based on more than a sense of solidarity among those who labor and suffer together. In America he found

...an historic and history-making striving toward a culture which is to be something serious, something marked by the same earnestness that presides over the life of work....American society is dominated, at least in its more valuable segments, by the psychology of the worker—that is, by a fundamental disposition characteristic of people who do something socially useful and who are dedicated to serious life.[34]

Attributing this psychology of the worker to the Puritan work ethic Simon calls a perfect example of the abuse of a key idea in the explanation of history. Social utility, he says, is a metaphysical characteristic of work and is part of our philosophical understanding of work as a human activity. This is so because work by its very nature is never a terminal activity but always leads to something else;[35] it is directed primarily toward the transformation of physical nature for the good of man;[36] and what Simon means by *man* in this context is not an atomized individual, but man in the generic sense, that is, society as a whole.

Simon recognizes the difficulties and limitations arising from a too literal and absolute identification of work with the *useful* exploitation of *physical* nature for the *purposes of man*.[37] Such an interpretation would leave no ground to justify the activity of contemplatives, philosophers, pure scientists, or even politicians. Such activity has no place in "bour-

---

[33]Simone Weil, *Réflexions sur les Causes de la Liberté et de l'Oppression Sociale*, 123.
[34]Yves R. Simon, *Work, Society and Culture*, 113.
[35]*Ibid.*, 109.
[36]*Ibid.*, 113.
[37]*Ibid.*, 45.

geois industrialist liberal society with all its emphasis on individualism and private rights" [says Simon][38] or in contemporary philosophy, because neither recognizes "the goodness of things that have nothing to do with social utility."

> Contemplative life can easily be justified in Aristotle's philosophy, because he has an idea of the good that is not merely useful but is better than useful, because it is desirable in itself, because it is an end in itself.[39]

Yet, Aristotle does judge the citizen according to his contribution to the common good.[40] For Simon it is clear that

> ...one cannot be alive and active, healthy, trained, educated and protected, at least most of the time, without incurring some sort of obligation to society, the proper repayment of which might well be in activities that are socially useful. In the ethic of the worker, this proposition has the rank of the first principle.[41]

What is the consequence of this first principle? asks Simon. The consequence is another essential characteristic of work. To be a truly human and humanizing activity, work must have as its object, as its purpose, not profit, not self-aggrandizement, but service. The subordination of profit to service is the proper, the civilized relationship.

> ...the real wealth produced by work is above all destined to serve [wrote Simon]; profit is but a counterpart of service, a result annexed to the essential product of labor activity.[42]

Weil bemoans the reversal of the roles of service and profit in modern culture.

---

[38]*Ibid.*, 44.
[39]*Ibid.*, 55.
[40]*Ibid.*, 54.
[41]*Ibid.*, 42.
[42]*Ibid.*, 121.

[This] reversal consists in the fact that signs..., money and symbol of credit in economic life, take on the function of realities of which the real things [services] become the mere shadows.[43]

This concept of the priority of service requires an understanding of human nature and of what is good for man, an understanding of the difference between genuine and illusory human needs. The sole purpose of the market place is not to give the public what it wants: bread and circuses, even if that is all it wants. Weil insists that only those things should be produced which are needed for human consumption, and among them she includes the useful and the agreeable, provided, of course, that there is question of true usefulness and pure pleasure.[44] A solution to the problem of work and wealth, service and profit depends on the recognition of what many economists, according to Simon, want to leave out of the picture altogether, namely, the possibility of a discrepancy between human desire and genuine human need.[45]

This concept of service brings us to a final essential characteristic of work: *Arbeit macht frei*, work shall make you free. Despite its cynical placement in crooked letters above the entrance to the Auschwitz death camp, this ancient dictum announces a profound and important truth ; but it is only true work, Weil's human activity *par excellence*, not servile work or slave labor, that liberates man. Subjection and exploitation, as we have seen, and not poverty, are the essential characteristics of that work which enslaves the proletariat. For both Weil and Simon, work liberates man only to the degree that intelligent choice enters into his work, intelligent choice with regard to the *kind* of work he does, the conditions under which he works, and the *end product* of his labor. Maritain praises the American labor unions, as he knew them, for their role in beginning the immense and difficult task of humanizing the industrial capitalist regime.[46] Their efforts toward the reform of the conditions of labor, particularly in the area of compensation, enabled the worker to put aside

---

[43]Simone Weil, *Réflexions sur les Causes de la Liberté et de l'Oppression Sociale*, 130.

[44]Simone Weil, *La Condition Ouvrière*, 234.

[45]Yves R. Simon, *Work, Society and Culture*, 124.

[46]Jacques Maritain, *Reflections on America*, 58ff.

enough in savings to enable him to choose another kind of work, if he so desired. For Weil and Simon, and also for Pope John Paul II, this intelligent choice must extend as well to the organization and management and to the *end product* of his work.

> ...It is necessary [wrote Weil] that the worker keep ever present in his mind the directing conception of the work he is carrying out, in such a way as to be able to apply it intelligently to continually changing particular situations...It is necessary also that all the notions made use of in the course of work be clear enough that the worker can recall them in their entirety in the blink of an eye.[47]

Weil reproached the present industrial system with subjecting workers

> ...in growing numbers and to an ever greater degree to a form of work which permits them to carry out the necessary gestures with no idea of their connection with the final result.[48]

The less workers have the possibility of such intelligent choices, the more they have the sense that their destiny is predetermined and that they are no longer in control of their lives. Simon finds a philosophical basis for the necessity of intelligent choice in the workplace in Aristotle's definition of art. Noting that Aristotle obviously refused to include the skills of the artisans of the Acropolis in his definition of art because of the contempt with which manual labor was looked upon in his society, Simon maintains that work, as well as art,

> ...is the ability to perform operations relative to the things to be made....In so far as a skill is an art, it comprises a grasp of the relation between the means and the end; art [or work] thus involves an apprehension of universal necessities 'in a true course of reasoning.'[49]

---

[47]Simone Weil, *Réflexions sue les Causes de la Liberté et de l'Oppression Sociale*, 103.

[48]*Ibid.*, 127.

[49]Yves R. Simon, *Work, Society and Culture*, 147ff.

Paradoxically, for Weil one of the sources of freedom in work is, as has been pointed out, a conscious and loving submission to the laws of the universe by which the worker achieves a victorious conquest over matter and over himself.[50] She says that Francis Bacon's remark that "Man commands nature by obeying it" is "all that is needed to define true work, the kind of work that makes man free to the very degree in which it is an act of conscious submission to necessity."[51] These then are the main characteristics of that work which, according to Maritain, Weil and Simon, must be the foundation and center of the new civilization. What if today Maritain and Simon returned to America where forty years ago, with enthusiasm and admiration, they recognized a society which had taken its first steps toward the realization of an integrally humane civilization?

What would be their reaction in the face of a society where the "little people of God," especially the Blacks, the Hispanics, and the elderly, find it harder and harder to escape from their lowly state, and deprived of any functional participation in the common good, tend more and more to drop out of that society, where the capacity and willingness of that society to exist co-naturally and in compassion with the poor who have the beatitudes promised to them, but who receive nothing of the promised trickle from the wealth amassed by the classes above them, can be measured by the growing problem of homelessness and the obscenity of the scandals at HUD; where, if we are to believe Bellah and the people he and his colleagues interviewed, the object of work is more and more, not service or personal satisfaction, but money, profits, and steady progress up the corporate ladder to economic power; where a new ruling class has come into control, the *arbitrageur*, whose object, pure profit, has nothing to do with production or service (someone has noted that with the hostile take-over of Nabisco huge profits were siphoned off from an enterprise newly encumbered with enormous debts, but that not one more Oreo cookie was produced, where the products of work are subordinated to profits, reality to the signs of reality, the irreality of the latest sign being indicated by the very name invented for it by its proponents — junk bonds; where small-scale production, whether in factory or on the farm, is systematically *annihilated* by huge diversified conglomerates

---

[50]Simone Weil, *Réflexions sur les Causes de l'Oppression Sociale*, 122.
[51]*Ibid*.

and agri-business; where truly productive jobs are farmed out to a lean and hungry proletariat in under-developed countries to cut costs and maximize profits at the expense of the indigenous working classes, where the object of advertising and marketing is not only to fulfill a need but also to create illusory needs; but why continue?

I suspect that if Maritain and Simon returned to America today, they would have difficulty recognizing it as the America they loved and admired in the fifties. Simon wrote:

> Once [civilizations] are cut off from the principles [of work] which make up the deep life of the soul, the blossoming externals of culture can only bring about a vacuum in which some kind of devastating frenzy is likely to develop.[52]

He warned:

> The immediate task before us, therefore, appears to be the development of a theory of culture centered not on leisure but on work in the broadest sense, 'including moral, social, and intellectual, as well as technical and manual work.'[53]

If his warning is not heeded, if the trends pointed out by Bellah and his associates, trends which have become even more obvious in the last eight years, continue in their present course, the America we have known in our youth may well be unrecognizable in the America of our grandchildren.

---

[52]Yves R. Simon, *Work, Society and Culture*, 186.
[53]*Ibid.*, 185.

Part III
God and Caesar

Charles P. O'Donnell

Maritain and the Future of Democratic Authority

The world today welcomes popular movements toward democracy and the widening demands for human rights, political, social, and economic freedom among Communist and other nations seeking to be rid of dictators. Although the Soviet Union is torn by the trauma of change, the response of its people to openness and reform raises hope for democracy there and in Eastern Europe. The popular 1989 uprising in Beijing, smothered by government terrorism, lamentably rescheduled the arrival of Chinese democracy. Hampered by class and tribal cleavages, economic misery, and inadequacies of political authorities, Third World nations struggle for democracy and more serious international attention.

Dramatic changes in Poland, Hungary and the Baltic states are in the early stages of liberalization. However, further advances in democracy there and elsewhere might be very difficult and might extend over many decades or longer. In particular, the tempo of democratic change might be delayed by internal ethnic dissension, economic crises, authoritarian resistance to freedom and a long-standing unwillingness to accept moral and spiritual values over purely political ones.

Since the last Great War democratic nations witnessed the triumph of benevolent technologies and higher levels of national economic prosperity along with a resurgence of the bourgeois ideal of wealth and power. The perils of modernized nuclear weapons and the onus of costly military outlays remain. A cluster of social ills--including poverty, drugs, violence, racism, pollution, and a decline in the quality of education-- challenge the democratic authorities of the future.

The next century will soon inherit these problems. Meanwhile, our times await the beginnings of a moral and political revolution that will reconcile antagonisms between political freedom and political authority and will inspire the vision of a new democracy. Such a vision draws more than ever on the latent resources of popular political aspirations, the wisdom and courage of elected political authorities and the promptings of spiritual life.

Maritain had such a vision. Building on the political wisdom of Aristotle and Aquinas and on the inherited experience of the free governments of his lifetime, he patiently developed a practical, historical, moral and spiritually inspired ideal of a new democracy capable of transforming democratic thought and practices. His contributions to political philosophy and to democracy are formidable. Henry Bars listed 35 of his books that in whole or in part relate to political thought and action.[1] His critical studies of modern moral and political philosophy enriched his political thinking. His genius discerned the connectedness of ideas and reality, of ideas and action which he expressed in *Les Degrés du Savoir* and in his wise applications of distinctions and analogies to political philosophy and practices. His personal involvement in the political events of the thirties and forties, especially during the Spanish Civil War and World War II, as well as his long sojourn in the United States and Canada, are significantly reflected in his political writings.

In this short paper I limit myself to certain salient problems of democratic authority particularly relevant to our world. The main topics are freedom and authority, political authority and power, the role of the people in democracy and Christian influences on the democratic ideal of civilized life. What I have to say here briefly cannot do justice to the richness and profundity of Maritain's political philosophy in which he dealt with basic related ideas as person, pluralism, equality, common good, virtues, natural and positive law, and sovereignty to mention a few.

The widely held ideology that democratic political authority must conflict with political freedom accounts for much of the confusion of democratic thinking. The fundamental premise of Maritain's personalist and pluralist philosophy of democracy holds that political authority is not morally and practically realizable in the absence of a spiritually oriented freedom of the persons who constitute the people of political

---

[1]Henry Bars, *La Politique selon Jacques Maritain* (Paris: Les Editions Ouvrières, 1961), 20-21; Gerald McCool, "Maritain's Defense of Democracy," *Thought* 54 (June 1979): 132-142.

society. Equally such freedom cannot realistically be achieved without a morally committed political authority.[2] This interpretation recognizes that freedom, as an internal dynamism of persons, although of primary concern for their eternal destiny, also substantially influences their political future as a people. The external dynamism of political authority, that derives its character from natural law, serves the common good of political society and its people so long as people are free from authoritarian or Machiavellian rule.[3]

The modern world, Maritain observed, is dominated by three conflicting ideas of the political freedom of man. One freedom centered on "freedom of choice as an end in itself eclipses the social and political primacy of social justice and the common good."[4] In reaction to the excesses of classical political liberalism a second philosophy of politics claimed the core of social and political life must focus on a freedom of autonomy that makes man the master of life.[5] This idea in Hegelian form "sought its realization in history through the State understood to be the highest expression of the immanent forces of being." This idea ends up in dictatorship.[6]

---

[2]Jacques Maritain, "*Démocratie et Autorité*," *Annales de Philosophie Politique: Le Pouvoir*, vol. 2 (Paris: Presse Universitaires de France, 1957), 34-36, 44-45; also Jacques Maritain, "*Principles d'une politique humaniste*" in *Jacques and Raïssa Maritain Oeuvres Complètes*, Vol. 8 (Fribourg: Editions Universitaires and Paris: Editions St. Paul, 1944), 207-244, and Jacques Maritain, *Scholasticism and Politics*, trans. Mortimer J. Adler (Garden City, NY: Doubleday Image Books, 1965), Chapter 2; Jacques Maritain, *Man and the State* (Chicago: University of Chicago, 1951), 126-129; see Yves R. Simon, *The Community of the Free* (Lanham, MD: University Press of America, 1984), Chapter on "Freedom and Authority"; Yves R. Simon, *Philosophy of Democratic Government* (Chicago: University of Chicago Press, 1951, Midway edition, 1989), 72-144.

[3]Jacques Maritain, *Du Régime Temporel et la Liberté* (Paris: Desclée de Brouwer, 1933), 50-64; Maritain, *Man and the State*, 32; Jacques Maritain, *Some Reflections on Culture and Liberty* (Chicago: University of Chicago Press, 1933), 18-20.

[4]Jacques Maritain, *Du Regime*, 47.

[5]*Ibid.*, 48-49.

[6]*Ibid.*, 49 footnote.

Maritain's third idea is that the essential purpose of political society is not the freedom of choice of each individual (which freedom man possesses as a reasonable being) but the political and common good of the people. The freedom "ordained to the good of the person" would aim at providing a truly human condition for all people. In such a good society "the dynamics of freedom will tend from the freedom of choice to the freedom of autonomy." The favorable conditions produced by the authority of that kind of political society would, in turn, foster the autonomy of persons known for their independence and generosity.[7]

Contemporary political authority is sometimes described in terms of minimal or maximal exercise of power. The minimal thesis favored by many conservatives includes a list of ideas borrowed from the book of classical economic liberalism. Maximal authority is a demand of communist ideology and of military dictators. Other standing views of authority include those so-called "realists" who see political power as a game of sophisticated political players. Its temporary successes are kept alive by the interventions of economic power brokers and with the aid of deftly managed propaganda programs which undermine democracy. From a similar perspective democratic authorities are tempted to concur with Machiavellians that the ambiguity of some evil means guaranteed success while respect for justice places an intolerable limit on reasons of State.

Democratic political authority for Maritain is neither minimal nor maximal, not a game, nor an end to be achieved by any technical means whatsoever. On the contrary, for him that authority is vested in a government or State with the right to act (under God's sovereignty) in accordance with the principles and processes of a popular Constitution, periodical popular elections, common action, and the common good.[8]

In the structure of democracy, Maritain held that the government or State occupies the highest level of political authority. It enacts and administers laws as the representatives of the people who are the immediate source of its right to rule.[9] The people retain that capacity at all

---

[7]*Ibid.*, 50-54.
[8]*Ibid.*, Maritain, *Man and the State*, 24, 25, 133-136.
[9]*Ibid.*, 12, 13, 25.

times. It is in this sense of self-government that Maritain quotes the words of President Abraham Lincoln, "a government of, for and by the people."[10]

The right of representative government to rule is accompanied by its power to exercise that right. "Authority and Power are two different things. Power is the force by means of which you can oblige others to obey you. Authority requests Power. Power without authority is tyranny."[11] Power, therefore, is subject to the moral and political purposes of authority.

As the use of force by political authority poses a problem of ends and means, Maritain indicated that political means must be proportioned and appropriate to the end of political society–its common good. That good

> is to better the condition of human life itself or to preserve the
> common good of the people...so that each concrete person...
> throughout the whole mass may truly reach a measure of
> independence proper to civilized life and is ensured alike by eco-
> nomic guarantees of work as property, political rights, civil virtues,
> and the cultivation of the mind.[12]

A second aspect of the problem of political means, Maritain notes, "relates to the means by which the people can supervise and control the State." Before taking up specific means of control the people may employ, the significance Maritain attributed to the idea of people is pertinent to their role as judicious evaluators of government actions. "The concept of the people," Maritain wrote, "is the highest and most noble of the concepts that we are analyzing. The people are the very substance, the living and free substance of the body politic. The people are above the State, the people are not the State, the State is for the people."[13]

His concept of the people includes all of the people but attaches particularly to the marginalized members of society and to manual workers. "Among the common people there is a huge variety of levels

---

[10]*Ibid.*, 25.
[11]*Ibid.*, 126.
[12]*Ibid.*, 54.
[13]*Ibid.*, 26.

and degrees. Superficially they may be moved by the winds of opinion, passions and special interests, At a deeper level there is a will to live together and the obscure consciousness of a common destiny and vocation and finally the natural trend of human will, considered in its essence, toward the good.[14]

The political participation of people united under just laws in a democratic political society, Maritain stressed, is based on the principle that the development of society and civilization moves from the bottom upwards to the State. In today's non-democratic societies where authority reaches from the top downward the development of people is brutally limited.[15]

Aware that democracies have over time improved their methods of controlling governments, Maritain also saw the continuing need for more education in public understanding, greater respect for and enforcement of human rights, and a deeper appreciation of the value of pluralism. Regarding other ongoing means of controlling abuses or delinquencies of authority, Maritain strongly supported the freedom of privately owned communication media, in spite of their shortcomings. He commended the use of private pressure groups, although they sometimes engage in private warfare. They can be of service to the public good if they do not encourage violence or provoke it. Maritain greatly admired the Saul Alinsky model of small groups working at local levels to correct commonly occurring abuses of power by private or public organizations. He supported the use of Gandhian techniques of nonviolence as a means of spiritual warfare.[16]

Present day experience with political parties in democracies indicate that to the extent ideologies and technologies become a passion for sheer partisan success the progress of democracy is jeopardized. Maritain urged political parties as representatives of the people to attend more seriously to the practical principles and goals they propose to support. He was not sympathetic to the formation of religious political parties either because they have often proved divisive or have been unable to fulfill their mission.[17]

---

[14]*Ibid.*, 137.
[15]*Ibid.*, 24.
[16]*Ibid.*, 64-171.
[17]Jacques Maritain, "Lettre sur l'Independance" (*Oeuvres Complètes,*

One of the little appreciated ways that the people can prevent abuses of government or private group actions is by their dedication to civic friendship which recognizes the essential equality of all citizens and respects differences among fellow citizens with regard to religion, race, and status in life. Civic amity, a companion of justice, is greatly enhanced by good argument among informed and responsible persons to whom the people attend.[18]

Maritain's idea of a Democratic Charter can contribute importantly to a people's democracy. It provides a framework of a practical political faith in a democratic ideal. It is, Maritain said, a statement of a "civic or secular faith, not a religious one." A democracy has no right to impose the creed on citizens as a condition of citizenship. It has the right and duty to educate them in this set of "practical tenets which the human mind can try to justify from quite different philosophical outlooks." The Charter which includes such principles as human, political, and social rights and their corresponding duties, justice, civic amity, and religious freedom invite a conscious agreement among people to assist them in the advocacy and defense of democratic conduct.[19]

A democratic educational system would, among other challenges, teach people not only the principles of the Democratic Charter but also the making of judgments which apply principles to the changing realities of social and political life. These judgments are of two kinds: one supportive of the just actions of social and political authorities, the other, as if in service of a loyal opposition, enabling citizens to criticize laws, policies, and practices contrary to justice and the common good. Both types of judgments involve popular reflection on public information and debates which yield a basis for public cooperation. They also recognize that the legitimacy of democratic authority depends on the support of a public consensus.[20]

Historically a moral conscience, that is a knowledge of political good

Vol. VI), 271-288: Jacques Maritain, *Integral Humanism*, trans. Joseph W. Evans (Notre Dame: University of Notre Dame Press, 1968), 261-264.

[18]*Ibid.*, 203-204; Gerald B. Phelan, "Justice and Friendship," *The Thomist* (January, 1943), 152-160.

[19]Jacqeus Maritain, *Man and the State*, 108-113.

[20]Jacques Maritain, *Existence and the Existent* (Garden City, NY: Doubleday Image Books, 1956), 56-59; also Bars, *La Politique*, 69-86.

and evil, aided by the energies of the Gospel, has slowly progressed among people during the past centuries.[21] Beyond that progress, Maritain pointed out that people will from time to time need prophetic persons or minorities to "awaken people to something better than everyone's daily business."[22]

The public virtues, an important qualification of persons holding public office, including political advisors, attest to the presence of a competence to judge well and of a conscience sensitive to the moral and political good. The moral conscience of political decision-makers has to be complemented by a religious conscience because the ethical nature a political society enjoins "the aid and comfort of religious faith" in order for political leaders to cope with the human condition.[23]

Maritain once remarked that "the tragedy of modern democracies is that they have not succeeded in realizing democracy," and that "the causes of this block are numerous...The main cause is of the spiritual order." His observation is a reminder that the unresolved centuries-old problematic of the relations between religion and politics is a key element in the failure of democracies to realize themselves. Some democracies established the facade of a Church-State, others yielded to encounters with popular religious indifference or to a polite and bland acceptance of religious freedom. Contemporary democracies still do not understand the extent to which religious freedom, one of the acknowledged human rights, serves to enrich democratic life.[24] Meanwhile the world is aghast at the spectacle of the power politics of religious extremists who provoke and encourage participation in inhuman warfare.

Democracy for Maritain is more than a set of institutions and their immediate successes. It is a spirit and a way of life which lies in the common hope for freedom, respect for authority, human rights and duties of persons, and a large measure of civic friendship. These and

---

[21]Jacques Maritain, "Questions de Conscience" (*Oeuvres Complètes*, Vol. VI), 648-651; Jacques Maritain, *Christianity and Democracy and the Rights of Man and Natural Law*, trans. Doris C. Anson (San Francisco: Ignatius Press, 1986), 11-17.

[22]Maritain, *Man and the State*, 142.

[23]Jacques Maritain, *Principles d' une Politique Humaniste* (Paris: Hartmann, 1945). 182-183.

[24]Maritain, *Christianity and Democracy*, 18-32.

other values are an integral part of the evangelical tradition which cautiously and confidently progresses in history in spite of interpretations of its ideas and practices.[25]

The Christianly inspired democratic political ideal foreshadowed by Maritain is not a Churchy State, nor a Church-State, nor a *Res Publica Christiana*. It is a secular political society inspired by a personalist and pluralist political philosophy whose contribution includes its advocacy of religious freedom and of spiritual over material values. It is a broadly ecumenical ideal.[26] A secular political society where members are inspired to perfect their freedom would grant that each citizen would possess human rights whether or not they are members of a Church because all citizens are equal politically and faith cannot be inspired by force.[27]

The Christianly influence on political society and its authority "is not automatic and necessary, it is menaced and contradicted. It is a heritage which is to be developed by the labor of all that is human and divine in man."[28]

Maritain's historical ideal of democracy is not utopian, his vision does not seek to redeem the world but to salvage justice and the common good of political society and its people. His vision is a *long-range hope* for a new age which, as Monsignor George Higgins recently pointed out is a hope which "rests on the knowledge that God is at work in the world."[29]

Do we rightly read the signs of the times--demand for political freedom in the world, a United Europe, a world order, a new age of democracy and, above all, a renaissance of religious faith?

---

[25]Jacques Maritain, *Man and the State*, 152-154, 167-171; re religious freedom in the United States see John Courtney Murray, *We Hold These Truths* (New York: Sheed and Ward, 1960), 27-142.

[26]Jacques Maritain, *Man and the State*, 159-161.

[27]*Ibid.*, 161-162.

[28]Jacques Maritain, *Christianity and Democracy*, 37.

[29]Jacques Maritain, *Man and the State*, 159; Msgr. George Higgins, *The New World* (Chicago), 30 June 1989.

William Bush

Bernanosian Barbs and Maritain's Marigny Lecture

Though also a Parisian, Georges Bernanos was not, like Jacques Maritain, born into the upper Parisian bourgeois with an illustrious maternal grandfather such as Jules Favre to emulate. Six years younger than the philosopher, his birth in 1888 was to a peasant mother from Berry, married to a highly successful, self-made interior decorator, whose father had been a humble cobbler from Lorraine, reduced to becoming a mere day-laborer in the capital. Nonetheless, in the apartment above his father's interior decorating shop, it was the traditional values of a Christian, monarchist France which were maintained. Thus, unlike Maritain, Bernanos did not drink in eighteenth century republican idealism with his mother's milk. His successful father, moreover, sent his only son to be educated by the Jesuits, along with the sons of the Parisian aristocracy.

When Bernanos met Maritain in 1926, he was 38 years of age, Maritain, 44. His first novel, *Under the Sun of Satan,* was about to become the all-time best-seller in Maritain's new, prestigious series, *Le Roseau d'or.* Bernanos, a modest regional inspector for an insurance company, was virtually unknown.

In contrast, Maritain's prestige could not have been higher. Convert of Léon Bloy, Professor at the *Institut Catholique,* well-known and honored at Rome, founder of the Thomist Study Circle, and philosophical editor of Charles Maurras's *Action Française* organ, *La Revue universelle,* Maritain's success at literary conversions in 1926 was legendary. Bernanos's naive wonder at finding himself catapulted into professional intimacy with such a notable Catholic figure was to prove disastrous however. He was constrained by Maritain to tone down his first novel so as not to risk, as Maritain put it, "wounding any Catholic conscience." This Maritain-inspired censorship of Bernanos's very Christian understanding of evil and sanctity provides irrefutable evidence of the limitations of Maritain's understanding of Christianity in 1926.

Ironically, both men lived World War II in exile. Unlike Maritain, who found himself stranded in North America on a lecture tour, Bernanos, with his wife and six children, had embarked from Marseilles for Paraguay in July of 1938, seeking that remote Eden where, Bernanos naively hoped, there would be no serpent lurking to seduce his six offspring. Two and a half years in Spanish Majorca from 1934 to 1937 had given him cause to worry about acceptable outlets for the very Bernanosian exuberance of his three older children, now aged 21, 19, and 17. In any case, a South American Eden—with or without the serpent—was an old dream, carried over from Bernanos's pre-World War I youth, when two friends had brought back reports of easy living in Paraguay, and the possibility of founding a French colony there to preserve the Christian values of old France.

That Bernanos immediately discovered life impossible in Paraguay, and that he opted for Brazil rather than Argentina, where Maritain's circle had warmly received him on his way to Paraguay, need not concern us here. What is more important is that his private humiliation as father of a noisy tribe of offspring upon having his youthful dream of Paraguay shattered, cruelly coincided with a yet more public humiliation as a Frenchman at France's signing the Munich Pact.

Installed in Brazil he thus began writing a long apology for the French entitled "We French," interrupting it, however, for the composition of a burning denunciation of the pro-Munich stance of Charles Maurras, just elected to the French Academy. In writing this little volume, published as "The Scandal of Truth" just prior to the war, Bernanos actually had the text of Maritain's 1937 *Ambassadeurs* lecture on Jews, "*Les Juifs Parmi les Nations*," before him. He thus in this text launched a number of barbs, still censored out of all editions, at Maritain's explanations of the role of Jews in modern society.

Wartime exile in the Western Hemisphere allowed both Bernanos and Maritain to soar to lyrical heights about civilization being saved by eternal France. Bernanos believed firmly in the predominant role France would be called upon to play in the modern world, insisting until his death in 1948 that the spiritual revolution he proclaimed as necessary to save western civilization from technology—a preoccupation he shared with Simone Weil—could come from France alone.

Maritain and Bernanos thus shared much more than just a common period in history. It was in fact usually their mutual Christian preoccupations which gave rise to those frequent barbs which, directly or indirectly, consciously or subconsciously Bernanos could not resist aiming in Maritain's direction from even before their first meeting in 1926; and, even twenty-one years later in his last lecture in October 1947, just nine months before his death, Bernanos was still aiming barbs at Maritain.

What concerns us here, however, is the fact that it was Bernanos's stance as a Christian which inevitably caused him to aim barbs at Maritain, and, more specifically, to take exception to all three of the dominant themes of Maritain's *The Twilight of Civilization*. This text, given in 1938 as a lecture at the Marigny theatre in Paris, does indeed dwell upon three basic Maritainian concepts, any one of which was capable of sending Bernanos into a prophetic rage--that is, progress, racism, and Christian democracy.

I

Certainly Maritain gives a very large place in his lecture to human progress, an idea in which he had been conceived and which he did not renounce at his conversion to Christianity. This idea was of course totally anathema to Bernanos as a Christian. Bernanos insisted, even from his youth, that belief in human progress allows its partisans to forget both "original sin and man's great dilemma"--that is, our common fall as a race from Paradise--indeed, our common status as human creatures who have fallen into a state of sin and mortality.

Thought about man's great and common dilemma seems far removed from Maritain, however, when, at the end of the first section of his Marigny lecture he speaks of "the horizontal movement through which is progressively revealed the substance and creative strengths of man in history."[1] This "progressively revealed" "horizontal movement," according to Maritain, "prepares the kingdom of God in history."[2] In the last section he even speaks of "the slow and difficult march towards an historical ideal of fraternal friendship amongst the poor, wounded

---

[1] Jacques Maritain, *Le Crépuscule de la Civilisation* (Montreal: Editions de l'Arbre, 1941), 27.
[2] *Ibid.*, 28-29.

children of an unhappy species made for absolute happiness."[3] That Maritain chose to believe in such an "historical ideal" is further implied in the middle of his lecture where he speaks of a "humanism of the Incarnation which seems to me invoked by our period in history as the only thing capable of coming to the aid of a world's sufferings."[4]

The idea of some such special application of Christianity being destined for a particular period in history is, of course, very far removed from Bernanos's more timeless view; for his application of Christianity was, I believe it fair to say, somewhat less parochial than Maritain's. He could never forget that according to unbroken Christian tradition the reign of the Prince of this World can be overcome finally on this fallen planet only by the coming again in glory of Jesus Christ.

Bernanos thus refused to be seduced by the demonic illusion that the Church of God could ever possibly manage to turn this world into a realm of fraternal charity. What he did allow—and this is an historic element I find singularly lacking in Maritain's thought on France and Christianity—was that in 496 France had entered into a national pact with the Christian God at the baptism of Clovis by St. Remi as first Christian King of France. This pact had resulted in the glory of French civilization without which we should all be the poorer.

A truly Christian culture for Bernanos is thus not to be derived from intellectuals and philosophers such as ourselves trying to shape a future by heady ideals, but rather from the humble, daily living of a whole baptized people where a common allegiance to the crucified and resurrected God-Man, Jesus Christ, determines the common man's attitudes as to what is and what is not of God, as to what is and what is not to be loved and honoured.

Certainly Maritain has a sense of this personal involvement with Christ when he speaks of the difference between the "anti-Christian spirit" and the "spirit which is against Christ Himself."[5] Even so, his highly intellectual bent tends to take the upper hand, prevailing even perhaps until *The Peasant of the Garonne.* For, whatever we may think of it, Maritain was unable not to take being a philosopher terribly seriously.

Bernanos, on the other hand, never wrote to prove his quite excep-

---

[3]*Ibid.*, 84.
[4]*Ibid.*, 44.
[5]*Ibid.*, 33.

tional intellectualism. Rather did he write from a profound personal need to exorcise his inner struggle, hoping thereby to lessen that terrible anguish of soul, that hideous inner pain caused by his visionary grasp of people and events. A tearing sense of urgency thus often disturbs Bernanos's disconcerted reader who, for the first time in his life, finds himself encountering an author who dares expose the depths of his heart before God.

Bernanos's writings, however, represent far more than the visceral ventings of a visionary. They are, in fact, rooted in an unusually keen knowledge of history, revealing the author's noble, but not always successful attempt at a truly cosmic application of the one Truth he prized above all others: God had become Man in Jesus Christ. Given that that one, unique, and time-severing Incarnation of the Second Person of the Holy Trinity had taken place through the Holy Spirit and the Virgin Mary to save man from sin and death, how, afterward, could the human race be said to progress? Only to the extent that Jesus Christ became all in all could there be any real progress for the Christian.

II

As for Maritain's treatment of racism, I believe that it was this Marigny lecture, even more than his 1937 lecture on the Jews, which weighed heavily on Bernanos in early 1940 as he wrote his own long article entitled "Race Against Nation."

In the first part of his Marigny text, Maritain speaks of racism as an example of that tidal wave of irrationality he identifies as trying to sweep away his perennial ideal of integral humanism.[6] In the second section, he ties racism to a demonic pseudo-theism;[7] in the third he maintains that racism is attached to "hatred of the God of Calvary and of the God of Sinai."[8]

Certainly Maritain's use of "racism" sounds familiar. Is it not similar to the use that still prevails today? A half-century following the attempted genocide of European Jewry, the thought and speech-patterns of European culture have become so completely conditioned by those

---

[6]*Ibid.*, 18-19.
[7]*Ibid.*, 37.
[8]*Ibid.*, 61.

tragic events that the word "racism," unless it have to do with the tension between blacks and whites, almost automatically invokes in us images of Jewish persecution.

Bernanos's use of "racism" in his article "Race Against Nation" is thus startling for us, being more thorough going, far more nuanced, and much less subject to recent linguistic conditioning. Racism, he allowed, was quite natural to man, just as are tribal allegiances, constituting a sort of basic natural virtue. As for the Jews, Bernanos always maintained, with remarkable lucidity, that they are certainly the world's foremost racists. Do they not insist on retaining their identity, regardless of the cost? This was moreover something which Bernanos sincerely respected, holding it in very high honour for he was aware of the sacrifices necessary to maintain such a feat of identity over three millennia of migrations, conflicts and persecutions, repeated exiles and dispersions; but, being Christian, Bernanos stated simply that such racism is historically totally against Christian tradition.

Unlike Maritain, Bernanos did not over-simplify, denouncing racism because he thought it to be irrational. Rather does he appeal to history where he saw the Christian genius as always being against it. Had that Christian genius not given birth to the glory of French civilization? Had it not shaped the blending of numerous European races into a single nation where, though a Breton was not a Norman, a common belief that God became flesh in Jesus Christ and calls man to become a partaker in His divinity was nonetheless shared—even among fighting factions?

The big thrust in Bernanos's "Race Against Nation" is, moreover, provided by observations on Hitler's belief in the superiority of the Germanic races—which includes the Franks, of course. This belief, Bernanos insisted, was actually a spiritual rebirth of paganism. It was, hence, completely contrary to the whole tradition of baptized Europe. Was Christianity's historic role not that of effecting a coming together, a spiritual blending, a mystical fusion of men in the humanity of Christ whereby they might become something none of them were before: sons of God through Jesus Christ by the power of the Holy Spirit?

Apart from Hitlerian racism's representing a spiritual rebirth of paganism, Bernanos would undoubtedly also have mercilessly mocked Maritain's ill-begotten idea of coupling his accurate statement that racism was contrary to the love of the post-Incarnation God of Calvary with that much more questionable statement of its being equally contrary to the pre-Incarnation God of Sinai.[9] Historically, how could Maritain get around the cruel fact that the servants of the God of Sinai massacred the native inhabitants of the Promised Land (an attitude of racial superiority which, regardless of its cause, still mysteriously, disquietingly, persists in our headlines today)?

Certainly, Bernanos, just as Maritain, was concerned about those too-numerous French Catholics who welcomed Hitler's racist regime since it promised to rid society of Jews and Free Masons. Yet, for Bernanos, the great tragedy taking place was that French Christians had abandoned their pact made with the Christian God in 496 with the baptism of Clovis. Thus the very heart, the very soul of France was being swept aside by the rebirth of pagan racism which, of necessity, must always be totalitarian and, thereby, always at war with all other races, something confirmed by the Nazi's clashes not only with the Jews, but also with the Slavs and the Gypsies. Bernanos puts it thus:

> The Church made Europe into a community of nations. Often divided among themselves, often enemies, they nonetheless remained conscious of their original fraternity. Through what is now happening, and through a change of spirit in their consciences, Christians now stand by, watching the destruction of one of History's most precious concepts.[10]

Then, in a typically acerbic Bernanosian thrust at his fellow-countrymen who, under guise of Christianity, welcomed a racist regime, he added:

> But then maybe Christians, through some clever manoeuvre, still hope to profit from this rising paganism by letting it get on with exterminating the Jews and the Free Masons? Such a tactic is like setting your house on fire to get rid of a burglar![11]

Bernanos's use of the word "racism" thus stretches well beyond Maritain's limited and rather emotional use of the word.

---

[9]*Ibid.*

[10]Georges Bernanos, *Le Chemin de la Croix des Ames* (Paris: Gallimard, 1948), 18.

[11]*Ibid.*

III

The real and most abiding difference between Maritain and Bernanos, however, has to do with "Christian Democracy." Like a sign-off tune, this topic surges up in the last pages of the Marigny lecture, reminding us that it was ever sweet to the ears of the son of Paul Maritain and Geneviève Favre. The slightest mention of Christian democracy however, sufficed to send Bernanos into a paroxysm of vituperation—he who at eighteen had written a priest-friend regarding Christian democrats: "They take equality, liberty and fraternity for theology.... Scratch a democrat and you'll get a theologian."[12]

Before we try to explain why Bernanos was so dead-set against Christian democracy's pretenses, let us note that Maritain does indeed attempt, in the last section of his Marigny lecture, to fuse his idea of Christian democracy with the witness of the Church of God. He quotes a statement made in October 1937 by the American Catholic episcopate in regard to Pope Leo XIII's use of the term "Christian democracy":

> His Holiness summons us to the defense of our democratic institutions, governed by a constitution protecting the inalienable rights of man...The accomplishment of this order of the Holy Father requires that our people, from childhood through maturity, be instructed in a more thorough manner in the true nature of Christian democracy...[13]

In addition to citing this pro-democratic text, Maritain also praises the American Catholic episcopate for re-introducing the term "Christian democracy" into its ecclesiastical vocabulary. Moreover, as a sort of trump card, he throws in the fact that the non-Catholic President Roosevelt himself had viewed democracy, with its respect of the human person, its liberty, and its good faith, as being rooted in religion, something Walter Lippmann saw as a complete break with past history where religion had not been regarded as the source of American democracy.

It is, nonetheless, striking—not to say actually peculiar—that after all

---

[12]Georges Bernanos, *Oeuvres Romanesque. Dialogues des Carmélites* (Paris, Bibliothéque de la Pléciade: Gallimard, 1961), 1736.

[13]Jacques Maritain, *The Twilight of Civilization*, 76.

these bouquets thrown at America in general, and at the American Catholic episcopate in particular, Maritain, at the end, suddenly does an about face, pirouetting away from the key role the United States is to play in saving Western civilization. Instead, we find him suddenly fixing a mystical gaze on eternal France as that civilization's real leader, citing as evidence what a desperate Cardinal Verdier in January 1939 had feebly called a *new axis*.[14]

What sort of deep and psychic Maritainian dichotomy are we confronting in this initial idealization of American democracy's fusion with Catholicism on one hand, and, on the other, the final parting gesture of praise and confidence in France? I do not ask this question lightly. Like it or not, it reminds me of a bizarre, but rather fascinating after-dinner story I was told in 1981 in the chateau of Kolbsheim by Maritain's own devoted God-daughter, the gracious Baroness Grunelius, who, with her wonted kindness, had offered me over night hospitality. It was from her own lips that I learned of how, after Raïssa's burial at Kolbsheim and the resulting necessity that Jacques too be buried in France, Maritain had expressed his desire that at his death his heart be cut from his body to be enshrined in America's heartland at Notre Dame University whither, following his burial in France, the Baroness Grunelius, a most reluctant emissary, was to convey it. In a tone nuanced by considerable relief, Madame Grunelius reported to me that her happy discovery of a French law forbidding international transport of parts of the human body had alone saved her from that distasteful and lugubrious trans-Atlantic journey.

As a literary critic, I cannot but relate this rather uncommon story to Maritain's literary about-face in the last pages of *The Twilight of Civilization*. In passing from an American-oriented hope to a French one is Maritain not actually reflecting that same deep-seated dichotomy which dictated that his heart be buried in America and his body in France?

Be that as it may, Maritain was not alone in being seduced by the idea of Christian democracy in America. The normal American reader, indeed, I would venture that most of us here, would tend to find optimism about the future of democracy something uplifting.

Bernanos took a more pessimistic view. With a certain accuracy he

---

[14]*Ibid.*, 89.

regarded democracy as being as good a school for totalitarian dictatorship as any other, something which may perhaps explain his lack of success in English-speaking countries. For Bernanos lucidly maintained that democracy can succeed only if there is some sort of economic success, a hard fact the idealists tend to gloss over as they abstract the democratic ideal from its basic lifeline of selfish economic gain. In an article from November 1944, Bernanos, no doubt thinking of Maritain, observes:

> ... naive persons don't seem to realize that the existence of the democracy of their dreams in a world such as ours is no less conceivable than the existence of a XVI. century army in modern warfare, and that it is as ridiculous to hope for the inauguration of true democracy as for me to wait for the restoration of the monarchy of St. Louis.

Then, as if echoing Maritain, he says he hears them saying, "Democracy will be this; democracy will be that. Churchill said; Roosevelt stated,"[15] before concluding:

> What difference is made by the definition? Even an idiot ought to understand that in a capitalist regime universal suffrage must become just another business, just like the others, while in a socialist regime with totalitarian tendencies, it becomes just what it was in Germany—a powerful, state-serving instrument. A plebiscite made Hitler. Hitler emerged from the womb of the people, for the people also produce monsters and no doubt only they are capable of producing them.[16]

Bernanos's conviction that it is usually economic concerns which dictate the popular vote and that democracies can thrive only from economic progress thus led him to understand that the trump card of the economic world can only be the treacherous concept of efficiency. Nor did he count on rank and file Christians as being in any way immune to

---

[15]Georges Bernanos, *La France Contre les Robots, Suivi de Texts Inédits. Présentation et Notes de Georges Bernanos* (Paris: Plon, 1970), 218.
[16]*Ibid.*, 218-19.

the hard fact that in spite of being created in the image of God and, through the Incarnation of God in Jesus Christ, made sons of God, they also, since efficiency is vital for the success of democracy, infallibly would be constrained with the non-Christians to become equally enslaved to machines. This is, in fact, the basic argument of Bernanos's last book written in Brazil, *France Against the Robots*.

Thus, unlike Maritain, Bernanos would never look to the United States to provide an answer. He was, indeed, not convinced that after less than two centuries of existence the young American phenomenon had really yet proven itself as a pinnacle of either freedom or democracy.

Bernanos's theology, based on his analysis of man's basic fallen nature and rejecting the illusion of human progress, thus proves much finer and more comprehensive than Maritain's highly intellectual view. I believe that it might even be demonstrated quite convincingly by some young theologian more adept at such tasks than myself, that Bernanos's Christianity was always much more thorough going and solid than Maritain's. Certainly it was freed from all Maritainian illusions regarding humanism, rationalism, and, need I say, Thomism....Just as the faith of Péguy, it was the Christianity of old France before the rise of the universities, professional intellectuals, and scholasticism, the Christianity of a St. Hilary of Poitiers, a St. Martin of Tours, a St. Germain, or a St. Geneviève, not that travesty of Christianity offered us by those learned doctors in theology of the Sorbonne who condemned the anointed of God, Joan of Arc, as a relapsed heretic, sorceress, and witch.

V

As for Bernanosian barbs, let us close by observing that when *Under the Sun of Satan* was about to appear, Bernanos, mindful of the much-publicized but short-lived conversions of Jean Cocteau and Maurice Sachs, launched his first barb at Maritain in filling out the author's information form for his publisher. Under "Religion" he wrote, terminating with an exclamation point: "Christian since his baptism. Not even converted!" Obviously he assumed that Maritain, whom he had not yet met, would read this form, for he also used a Léon Bloy quote to explain his purpose in writing, explicitly naming its source: "A horrible complaint about sin, but orthodox and of an uncompromising veracity, with neither bitterness nor solemnity (Léon Bloy)." Moreover, even in his last lecture nine months before his death, Bernanos was still comparing Maritain's literary conversions to works of high fashion, to garments of *haute couture*, signed by their author; and, regarding those short-lived conversions of Cocteau and Sachs, Bernanos observed in that same lecture that ironically they were like rare, exotic hot-house flowers. They had been forced into bloom by Maritain in the rarefied, climate-controlled greenhouse of Raïssa's salon at Meudon, but, alas! were totally incapable of survival in the world outside...

Behind all Bernanos's barbs, however, lies a great and touching irony, bitter even if one be a disciple of Maritain. It was he, Bernanos, and not Maritain who was the true disciple of Léon Bloy whether by his unpredictable behavior, his visionary gifts, or his all-encompassing Christianity where no philosophy was needed to justify it. Certainly, just as it would be hard to have imagined Bloy on a Sunday afternoon at Meudon amidst the faithful of the Thomist Study Circle, chatting about spirituality in hushed tone over tea, even so did Bernanos's rare presence there prove an uncomfortable one.

Dare we allow ourselves to imagine Bernanos there on some rare Sunday afternoon—as, indeed, he was, in fact. Certainly I have no difficulty in conjuring up such a fantasy, full of explosive possibilities. How not imagine Bernanos rather uncomfortably ensconced beside the most attractive female present, engaging her in animated conversation? Realizing that in spite of herself, his neighbor is fascinated by his great charm and wit, Bernanos sets down his cup of tea and, with great and characteristic gesticulations starts to pooh-pooh, with irresistible, good-natured mockery, the naive pomposity of the Thomist Study Circle's having categorically enshrined St. Thomas Aquinas as "leader and guide in the knowledge of truth." Throwing his hands wide in despair, his face full of astonishment, Bernanos asks rhetorically, in much too loud a voice, how all those unfortunate Christians in the twelve centuries before St. Thomas Aquinas had managed to get by without such a leader and guide to truth! How deprived they must have felt! At the very absurdity of such a ridiculous idea Bernanos erupts with his famous great laugh, shattering the reverent, hushed gentility of Raïssa's semi-monastic salon. Yet, alas! Bernanos being Bernanos, he's only started, for he's going farther still. Pouring forth his deepest Christian convictions, much to the now-obvious delight of his attractive blonde neighbor's adoring gaze, he decides that the moment has come for him to make himself heard by everyone present in a propitious quote from Léon Bloy.

One can imagine Vera, having just poured a cup of tea for a bearded Russian emigré, looking up, alarmed and scandalized. Jacques too, who had just quietly bent forward to present a new American convert to

Raïssa on her corner of the sofa, also looks up uneasily. As for Raïssa, she jerks around in defiant disbelief, glaring in the direction of Bernanos and his blonde neighbor, her eyes flashing, visibly pierced to the heart by such an affront as that quote.

Indeed, all three of these Benedictine oblate Godchildren of Léon Bloy have recognized that quote; for it is, indeed, a quote of their incorrigible and so conveniently dead old master. It is, moreover, alas! one of those very awkward, impossible, best-to-be-forgotten quotes which he was ever wont to make; and now, for the very first time, it has been uttered in the salon of Meudon, challenging all Meudon stood for! Who, but that indelicate, semi-barbarian, and wild Bernanos, would have had the effrontery to utter it here, of all places?

Worse still, it was much more than a mere utterance. In the twilight of that afternoon, itself so poignantly a part of th twilight of pre-World War II French Catholic social idealism, Bernanos had shouted his challenging quote. Indeed, he had proclaimed it; and it resonated like the voice of doom as he uncompromisingly announced not only for the benefit of his blonde neighbor, but especially for Maritain, his and Léon Bloy's preferences where Christianity was concerned: "I'm for UN-civilized Christianity!"

John Hellman

World War II and the Anti-Democratic Impulse in Catholicism

On 12 June 1940, as apparently invulnerable Panzer divisions rolled across Belgium and France, Yves R. Simon, a militantly anti-Fascist French philosopher in exile at Notre Dame University, wrote a remarkable prophetic letter to his mentor, Jacques Maritain, who had just fled to New York. Simon thought that though Paris might probably be burned "the Nazis will not win the war. The war will be won by the USA"; but he warned Maritain since arriving in South Bend some months earlier he had discovered, to his great shock and dismay, that the struggle against Fascism was not being supported by the Catholics in the United States as one might have assumed. In fact, he told Maritain, the most important counter weight to the anti-Fascist movement in the United States was "centered in the American Catholic milieu." Recalling for Maritain their struggles in France a few years before against Catholic sympathizers of Mussolini's invasion of Ethiopia, or Franco's coup against the Spanish Republic, he concluded that the situation was "*Just the same!* All of the countries will have been betrayed by their Catholics." "Imbeciles have been in key positions [in] the Vatican, the bishoprics, the universities, the Catholic press," he charged, and they simply gave "free reign to criminals."[1] Simon and Maritain soon discovered that their uncompromising anti-Fascism isolated and alienated them from their fellow Catholics in the United States as well as in Europe, to a painful, and unexpected, degree; but, in those days, there was such a concern for defending Catholicism's public image that we are only now discovering the fierce

---

[1] Yves R. Simon to Jacques Maritain, 12 June 1940.

95

secret battle being waged for the Church's soul by men like Maritain and Simon, and Free French leaders like Charles de Gaulle.

Rather than burn, Paris surrendered; and on 15 June 1940, as the French Prime Minister, Paul Reynaud, appealed to the U.S. for support, Jacques Maritain telegraphed Roosevelt, whose guest he had been not long before. The philosopher urged the President to make a public declaration against Nazism to support French morale or that country would make a separate peace. He begged Roosevelt to act "that the great American democracy assure the triumph of democracy over barbarism."[2] Thus Maritain went on record opposing the surrender and neutralization of France even before Charles de Gaulle's famous, historic appeal on the 18th of June.

Since Maritain was considered the world's most important Catholic thinker at the time, his call for resistance had a certain importance—although de Gaulle's appeal seemed to have little effect, at least in the United States. While often sympathetically interested in Maritain's opposition to the armistice, Frenchmen in the U.S. overwhelmingly refused to support de Gaulle's claim to represent France for the same reason that Roosevelt (with Maritain's support) withheld his recognition of the General's movement: political legitimacy required the support from the people. Prominent Frenchmen in America—Alexis Leger (the poet Saint-Jean Perse)[3], the great *Europeanist* Jean Monnet, Antoine de Saint Exupery—as well as Maritain—confirmed Roosevelt's perception of this unknown young general as a potential dictator.[4] A lonely exception to the indifference to de Gaulle was Yves R. Simon who urged his mentor Maritain to find out more about the General and to consider backing him if he and his compatriots seemed worthy of confidence.[5] Simon was following a sort of Jacobin instinct since information about the de Gaulle movement was very scarce, and it was years away from being equated with the "Re-

---

[2]Jacques Maritain to President Roosevelt, 15 June 1940.

[3]Leger was one of France's most important diplomats, having served as secretary of the *Quai d'Orsay* during the prewar period. He fled to the U.S. just days before the armistice, and felt the armistice "did not invest the General with any political power."

[4]Raoul Aglion, *Roosevelt and De Gaulle: Allies in Conflict* (New York: 1988), 35.

[5]Yves R. Simon to Jacques Maritain, 26 June, 10 August 1940.

sistance" as a whole. The American government concluded that de Gaulle was simply not that important—his movement was a mere symbol of resistance capable of a negligible military contribution.[6] So the General's movement came under the tutelage of Churchill (who identified with the romantic "prophet in the wilderness" side of de Gaulle) while it remained "an unfortunate diversion" for Franklin Roosevelt.[7]

In the United States, only a few prescient individuals, such as Yves R. Simon, remained vividly interested in the Free French as, from Notre Dame, he prodded Maritain to seek more information about them in New York; but Maritain answered that "things are more complicated here than you seem to think....And sadder. France has not only been betrayed in a terrible way, she betrayed herself; and the French bourgeoisie actually has the government they deserve." Their own role in the United States, Maritain suggested, was not to search for charismatic leaders to overturn the government in France but rather "to prepare the moral and political revival of the French *population* itself, which is much more complicated than struggling against a government." Among their most urgent tasks was the preparation of the "political philosophy and social disposition and practical politics which France will need--in two or three years perhaps."[8] So, while the two men may have differed on de Gaulle, both had already refused the possibility that, in the long run, totalitarianism would prevail.

In September 1940, Maritain decided to lecture at Columbia University in the first semester and Princeton in the second, as he learned that the Gestapo had searched his home in the Parisian suburb of Meudon; and so Paris was closed to him.[9] That same month also brought news of de Gaulle's first, spectacular, failure: in September the General had persuaded Churchill that the people of Dakar would rally to him if he launched an Anglo/French attack. So, after that ill-conceived fiasco, the self-proclaimed leader of the Free French lost credibility, as it was then

---

[6]William Langer, *Our Vichy Gamble* (Hampden, CT: 1965), 289-99.

[7]Julian G. Hurstfield, *America and the French Nation, 1939-1945* (Chapel Hill, NC, 1986), 29.

[8]Jacques Maritain to Yves R. Simon, 10 August 1940; 31 August 1940.

[9]René Mougel, "*Les Années de New York*," *Cahiers Jacques Maritain*, 16-17 (April 1988), 15.

clear that the French army and navy were behind Vichy, not him. Thus, in the short term, de Gaulle was completely useless, apparently incapable of any significant military or inspirational contribution to the war effort.[10]

On 27 September Maritain wrote Simon about what he called "the Dakar escapade," remarking that it "reawakens an old instinct in me which tells me that generals...are bad politicians (with Bonaparte an exception)....In the end one is always brought back to hoping...in the people. But our poor people without star and without guide!" Maritain also signaled "the discrete warnings being given to the *New York Times* by its London correspondent. He has called the Dakar adventure a tragicomedy. And seems to suggest that de Gaulle is an export-item for the English" and that their confidence in him does not go beyond inviting him to official ceremonies, dinners, and receptions.[11] As for Maritain, his book, *A Travers le Désastre*, composed from September to October 1940, was a decisive and inaugural text,[12] as with that book Maritain became "the moral beacon for those in exile."[13] In it he maintained that "it is not in a man, it is in the people of our country that we have our best hope."[14] Thus Maritain placed his confidence in "the people" and not in a savior on horseback, neither in Pétain...nor in de Gaulle. So with the philosophers and the majority of Frenchmen in the U.S. against de Gaulle (85% according to an estimate made as late as May 1942), the already weak prospects of recognition for his movement became even more remote.[15]

Yves R. Simon remained interested in de Gaulle, but from a different, intensely personal perspective, as he wrote to Maritain on 20 December:

I am in the midst of effecting...in the depths of my soul,...a work of political adjustment, a great revision, and I don't yet know the results. I am more and more persuaded that even the healthiest

[10]Raoul Aglion, *Roosevelt and De Gaulle*, 115.

[11]Jacques Maritain to Yves R. Simon, 27 September 1940.

[12]Charles Blanchet, *"Jacques Maritain, 1940-1944: le Refus de la Défaite et ses Relations avec le Général de Gaulle," Cahiers Jacques Maritain*, 16-17, 40.

[13]Raoul Aglion, *Roosevelt and De Gaulle*, 36.

[14]Jacques Maritain, *A Travers le Désastre* (New York, 1944), 115.

[15]Raoul Aglion, *Roosevelt and De Gaulle*, 115.

results. I am more and more persuaded that even the healthiest theoretical work can...contribute to disasters in the immediately practical realm because when the house is burning with the inhabitants locked inside, what is important is the immediate practical....[W]hat has been subtracted from the heritage of the French Revolution, from the rights of man and the citizen, has gone, not to St.Thomas, but to Hitler. I had my small part of responsibility inthat game and I intend to participate in it no longer. ...The spirit of lies and treason is flourishing in the catholic center where we live. It breaks the heart to think that it is fortunate, for the...U.S.A., that there are only 23 million Catholics in that great country....There is no encyclical to say how a state which is betrayed by its Catholics ought to react.....[16]

Maritain's *A Travers le Désastre*, which appeared during January 1941, gave him a very high profile. That same year it was published in South America, in Spanish and Portuguese, and appeared in German in the United States. It was translated into Polish by the great poet Czeslaw Milosz who explained how it constituted a powerful, lucid analysis of the French defeat by "the most celebrated representative of contemporary Catholic philosophy" which would serve a world in the throes of an *international civil war* as a powerful antidote to the Hitlerite claim that France fell because of the decadence of democracy.[17]

In France Maritain's book was copied, mimeographed, and printed several times in the southern zone, before being reprinted at Paris--the second publication of *Editions du Minuit*, the famous clandestine Resistance publishers.[18] Back in France, a Catholic journalist sympathetic to the Resistance recorded in his diary how he "read Maritain's *A Travers le Désastre* in a copy which came from America, slipping into France under the nose of the customs officers at the Pyrenees frontier. Many, here, had confidence in the author, but it was difficult to imagine that a compatriot

---

[16]Yves R. Simon to Jacques Maritain, 20 December 1940.

[17]Czeslaw Milosz, "'A Travers le Désastre,' Clandestin Varsovie," Cahiers Jacques Maritain, 16-17, 29-33.

[18]René Mougel, "Les Années de New York, 1940-1945," Cahiers Jacques Maritain, 16-17; cf., Le Bataille du Silence. Souvenir de Minuit (Paris: Vercors, 1967).

outside the country could put himself in our place so perfectly."[19] As *Le Désastre* gave Maritain immense moral authority, officials of the Free French from London visited him on their way through New York to Washington to organize the services of the *Comité Français de Liberation.* He was invited to communicate directly with the head of the Free French, and charged with directing the *Université française libre* just being founded in New York.

Yves R. Simon quickly noticed and told Maritain that what he had written about the de Gaulle movement in *A Travers le Désastre*[20] seemed "terribly embarrassed."[21] Maritain responded:

> One must show that Thomism is what is strongest against false democracy....It is a question of aiding America to (discover?) a new democracy....one must distinguish clearly democracy as a general political philosophy founded on respect for the human person and the vocation for liberation rooted in human per-sonality (inthis sense... St. Thomas was a democrat, in this sense... the Gospel works in history in a democratic direction).

Simon, who had rarely contradicted his *maître* in the past, could not agree that Thomism was the best instrument in the circumstances, and contended:

> ...if St. Thomas were alive today he would be for Franco, for Tizo, forPétain; that's evident. St. Thomas, that's Garrigou. To do some-thing practical in 1941, with St. Thomas, in politics, is a joke. And that is why...late in the night...I am reading 'The History of the French Revolution'...trying to understand practical things which my understanding of Thomism doesn't explain to me....

If Simon's Thomistic background had failed him, so had many of his con-temporaries who had been influenced by Thomism:

> I surely hope to find...a political spirit not made to please Franco,

---

[19]Pierre Limagne (30 July 1941), *Ephemerides de Quatre Années Tra-giques*, 1940-1944, I (Lavilledieu, 1987), 218.

[20]Jacques Maritain, *A Travers le Désastre*, 115.

[21]Yves R. Simon to Jacques Maritain, 11 February 1941.

Tizo, Pétain and Garrigou....But you know that the [notion of] 'the democracy of the person' has always seemed very vague to me. And...I am strongly discouraged by the...political gestures of the most intelligent Thomists during these last years.

These things led Simon to a critical analysis of his own past:

There was my idiotic, but so Thomist, book on the war in Ethiopia where I dismissed with a virtuous severity...clairvoyant people who...wanted...an antifascist crusade. — Perhaps that is what has contributed the most to separating us for the last two or three years: I broke with my past...while I don't think there has been an analogous rupture in you....I don't see a break in you. There is one in me.[22]

Maritain responded by arguing that, contrary to what Simon had glibly suggested, he had accomplished *a break* with his past--one which opened up in the mid-1920s:

To have believed for a certain time in a parallelism of action between the people of the *Action Française* and the Thomist renaissance is one of the greatest scourges of my life....I had an instinctive horror of those well-dressed savages, but had never read the books of Maurras, and I confided myself to the wisdom of my director, he whointroduced me to St. Thomas. I dearly paid for that error. The rupture in question began a bit before the condemnation [of the *Action Française*], and...since that time I have undertaken the liquidation of the errors of the past with perseverance. [23]

Simon, however, would not let the issue die; raised questions not only about the "democracy of the person" but also about the larger implications of the *Christian Personalism* which was becoming fashionable in Catholic circles. "Last winter," he wrote Maritain, "our seniors did a treatise on the subject: Thomistic personalism: true internationalism. It

---

[22]Yves R. Simon to Jacques Maritain, 16 July 1941.
[23]Jacques Maritain to Yves R. Simon, 31 August 1941.

was polished folly: everything idiotic was individualism, everything nice was personalism';[24] and so, Simon implied, in an international civil war betseen authoritarian powers and the liberal democracies, good Thomist Personalists would be inclined to side with "anti-individualist" forces. Two months later, on November 6, commenting on Cardinal Baudrillart's speech describing a "Holy War" against the Communists in Russia, Simon claimed:

> ...totalitarian regimes,...above all in the apparently less radical forms which they have taken on in Italy, Spain, in Slovakia, in France, are accomplishing with a growing efficacy a more redoubtable infamy than any persecution: *the corruption of the Catholic world from within, what the Patriarch of Lisbon called the dechristianization of the Church itself*.....[W]e are in full Catholic crisis. The thought that one of my sons could be called to the sacerdotal vocation, and that that immense honour could be accompanied by the danger of seeing him tied hands and feet to those corrupters of conscience, the thought that I could be the father of priests like Alfred Baudrillart, Gillet, Gemelli, Tizo, O'Brian, etc. sends a chill down my spine. I would rather put my daughter in a bordello.[25]

Some weeks later, Simon added that, in his view:

> 'Catholic democracy' is condemned to only producing rubbish... Better to work in the framework of just plain democracy. There at least we have dynamic and normative facts: the French Revolution, the American Revolution, Italian independence, etc.; these facts are generally of a questionable Catholicism; this is the problem we have to face. Garrigou never even tried.[26]

In a lengthy and thoughtful letter to General de Gaulle, which was dated on 21 November,1941, Jacques Maritain outlined his views of the French political situation. He began by warning the General that the Vichy government was pursuing a policy which, despite appearances,

---

[24]Yves R. Simon to Jacques Maritain, 3 September 1941.
[25]Yves R. Simon to Jacques Maritain, 6 November 1941.
[26]Yves R. Simon to Jacques Maritain, 26 December 1941.

could have disastrous effects on the Church in France. For, he argued:
> ...the Vichy government is the blind agent of incalculable dis-
> asters. In officially compromising the French Church...with the
> regime andthe myth of Marshall Pétain, it is preparing popular
> resentments in the wake of the victory, and perhaps a religious
> war, which will be a second catastrophe for the country....It in-
> vokes the teachings of the popes and of the social Catholic school
> which it corrupts in dechristianizing and in tying the errors to a
> Maurrasian, or fascist, or childishly reactionary political philo-
> sophy, and class revenge. [Thus it] risks ruining in advance all
> effort of reconstruction capable of reconciling the French in a work
> of political and social regeneration with a truly, and authentically
> and vitally Christian inspiration.

Maritain told de Gaulle that the resistance movement should not only be concerned with military victory, but focus on deeper aspirations of the masses of the French population as well:

> ...it is in the French people, in the young and healthy elements of a
> bourgeoisie which has experienced a horrible bankruptcy as a
> class,that all of our temporal hope now resides....It would clearly
> be vain to propose a return to the pre-war regime to France; but it
> is no less evident that it would be folly to renounce the victories,
> hopes and historical ideal of democracy,...fundamentally renewed
> ..., reestablished in its evangelical sources and with a new self-
> confidence....We need a new language...a new declaration of the
> rights of man, the hope of a new Republic....[S]uch a promise could
> ...reawaken our people and help them to regain their energies and
> virtues. These hopes are centered in Free France and its leader.[27]

The philosopher urged the Free French to disprove the anti-liberal

---

[27]This admonition to de Gaulle was similar to those made in the same period by Simone Weil who also thought that the imperious General often missed the point of resistance against Fascism and authoritarianism. Cf. John Hellman, *Simone Weil: An Introduction to Her Thought* (Philadelphia: Fortress Press, 1984), 27-43.

rhetoric of Vichy by demonstrating that an attachment to French religious traditions and to the French revolutionary and democratic traditions were not incompatible but complementary:

> ...I think that the immense mission which Providence has delegated to the movement which you lead is to give to the French people, in this unprecedented historical conjuncture...an opportunity to reconcile...Christianity and liberty...those two traditions of spiritual fidelity and temporal emancipation, the tradition of Saint Louis and that of the Declaration of Rights,...opposed the one to the other...for so many years, but where there are...truths...precious to us in a parallel way."[28]

While Maritain was appealing to de Gaulle to embrace revolutionary and religious traditions, Roosevelt's advisors were warning him that de Gaulle was less a Resistance General than a radically ambitious politician who threatened the future of French democracy;[29] and soon Maritain, too, was tending toward that point of view.

When Martain's admonitory letters to de Gaulle in late 1941 and early 1942 recently came to light, Maurice Schumann, voice of the Free French in London and resolute champion of de Gaulle's legacy since that time, tried to explain and minimize their significance. In 1941-1942, Schumann explained in 1988, Maritain had been "un gaulliste inconditionnel" (an unconditional Gaullist)..."but, rather than obscuring his liberty of examination, his gaullism impelled him to make scrupulous use of it to the point of meticulousness." Schumann admitted there was a striking change in tone in Maritain's letters to the General between autumn 1941 and spring 1942, but he blamed it on two or three self-styled Maritain disciples who had escaped France at the time. These men had gone neither to London nor Algiers (like the quasi-totality of such refugees) but to the United States where they justified their itinerary by arguments which Maritain repeated practically word for word: "the missionaries sent out from England are too often men of the extreme-right"; Free France seemed oriented toward "a sort of Moral Order"... "the

---

[28]Jacques Maritain to Charles de Gaulle, 21 November 1941.

[29]Leahy to Hull, 12 September 1941, in *Papers of the Foreign Relations of the United States: 1939-1945*, I, 2: 431.

domestic politics of the Marshall without the Marshall." Those tales did not convince Maritain, Schumann insisted, but "they bothered him to the point where a real disagreement grew up between him and de Gaulle," even leading Maritain to write those harsh words that while "*Il est vrai de dire que la France Combattante represente moralement la France, il serait vain de pretendre qu'elle la represente Politiquement,*" but, Schumann implied, Maritain soon learned better and went to work for de Gaulle like everyone else.[30]

In fact, however, these Maritain letters were written in a climate of tension between the United States and the Free French precipitated by the Saint Pierre and Miquelon incident in December 1941. On the spur of the moment de Gaulle ordered Admiral Muselier to seize the Vichy controlled islands off the North American coast without informing anyone. On 17 December he had told the American Foreign Office in Canada, preoccupied with America's sudden entry into the war, that a proposed Muselier mission to Canada would not proceed without prior American approval, but seven days later he ordered Muselier to proceed without consulting them. Muselier's subsequent resignation from the French National Committee precipitated rifts among the Free French, and de Gaulle's moral and diplomatic standing with the U.S. understandably plummeted once again.[31]

Just after the Saint-Pierre and Miquelon incidents, on the seventh of January 1942, de Gaulle wrote a peculiar, highly charged letter to Maritain. He agreed that France should have a new "interior national ideal" and insisted:

> But it is in this area above all that we have much to expect from you, Jacques Maritain. You have begun so well! You must continue. There should be one basis for salvation: disinterestedness and people have now been prepared to embrace it by disgust and holy misery....Each person will only find his place in each person's self-abnegation.We need a people in workers' smocks, laboring in the light and playing in full sunshine. We will try to

---

[30]"Temoignage de Maurice Schumann," *Cahiers Jacques Maritain,* 1617, 36-37.

[31]Julian G. Hurstfield, *America and the French Nation, 1939-1945,* 120-125.

draw that out of that war-revolution. I know that everything which is young wants it. We don't expect anything at all from academies.

Did de Gaulle's glowing vision of war-revolution, in any way, disturb Maritain? The General sought to reassure the philosopher: "I am not worried about democracy. Its only enemies at home are puppets. I am not at all afraid for religion. The Bishops played the wrong game, but the good cures, the simple priests, are saving everything."[32]

When Maritain did not respond, de Gaulle cabled him to come to London as soon as possible: they had many things to discuss.[33] Maritain cabled back, politely but cryptically, that he was prevented from dropping everything and going to see the general by his obligations to American universities.[34]

On 21 March Maritain explained himself to de Gaulle sternly and at length. From the information he had received, he wrote:

'Gaullism' has not summoned as profound and vast a movement of sympathy as is necessary; a large part of resistant elements, notably in workers' milieu, are keeping their distance. I am told that the slogan: deliver the *patrie* from the Nazi oppressors, does not suffice...because that same slogan is employed by the partisans of Marshall Pétain, who represent him as...gaining time and in fooling the Germans.....And the milieu of which I speak are asking themselves if the political ideal of Free France isn't oriented toward a sort of moral Order which would continue...after the... liberation, the interior politics of the Marshall without the Marshall....I am also told that the very way in which the propaganda of Free France is conducted in France gives credence to this, and that the missionaries of Free France sent from England are too often men of the extreme Right.

Once again Maritain confronted de Gaulle with the need for a firm and clear commitment on the part of the Free French to democracy, rather than raw political power:

---

[32]Charles de Gaulle to Jacques Maritain, 7 January 1942.
[33]Charles de Gaulle to Jacques Maritain, 3 March 1942.
[34]Jacques Maritain to Charles de Gaulle, 6 March 1942.

I am convinced that the essential factor...is the French people itself, notably the workers and peasants, because I believe that the
bourgeoisie as a class are bankrupt. But the people need leaders to
act in concert with them; if such leaders are to come forth, I suppose one must expect them from worker and peasant elites and
individual elements coming from the former directing classes and
decided to work with the people.

So Maritain's ideas were similar to de Gaulle's (and Vichy's[35]) *elitism*, but different insofar as Maritain declared the potential bourgeois
elites corrupt. Maritain, more of a democrat and populist, told de Gaulle:

...it is a question of proposing a renewed democratic idea to
France, *more* profoundly and *more* truly democratic, more fervent
for liberty, for justice and fraternity, more truly republican than
that of the old liberalism,...conscious of its spiritual principles and
tied to radical reform of structures....If Providence give us the men
required for that...they will stress the evangelical inspiration of
democracy, in a new language accessible not only to Christians
but also to unbelievers.

Maritain said that a question which seemed more and more urgent to him
was the "ideological refurbishing of the French people," and he encouraged the General to familiarize himself with Yves R. Simon's *La Grande
Crise de la République Française* and the books in the forthcoming *Civilisation* series by Simon, Catholic trade union leader Paul Vignaux, and himself.[36]

---

[35]Especially in Vichy's institutions such as the National Leadership
school at Uriage. See John Hellman, "Maritain, Simon, and Vichy's Elite
Schools," *Freedom in the Modern World: Jacques Maritain, Yves R. Simon, and
Mortimer J. Adler*, ed. Michael D. Torre(Notre Dame: University of Notre
Dame Press, 1989), 165-180.

[36]He also recommended the *"Temoignage sur la Situation en France"*
by the anonymous *Dirigeant de l'Action Catholique* (in fact, Pierre Limagne, *Ephemerides de Quatre Années Tragiques, 1940-1944*, I) published
by Claude Hurtubise at the Editions de l'Arbre in Montreal. In that forthcoming collection, *Civilisation* Maritain cited the books *Les Droits de*

On 21 April de Gaulle, again, urged Maritain to come to London,[37] and then on 22 May telegraphed the Free French delegation in Washington to go to see Maritain in New York and press him to join the *Comité National* which was being set up (as almost a "government in exile"). This provoked another, even more cutting, response from Maritain who raised questions about the Resistance's general political inspiration:

> ...it would be in my opinion an irremediable fault to confuse [your] political *inspiration* with the political *power* or with a government in exile or with a provisional pre-government governing in the name of the French people. Because the will of the French people will only be able to express itself in a political way after France will be delivered from German oppression and the Government of Vichy.

Or, as he put it in another way:

> [while]...France *Combattante* represents France *morally*, it would be vain to pretend that it represents her *politically*. There is no mission more noble that such a moral mission, no mission more suited to arousing vast forces, but on the condition of not falling from what Péguy called the *mystique* into what he called the *politique*, and on the condition that eventhe hint of a demand for politiccal power be excluded. Can one imagine *Jeanne d'Arc* being concerned with taking on political power and of preparing a government?

Maritain even implied that de Gaulle might have missed the great lesson of the 1930s:

> It is from their own will and their own experience that the reconstruction...ought to spring up. On that question of the confidence of having or not having confidence in the French,...there is a

---

l'Homme et la Loi Naturelle" by himself, Yves R. Simon's *La Marche à la Délivrance*, and what became Paul Vignaux's *Traditionalisme et Syndicalisme*. Jacques Maritain to Charles de Gaulle, 21 March 1942.

[37]Charles de Gaulle to Jacques Maritain, 21 April 1942.

primary choice to pose in the depths of the conscience. As for me, I have chosen confidence.

While Maritain did express his gratitude to the General for the latter's speeches to the French people he also warned him that:

...a certain spirit of arrogant authoritarianism shown by many subordinate administrators, a certain concern for prestige among them ... a certain tone of moralizing superiority...are of the sort to undercut the movement in a serious way.

Maritain also warned about the Free French attitude toward the Americans:

If the State Department finished by accepting the *fait accompli* at Saint-Pierre and Miquelon, it would not be by democratic weakness, but by virtue of realistic considerations, and it has certainly retained a profound resentment.

This was not an isolated instance of de Gaulle's lack of politeness and judgment:

Since this letter [is]...written in complete frankness, allow me to tell you that the allusion to the *Gribouille*[short-sighted idiot] in one of your recent talks seemed catastrophic to me.
    Political inspiration to the exclusion of ... concern for political power,--liquidation of the idea of a diplomatic recognition of the movement-revision of the general attitude regarding America, --*voilà mon Général*, the three fundamental points on which I wanted to clarify my thinking for you.[38]

So Maritain's long letter of 25 May 1942 showed deep reservations about de Gaulle and the Free French which made it unthinkable for him to rejoin the *Comité National* in London, but de Gaulle did not break with Maritain even when the latter refused to adhere to the Gaullist group *France Forever* in June.[39]

---

[38]Jacques Maritain to Charles de Gaulle, 25 May 1942.
[39]Charles Blanchet, *"Relations," Cahiers Jacques Maritain*, 49.

At about this time, Maritain himself was reproached from a very different quarter. On 24 May 1942, the *prieure générale* of the Ursulines, returning to Rome from France, wrote of "disquiet" aroused in certain French and Roman milieu by "his current ideas."[40](She seemed to mean, particularly, his criticism of the Church's involvement with Vichy.) Maritain's response was much harsher than his rebuke to de Gaulle:

> You could answer [those who are worried about me]...it would be more appropriate for them to worry over...Cardinal Baudrillart associating his prestige...with the worst policy of collaboration with the enemy, Father Garrigou-Lagrange militating politically for the government of Vichy, a handful of traitors trying to corrupt French Catholic opinion by radio and the press. Moreover Father Louis of the Trinity (Provincial of the French Carmelites) had chosen, in his conscience as a religious and disciple of Saint John of the Cross, to continue the fight alongside General de Gaulle, and I haven't heard of his being asked to abandon his battleships for mystical studies.
>
> Finally, you know as I do...it is not only a question of our fatherland, but of the Holy Church, which is made vulnerable today by those who would compromise it with the fascist 'new order' a crisis no less serious than that of the great schism in the middle ages; it is no longer a question as it was at that time of choosing between a legitimate Pope and an illegitimate Pope, but rather between conceptions which maintain Christian truth in souls and those which lead..., as the Cardinal of Lisbonne said, to 'de-Christianize the Church herself.' When a Christian has understood that, he has to choose at the price of risks and perils, and not take refuge in a patronizing neutrality.[41]

De Gaulle then responded to Maritain's position via a spokesman, Christian Socialist André Philip. Maritain reported the result to Simon:

> I have just received a letter from André Philip who the general as-

---

[40]Charles Blanchet, *"Relations,"* *Cahiers Jacques Maritain*, 42.

[41]Jacques Maritain to *"Une Religieuse,"* 3 June 1942, reprinted in *Cahiers Jacques Maritain*, 16,17, 93.

signed to respond to me. The thesis is directly opposite [to that in my letter to de Gaulle]. The future provisional government is to be presided over by de Gaulle and created by him: that is the only way to save France from anarchy. (In my view that plan is good for a Lenin or a Maurras, when one wants to impose a revolution or a *coup de force* on a country. But I don't see the necessity in the present case.)[42]

Meanwhile de Gaulle tried to mollify the Americans. On 26 October 1942 he tried to explain to them (for the first time) the moral and political principles of the movement he had founded in June 1940. His letter to the State Department innocently announced that the newly formed French National Committee was obviously "bound" by the laws of the Third Republic because he was "not a political man." Not only was de Gaulle's avowal two years late, but his claim to be devoid of political ambitions contradicted two years of pursuing a recognition that was unrelated to military goals.[43] It also gainsaid the intentions clearly set out to Maritain...(who was probably confiding in Roosevelt).

Through all of this Jacques Maritain was trying to affirm his own democratic credentials. When a mutual friend sketched an outline of what he saw as the two main periods of Maritain's intellectual evolution, the philosopher admitted to Simon that he:

...would have preferred that he expose my...political philosophy... as a doctrinal synthesis,....in my 'second period.' Before that I was only concerned with metaphysics and speculative philosophy.... Even *Three Reformers*[44] was written from that point of view and political and social questions were...not the direct object of study. ...There is not, strictly speaking, a *Political Philosophy* of J.M. before *Religion et Culture*. I...admit the 'two periods' but the first was com manded by metaphysics, the political ideas were only a sketch. I hope that [he] will be able to indicate that....
   If our friend could further accentuate the democratic and 're-

[42]Jacques Maritain to Yves R. Simon, 21 August 1942.
[43]Raoul Aglion, *Roosevelt and De Gaulle*, 132, 134.
[44]This is an early *anti-individualistic* monograph done by Mari-

publican' character of my present positions I would be happy for it.[45]

Meanwhile, by the end of 1942, Roosevelt tried to deal directly with the duplicitous and ambitious Vichy figure Admiral Darlan, instead of de Gaulle, who went into a 'violent rage'[46] --thus further exasperating Maritain. On 4 December Maritain wrote Simon that, in his view:

...The Darlan affair is terrible for France, and it is possible that in a few months that wily character could create a dictatorship with democratic trappings,....he is consolidating his power....During that time de Gaulle is ...ruining his own cause. Philip's visit to the White House was catastrophic, as he played a game of prestige and insolence with the president. After that, when the President invited the general, the General, rather than arriving as quickly as possible, posed conditions....[I]n the meantime our friends are given over to the Gestapo, famine, and terrorism....[47]

Darlan's threat to de Gaulle's political power abruptly ended on 25 December when the Admiral was assassinated by a young Gaullist, Fernand Bonnier de la Chapelle. Did de Gaulle order Darlan's assassination? Roosevelt could not know and appeared with armed bodyguards for his meeting with de Gaulle at Casablanca a month later.[48] On 22 January 1943, the first day of that conference, de Gaulle told Roosevelt he conceived his role to be that of Jeanne d'Arc, and the next day remarked: "I must frankly tell you that I am no longer a military leader. I am the leader of a great political movement. I am today in the position of Clemenceau." When the amused Roosevelt asked who he wished to be, Jeanne d'Arc or Clemenceau, de Gaulle answered: "I am both," thus

---

tain which, as Yves R. Simon pointed out, was being approvingly cited by reactionaries at Vichy.

[45]Jacques Maritain to Yves R. Simon, 1 November 1942.
[46]Cf. Jacques Maritain to Yves R. Simon, 4 December 1942.
[47]Raoul Aglion, *Roosevelt and De Gaulle*, 147-48.
[48]Raoul Aglion, *Roosevelt and De Gaulle*, 148.

confirming the President's impression that he was a potential dictator.[49] Churchill commented to an approving Roosevelt that de Gaulle "has undoubtedly Fascist and dictatorial tendencies. At one time he represents himself as the sole barrier against Communism: at another, as enjoying Communist support."[50]

In the light of these developments, Maritain wrote Simon:

...The primordial position taken by de Gaulle...makes him more precious to us than ever, and obliges us to be more and more attached to the spirit (which ought to be, or might have been, that) of his movement. But at the same time he ruins all that by his absurd errors [of judgment]. The two great dangers which I see are: 1) Chauvinistic nationalism and demands for prestige; 2) Absurd anti-Americanism and anti-British feelings. To quarrel with a man as devoted to France as Churchill is a masterpiece of a gaffe for which France might have to pay the costs....There is one of the major reasons for American opposition to de Gaulle...[51]

In response, Simon granted that "there were in Gaullism, at its beginnings, people who would have liked a Pétain regime without the *Boches*" but now one had to focus on the common fight for the good cause, and how to revivify France. He recalled that the *Commune* shot less than 500 people while the victorious bourgeois who put it down shot over 17,000. While he hoped that Fighting France would not indulge in indiscriminate massacres he charged that the executions:

... would be more than 17,000. Incontestable traitors, plotters against state security, torturers, calumniators responsible for the deaths of a number of good people, dishonored characters who have to disappear from public life if public life is to be possible on French soil,...an enormous mass of Frenchmen. 100, 000, 500,000?

---

[49]*For the President. Personal and Secret: Correspondence Between Franklin D. Roosevelt and William C. Bullitt*, ed. O.H. Bullitt (Boston: 1972), 568.
[50]Julian G.Hurstfield, *America and the French*, 194.
[51]Jacques Maritain to Yves R. Simon, 13 April 1943.

We will not shoot all of them, but all must disappear or France will not be restored to life.

But who are these dozens, these hundreds of thousands of people who *will be* liquidated if fighting France isn't prevented from effecting the *great rupture* that it has promised? One finds an astonishingly high proportion of people belonging to the good, to the high society. Admirals, Generals, Bishops (with the exception of Msgr. Saliège, who among them hasn't been dishonored?)--if we can't reintegrate men like Darlan then neither can Cardinal Gerlier ...Cardinal Lienart, whom I loved so much....

May God have pity on his Church! The more I think about it, the more it seems to me that Catholic responsibilities in that war take a place immediately behind those of the Nazis.

...Among the factors blinding people...what was more efficacious than Catholic propaganda against Communism? Without that propaganda there would not have been the war.

In a letter several months later, Simon mused about "Social Catholicism," informing Maritain that he was, as he put it, evolving in a more and more egalitarian direction: [Take the case of Albert de Mun,]

That former officer of the Versailles army, who opposed amnesty for the *Communards* [hence 17,000 *Communards* died for 500]...that handsome fellow claimed that Leo XIII had encouraged him in his taking action in favor of the directing role of dominant classes, and I am convinced he was telling the truth.[52]

Meanwhile, President Roosevelt tried to recognize General Giraud as "the only French leader" in North Africa, but American attempts to prop him up failed. After Giraud and de Gaulle were appointed co-presidents of the French Committee of National Liberation on the insistence of Roosevelt, de Gaulle quickly relegated Giraud to military considerations and established near absolute political control,[53] and from that summer of 1944, de Gaulle continued to make as much trouble for

---

[52]Yves R. Simon to Jacques Maritain, 9 August 1944.
[53]Cf. Raoul Aglion, *Roosevelt and De Gaulle*, 155.

Roosevelt and Churchill as he possibly could.[54]

While de Gaulle was consolidating his power over the Free French movement, in May 1944, Maritain resigned from the presidency of the [Free French] school in New York--despite the urging of the Free French authorities to continue, pleading a need to return to philosophy; but a few weeks later General de Gaulle, in New York to coordinate Free French military initiatives with the Americans, urged him to accept the French ambassadorship at the Vatican.[55] On 28 July 1944, Maritain wrote to Simon: "I saw de Gaulle at New York and I had an *excellent* impression. But I am afraid that they will ask practical tasks of me."[56]

The consistent refusals of Roosevelt to recognize de Gaulle as the head of a provisional government of France, even after the liberation, only ended in October 1944 when Eisenhower conveyed his hope that a French government contribute to international efforts to subdue Germany. De Gaulle's visit to Washington in July was for reasons of military expediency as the State Department complied with Eisenhower's request for recognition.[57] In sum, the fears over de Gaulle's dictatorial tendencies were only overridden by military considerations.

Maritain returned to France on his way to Rome, but he was disappointed by what he saw. On 9 January 1945, Simon wrote to Maritain: "...what bothers me the most is that [same] lack of renewal which struck you [on your visit to France]....Social Catholic types, Duthoit [Bishop of Arras], Lienart, and company will always only do the dirty work for criminals."[58] Maritain "went to work for de Gaulle" but with a particular, consistent perspective on the situation, as he told Simon: "What the general has in view is less success in such or such diplomatic negotiation as the gesture of choosing me to represent France to the Vatican and which he regards as significant in itself.[59] Thus Maritain and Simon were disappointed by the lack of democratic renewal, of a break

---

[54]Cf. *Roosevelt and Churchill: Their Secret Wartime Correspondence*, ed. Francis Loewenheim, et. al. (New York, 1975), 534.

[55]Cf. René Mougel, "*Les Années*,"18-19.

[56]Jacques Maritain to Yves R. Simon, 28 July 1944.

[57]Timothy Maga, *United States, France, and the Refugee Problem. 1933-1947* (Ph.D. thesis, McGill University, 1981), 262.

[58]Yves R. Simon to Jacques Maritain, 9 January 1945.

[59]Jacques Maritain to Yves R. Simon, 29 January 1945.

or "rupture," in postwar France; but their lonely stance against the fascistization of the Church was vindicated by the philosopher's symbolic appointment to Rome.

What are the most important lessons of this episode? It is strikingly significant to learn how, in 1940-42, the "orthodox" Thomists were favorable to an authoritarian Europe. Maritain, who was the leading Thomist intellectual, was shocked by the comportment of American Catholic leaders as well as by great French scholars like the Pétainist Père Garrigou because it suggested where Thomism led, politically; and how and why had Maritain come to be so different? He had a Jewish wife, was a convert from Protestantism, had his house searched early in the war, his friends placed under surveillance, and he had been the object of a violently partisan attack for his very moderate *neutralist* stand on the Spanish Civil War. It was *not* his study of Thomism, much less Catholic doctrine, which led him--or Yves R. Simon--to oppose Fascism any more than Marxism led Walesa, Havel, or the other heroic Eastern Europeans of '89 to oppose totalitarianism. It was more a sense of human dignity and of right and wrong. De Gaulle had his own reasons, acted accordingly, and, on the surface at least, prevailed. The important point is that, as Yves R. Simon concluded, Thomism was the wrong formation to stimulate resistance to Fascism in 1940. So it was important to examine the tradition, and oneself, to find out what went wrong. As Havel has said, there is nopoint blaming others: self-examination is the prelude to inoculation against the poison of totalitarianism. Here it is not so much the fine points of the philosophy as the whole mental structure which was behind it: the seminary training, the dogma, the notion of authority, the sense of the human condition never essentially changing, the deference to authority of all sorts. A new kind of Christian democratic thinking would come out of this realization.

Part IV
Knowledge and
Its Foundations

D.T. Asselin

Foundationalism and Foundation in Strauss and Maritain

...[W]hen...[uncultured persons] argue about anything, they do not care what the truth is in the matters they are discussing, but are eager only to make their own views seem true to their hearers. Plato, *Phaedo*, 91A.

Today, democratic liberalism forms the premises of most competing political theories in the West because it comprises goods that most are eager to share, but celebrating democratic liberalism is not philosophy. Indeed, it need amount to no more than sophistic demagogy, "making one's own views seem true to one's hearers." In order to avoid begging the question, as a philosopher one must ultimately show "what the truth is in the matters [one is] discussing." To the extent of one's commitment to (a) liberal values or (b) some moral tradition that comprehends them, one must show how not the values themselves, but rather the realities on which they are based, can certify one's political agenda. Thus if one is to make sense of Leo Strauss's and Jacques Maritain's continued impact on political philosophy, one must analyze the discourse of democratic liberalism, insofar as it presupposes democratic-liberal values. This is our first and main task. In its wake, we shall indicate how Strauss and Maritain think that natural law philosophy rightly avoids begging the question of liberal values, and then more briefly compare Strauss and Maritain on two issues about natural law theory.

I. On Foundations in Foundationalism/Anti-Foundationalism

In order to introduce the distinctiveness of Strauss and Maritain, we shall first sketch today's foundations conflict through Alasdair MacIntyre's foundationalism and Richard Rorty's anti-foundationalism.

Because of the theory of objectivity within his concept of edifying philosophy, Rorty would reject natural law politics. For that implicates metaphysics of the type that he refers to as both traditional and Platonic. Rorty regards this metaphysics as false, because, among other reasons, it depends upon a discredited view of objectivity. His concept of objectivity is axiological and praxiological: for him, knowledge is essentially a conversation aimed at preserving the values of individual freedom, creativity, and interpersonal communion. Knowledge is not, because for Rorty it cannot be, *adequatio intellectus ad rem.* So, in *Philosophy and the Mirror of Nature,* we find him rejecting the epistemological distinction between the objective as what is non-mental and the subjective as what is mental. Late in that same book, Rorty claims that "the distinction between epistemology and hermeneutics [which edifying philosophy is, in part] should not be thought of as paralleling a distinction between what is 'out there' and what we 'make up.'"[1] Rorty develops his notion of objectivity by (i) interpreting virtually the whole tradition of metaphysics and epistemology as based on the false premise of representationalism and (ii) replacing epistemic/doxastic representation with liberal values as the basis of philosophy. In its urgent sense philosophy is *edifying conversation*: it is dialogue and community because it is conversation; it edifies by recognizing and supporting those goods, as well as by affirming individual creativity. Philosophy so understood should aim at keeping a conversation going, generating new descriptions. That enables us creatively to deal with the world and ourselves as moral agents. Philosophy should not entail commitments to truth understood *Platonically* --namely, as being in contact with permanent, ahistorical objects and their qualities.[2] For Rorty, *Platonic* objectivity dehumanizes: it closes conversation, and so stifles individual freedom and creativity.[3]

---

[1]Richard Rorty, *Philosophy and the Mirror of Nature* (Princeton: Princeton University Press, 1979), 342.

[2]*Ibid.*, 3 73-79 .

[3]Thus although Rorty's critique of natural law politics would extend beyond Popper's, it flows from the same reaction to Plato: one should not try to erect a society based on objective knowledge (in the Platonic sense), because a perfect theory of reality is impossible. For an outline of Popper's reaction to Plato, see his *The Open Society and Its Enemies. The Spell of Plato,* fifth, rev. ed. (Princeton: Princeton University Press, 1966), 21-34.

Thus for Rorty, the liberal values mentioned simply are given. For him they are objective and foundational, because he replaces traditional foundations with them. So we note first that Rorty's anti-foundationalism is incomplete. It is a foundationalism of value, an anti-*episteme* foundationalism.

Alasdair MacIntyre has become a leading foundationalist in ethical theory, and our claim that Strauss and Maritain would object to his foundationalism might seem strange. For MacIntyre espouses virtue ethics, which bears close affinities to the natural law politics of Strauss and Maritain, but the following two passages from MacIntyre's *AfterVirtue* suggest the disagreement between him and Strauss and Maritain. First he writes: "[I]f my account of moral tradition is correct, a tradition is sustained and advanced by its own internal arguments and conflicts."[4] And second: [A]ny adequate teleological account [of virtue] must provide us with a clear account of the *telos*; and any adequate generally Aristotelian account must supply a teleological account which can replace Aristotle's metaphysical biology."[5]

Now, as we understand MacIntyre's concept of moral tradition, that object is either a political order or includes one; so it corresponds in part with a rational and humane politics in Maritain's and Strauss's sense. Furthermore, foundation in the sense that interests MacIntyre is the moral tradition itself, as opposed to the sort of Platonic-Aristotelian foundation that he challenges. For MacIntyre, a moral tradition sustains itself by its own elements and conflicts; so for him, moral traditions themselves are foundational to a sound politics. This ordering of foundation and structure reverses the Platonic model of *Republic*, Book Six, wherein "our constitution will have its perfect and definitive organization only when such a guardian, who knows these things, oversees it" (5O5E7-8).[6] In terms of today's foundations issues, Plato's image of the Divided Line means that a moral tradition is to be shaped by a sound philosophy, wherein not opinion (*doxa*), but only knowledge (*episteme*),

---

[4]Alasdaire MacIntyre, *After Virtue*, second ed. (Notre Dame: University of Notre Dame Press, 1984), 260.

[5]*Ibid.*, 163.

[6]Line reference to Burnet edition (Oxford: 1902); translation from *The Collected Dialogues of Plato* (Princeton: Princeton University Press, 1963).

can authorize a particular conception of the political good. By that account, a moral tradition is not self-sustaining and cannot be. Nor is a rational and humane politics self-sustaining. Plato and Aristotle are radically committed to true metaphysics as foundational. A moral tradition, or some form of government included in it, might provide conditions for one's pursuing first philosophy; but that does not mean a moral tradition actually includes first philosophy, or is one, or is directly responsible for the content of one.

True: MacIntyre targets Aristotle more than Plato, especially when he remarks that an adequate teleology of virtue requires clarity about the human *telos*, free of "Aristotle's metaphysical biology"; but Aristotle places theoretical and specifically metaphysical knowledge above practical cognition. This MacIntyre seems loath to do, because of his notion of a moral tradition as self-sustaining. More directly and more importantly, Aristotle's metaphysics grounds principles used in most of his natural treatises. In this case, MacIntyre's own foundationalism is ambiguous. MacIntyre appears to believe that theoretical knowing is prior in the intelligibility of its objects to practical, and he is nothing if not generally Aristotelian in his theory of virtue. Yet simultaneously, he doubts a principle of Aristotle's theory of virtue: that the good of an object is its natural *telos*, a principle that holds across the theoretical divisions of knowledge, from biology to theory of human nature and ethics.[7]

MacIntyre is, thus, a foundationalist within the sense of today's foundationalist/anti-foundationalist controversy. His own foundationalism notwithstanding, MacIntyre appears to believe, with Rorty, that the discourse of a moral tradition, rather than the objects of the discourse itself, adequately grounds politics.[8]

---

[7]For a recent discussion, see our *Human Nature and Eudaimonia in Aristotle* (New York: Lang Publishing Co., Inc., 1989), 24-47 and 63-85.

[8]MacIntyre's discussion of *prudentia* in St. Thomas Aquinas might appear to contradict this observation because he does outline conditions under which the content of that intellectual virtue can be generalized. See his *Whose Justice? Which Rationality?* (Notre Dame: University of Notre Dame Press, 1988), 192-98, esp. 196; but that discussion contains the same ambiguity in MacIntyre's understanding of the primacy of theoretical cognition, insofar as he observes that the Thomistic principle of justice "is ultimately grounded on a theological understanding of the ordering of

If that is so, then no matter how vigorously each might deny it, Rorty and MacIntyre are subjective idealists in the sense that they take beliefs in values and justifications of those beliefs (Rorty), or whole moral traditions constituted of the same (MacIntyre), as foundations. Thus insofar as Rorty and MacIntyre express its opposite poles, today's foundationalist/anti-foundationalist dichotomy is doxastic rather than epistemic. Accordingly, no apology for liberal democracy, or for the moral tradition supporting it, could be stronger than that doxastic basis.

This all suggests that, ultimately, neither Rorty's nor MacIntyre's is anything but a conventionalist position. That is what Plato, in the opening quotation of the *Phaedo* and the quotation of the *Republic*, 505E7-8, so strongly opposed. For as those dialogues, not to mention *Gorgias*, powerfully remind us, conventionalism is practically inseparable from power politics. Nor can a Rorty or a MacIntyre maintain his ethical-political position without adequately showing that an epistemic foundation for politics is in fact impossible. We turn now to those issues.

II. Foundation in Strauss and Maritain

Strauss's polemic against thought that, in his view, refracts the intelligibility of politics, indicates his rejection of doxastic foundationalism. Strauss believed that classical political philosophy, which he deems essentially Platonic,[9] has an objective, natural view of politics. If Strauss believed that his own thought was not distorted by modern rationalist egoism (Hobbes, Locke),[10] or revelation to the extent one's philosophic

---

things" and on a "metaphysical theology" (198). Other things being equal, that foundation should be subject to the same criticism as "Aristotle's metaphysical biology."

[9] See Leo Strauss, "Distinction between Facts and Values" in *Natural Right and History* (Chicago: University of Chicago Press, 1973), 78-80; and "What is Political Philosophy?" in *What is Political Philosophy?* (New York: Free Press, 1959; repr. Westport: Greenwood Press, 1973), 27-28.

[10] The following states Strauss's view that modern natural right differs essentially from that of Plato, Aristotle, or Aquinas, because Hobbes's and Locke's form(s) is egoistic, whereas their predecessors took human perfection, man's natural (and supernatural) *telos* as the immediate object of politics: [For Hobbes and Locke] "Death must then be the

position is inseparable from it (Aquinas),[11] or an incoherency in the fundamental premise of historicism (Hegel, Marx, Nietzsche, Heidegger, and others),[12] he believed so for one reason: nature is the only foundation of a rational and humane politics, the truly best politics.[13]

Strauss's development of that belief commits him to others outside

---

greatest evil: Not the natural sweetness of living but the terrors of death make us cling to life. What nature firmly establishes is that from which desire moves away, the point of departure of desire; the goal toward which we move is secondary. The primary fact is want. But this want, this lack, is no longer understood as pointing to something complete, perfect, whole." Leo Strauss, *Natural Right*, 250.

[11]Strauss distinguishes Socratic-Platonic natural right from Thomistic natural right (not to mention a third, Aristotelian version). This passage indicates the difference of the Thomistic from the Platonic form of natural right, which, as he argued in the work quoted here and many later writings, is the truest form because it was the original form of natural right: "...[T]he ultimate consequence of the Thomistic view of natural law is that natural law is practically inseparable not only from natural theology—i.e., from a natural theology which is, in fact, based on belief in biblical revelation—but even from revealed theology," Leo Strauss, *Natural Right*, 164 .

[12]Leo Strauss, *Political Philosophy*, 59-60: "The most common form of historicism expresses itself in the demand that the questions of the nature of political things, of the state, of the nature of man, and so forth, be replaced by the questions of the modern state, of modern government, of the present political situation, of modern man....Since it is hard to see, however, how one can speak adequately of the modern state, of our civilization, of modern man, etc., without first knowing what a state is, what civilization is, what man's nature is, the more thoughtful forms of historicism admit that the universal questions of traditional philosophy cannot be abandoned. Yet they assert that any answer to these questions, any attempt at clarifying or discussing them, and indeed any precise formulation of them, is bound to be 'historically conditioned,' i.e., to remain dependent on the specific situation in which it is suggested."

[13]This may be summarized under two headings: (i) Strauss's principles of philosophy and justice, and (ii) his principles of knowledge and virtue. Concerning the first: for Strauss the classic natural right of Plato

the mainstream of Platonic-Aristotelian-Thomistic natural law. We do note, in passing, that he distinguished those thinkers and, for his own part, believed that Plato's was the purest natural law theory.[14] His own foundationalism is a unique and, to some, compelling form of Platonism, wherein (i) the philosophic life is unequivocally the highest human good;

---

maintains (a) that politics and political objects (virtues; good and evil; human nature; governments, insofar as they reflect or deflect the necessary attributes of human nature) are intelligible to man *qua* philosopher and, in a qualified way, to man *qua* citizen; but political theories that abstract from such a canon of intelligiblity cannot lead to a rational, humane politics (See *Natural Right*, 78-80 and *Political Philosophy*, 27-28). This same natural right proposes (b) that only the good man (or the philosopher, if and when a true philosopher rules) properly judges politics, because virtue is the only proper claimant to political rule (See *Political Philosophy*, 36-38). Platonic natural right also requires (c) a strict political hierarchy, wherein the virtuous (that is, the philosopher or the good man) rule because the virtuous possess virtue in an active sense, whereas all others have a passive, obediential form of virtue. That is, a rational and humane politics requires the same hierarchy (See Leo Strauss, *Natural Right*, 130-44).

Strauss's principles of knowledge and virtue propose that true virtue is philosophic virtue, because philosophy is without qualification the highest human good. Citizen-morality merely clears the way for philosophy, although it is not necessarily, nor entirely, incompatible with philosophy (See Leo Strauss, *Natural Right*, 150, n. 24, and again, 130-44, especially 142 on the citizen's contempt of philosophy). Thus to repeat, true virtue is theoretic, not civic, and philosophic, not moral. Moral virtue, Aristotle's *ethike arete*, is, in fact, "merely political or vulgar virtue" (Leo Strauss, *Natural Right*, 151-52).

[14] See Leo Strauss, *Natural Right*, 146-64. For a detailed outline of this point of Strauss's interpretation of classic natural right, see Victor Gourevitch, "On Natural Right" in *The Crisis of Liberal Democracy*, ed. Kenneth L. Deutsch and Walter Soffer (Albany: State University of New York Press, 1987), 30-47, esp. 42. For reasons that become evident below and we have expressed elsewhere ("Review of Deutsch and Soffer," forthcoming in *The Thomist)*, Strauss's classification is incomplete and proceeds from questionable premises.

(ii) this same life is marked by a Socrates-like agnosticism about the paramount questions of philosophy; (iii) true justice is, correspondingly, a kind of Socratic self-examination;[15] and (iv) political justice, which is not necessarily true justice, is the rule of the philosophically enlightened. It is rule of the virtuous or, given a strict Socratic notion of virtue as knowledge, nearly virtuous, gentlemen.[16] Strauss believes that political justice can flow only from those objective features of the human situation. Because Strauss simply presumed that Plato accepted the Socratic pro-

---

[15]To summarize this consequence, which, to put it mildly, seems paradoxical to many students of Plato, let us only cite Strauss's beliefs that Xenophon, first, naturalized Plato's theory of Forms as subsistent entities, and, second, did so rightly. So, contrary to much evidence in the Platonic corpus, for the philosopher (that is, Plato's Socrates as corrected by Xenophon's pragmatic agnosticism), knowledge of the eternal ideas is no more than knowing certain "fundamental and permanent problems" that affect philosophic investigation. In essence, Strauss extends the aporetic quality of some Socratic dialogues of Plato to philosophy itself and to true philosophy. He justifies that logical move as follows. First, humans as humans--that is, potential philosophers--are torn between (i) imposing order on the cosmos by the norms of mathematical knowledge and the productive arts and (ii) "the charm of humble awe, which is engendered by meditation on the human soul and its experiences. Philosophy is characterized by the gentle, if firm, refusal to succumb to either charm" (*Political Philosophy*, 39-40). Second and correlatively, "philosophy as such is nothing but genuine awareness of the problems, i.e., of the fundamental and comprehensive problems. ...Therefore the philosopher ceases to be a philosopher at the moment at which the 'subjective certainty' of a solution becomes stronger than his awareness of the problematic character of that solution." (Leo Strauss, *On Tyranny* [Glencoe: Free Press, 1-63; repr. Ithaca: Cornell University Press, 1968], 210.)

[16]True virtue, again for Strauss, is philosophic knowledge. Given that strict Socratic notion, we can reasonably infer Strauss thinks that (i) the attitudes about life, philosophy, and politics and (ii) the corresponding moral habits, of those who are well-born, leisured, and liberally educated reflect true justice. Because for Strauss, the support of such people is necessary to all forms of political stability, true justice is imitated by this

fession of ignorance, he attributes, illicitly, metaphysical agnosticism to Plato.[17] His position is, in consequence, difficult to reconcile with Plato's belief that man can have knowledge (*episteme*) of absolute intelligibilities (for example: the second proof for the soul's immortality in *Phaedo*, especially 74A-75E; the view that the illumination of the Good certifies our knowledge of all other intelligibilities in the downward path of dialectic, *Republic*, VI, 511 C, VII, 533B-D; the parallel idea in *Symposium*, conjoined with the ascent to Beauty and all other true realities spoken of in *Phaedrus*, 246D-248C[18]). However all this may be, Strauss's Platonic foundation for politics is a foundation of things, rather than beliefs about

---

same rule of the well-born and the educated. Strauss seems to imply as much in his essay, "What Is Political Philosophy?" Therein, he concludes a discussion of the anti-democratic nature of Platonic and Aristotelian natural right by observing that it is good inasmuch as it allows the education and leads to the rule of gentlemen: "Now to the extent to which democracy is aware of these dangers [radical egalitarianism and conformism], to the same extent it sees itself compelled to think of elevating its level and its possibilities by a return to the classics' notion of education: a kind of education which can never be thought of as mass-education, but only as a higher and highest education of those who are by nature fit for it. It would be an understatement to call it royal education." *Political Philosophy*, 38; see 36-38 for the whole discussion. For compatible evidence suggesting this concept of political justice as over against true justice, see above, n. 13.

[17] Which attribution we have analyzed in detail in "Critical Discussion: Leo Strauss on First Philosophy, the Forms, and Politics in Plato," currently unpublished, and "Review of Deutsch and Soffer," *The Crisis of Liberal Democracy*," forthcoming in *The Thomist*, 23.

[18] Following Guthrie's lead on the interconnection of *Symposium* and *Phaedrus* on the intelligibility, to us, of the realities *(ta onta)*; see his A *History of Greek Philosophy. Plato: The Man and His Earlier Period* (Cambridge: Cambridge University Press, 1975), 392, 402-03. This is not to overlook that for Plato this intelligibility characterizes the fleeting *episteme* of man's incarnate state. Still, the weight of Plato's evidence requires that Plato not be the metaphysical agnostic whom Strauss believes he is, if only because Plato time and again uses *episteme* in reference to knowledge in our incarnate state: fleeting *episteme is* still *episteme*.

them. It is a foundation rooted in the facts of human nature. Attributing metaphysical agnosticism to Plato, Strauss implicates the matter or content of first philosophy; but he accepts the formal dependence of justice on first philosophy, as Plato indicated that foundation at *Republic*, VI, 505E7-8.[19] Strauss's position transcends today's foundationalist/anti-foundationalist dichotomy for that very reason. His is a foundation of real, as opposed to rationate, objects; it is an epistemic rather than doxastic foundationalism.

It goes without saying that the same is true of Jacques Maritain. Accordingly, let us focus both on his agreeing with Strauss (and natural law theorists generally) that only epistemic foundations suffice for sound politics, and also two nuances of his concept of foundation for politics.

The first of these nuances was foundation, understood ontologically. The basis that Maritain attributed to human rights indicates his ontology of the natural law. Rights derive from "the true idea of natural law, as looked upon in an ontological perspective and as conveying through the essential structures and requirements of created nature the wisdom of the Author of Being."[20] Maritain included the principles that (i) man has a specifically human and a permanent nature, identical in all men, which (ii) includes intelligence and free will, and to which (iii) there corresponds a specifically human supreme good, within this ontological foundation.[21] By the same term, Maritain pointed to "the normality of functioning which is grounded on the essence of that being: man."[22]

Maritain called the second aspect of foundation gnoseological. As expressed in *Man and the State*, this concept included at least three items. First, however complete and true the natural law might be in itself, i.e. ontologically, still that law as known admits of degrees of truth and certitude in the individuals who know it.[23] Second, the natural law is known *per inclinationem*. In order to know it, one needs an elaborate social network. Only that device allows the best human inclinations progres-

---

[19]Line reference to Burnet edition (Oxford: 1902).

[20]Jacques Maritain, *Man and the State* (Chicago: University of Chicago Press, 1951), 84.

[21]*Ibid.*, 85-86.

[22]*Ibid.*, 88.

[23]*Ibid.*, 89-90.

sively to emerge, and those inclinations are necessary conditions of moral illumination.[24] Third, the sole condition of the natural law's fulfillment occurs "[o]nly when the Gospel has penetrated to the very depth of human substance."[25]

Thus in their own minds, both Strauss and Maritain would anchor politics on *episteme* of human nature. Maritain no less than Strauss would deny the tacit premise of today's foundationalist dichotomy--namely, that beliefs and their justifications, rather than the objects of belief, constitute adequate foundations.

This gains importance when we notice that both Strauss and Maritain thought that our century's horrors signalled the political climax of a uniquely modern rationalism. In their view, that rationalism, initiated by Descartes, simply is subjective idealism. Doxastic foundationalism of the sort already discussed, including Rorty's variant of it, is one of its consequences. When its premises are unchecked, this idealism declines into intoxication with the self. Thus, if Strauss and Maritain are right, ultimately neither subjective idealism nor its foundationalist/anti-foundationalist offspring could avoid power politics, because in politics subjective idealism and its offspring form conventionalisms. More, they might even celebrate power politics, as we see in Nietzsche; and if it is plausible to view Nietzsche in that way, then whether it be a moral tradition in MacIntyre's sense, or liberal values in Rorty's sense, no mere doxastic constellation could adequately respond to power politics. Thus, to avoid begging the question in one's commitment to a moral tradition or liberal values, one must return to first philosophy with Strauss and Maritain.

True: Rorty denies the very possibility of doing so, and MacIntyre appears to deny it; but neither actually disqualifies an epistemic foundation of politics. Moreover, Rorty develops his critique on the basis that the traditional concept of objectivity is representationalism. Because he acknowledges that Aquinas, and perhaps Aristotle, escapes the fallacies of representationalism,[26] his not taking precise aim at them, too, merely is to dismiss a venerable strain of epistemic realism, however unpopular it might be currently. We do not here suggest that Strauss's or Maritain's epistemic realism is in fact right. That requires separate proof. We simply

---

[24]*Ibid.*, 91-94 .
[25]*Ibid.*, 90.
[26]Rorty, *Mirror of Nature*, 40-41 (and n. 8 therein), and 45.

have outlined some of their principles in that area and urged that, first, Rorty has not actually overcome them, and second, by his logic, he should have tried. Where MacIntyre is concerned, while he generally acknowledges the primacy of theoretical cognition, he does not cogently reject its obvious consequence for the moral tradition that impresses him most, the Aristotelian.

III. Postscript: Strauss and Maritain on Knowing the Natural Law

In 1988, Professor Mortimer J. Adler urged this association to consider whether Strauss's natural law position is itself adequately grounded.[27] Adler's challenge obviously requires another paper. Nevertheless, we have said enough here to draw two distinctions between Strauss and Maritain, and now we turn to stating them briefly.

As we saw for Strauss, true virtue is philosophic virtue. This results in a consequence that Strauss readily admits, namely, that either one knows the principles of the law as an agnostic Socratic-Platonic, or one knows a mere vulgar reflection of them. Maritain's distinction between the ontological and gnoseological aspect of the law provides a way around the Straussian dilemma. The reason is, in a word, context. For Maritain, historical circumstances form necessary conditions of the law as known, promulgated, and obeyed—the only sense in which the law actually functions as law. In other words, from a Maritainian perspective, Strauss would appear to overlook the reality-determining function of man's always being situated in a specific time and place. It is true that Strauss fought a particular understanding of context, that in the historicism of Hegel, Nietzsche, and Heidegger; but Strauss seems to have been unaware of a Maritainian notion of what we are calling context, according to which actual existence is the first perfection of the real, which existence includes the historical and contingent. From this viewpoint, Strauss's dichotomy would flow from an exaggerated Platonic rationalism, one that denies reality to the contingent.

This same oversight leads us to Strauss's and Maritain's different views of philosophy and revelation. For Maritain, the law as law is

---

[27] Our manuscript, "Strauss on First Philosophy," takes up the same question in detail, though in the narrower context of whether Strauss's natural law position is adequately grounded in Plato's thought.

ultimately perfectible only in terms of its ultimate foundation; it is perfectible only when the Gospel's message penetrates "the very depth of human substance"; but Strauss appears to have adopted a neo-Averroist position on the distinction between philosophy and faith.[28] Because he never directly acknowledged neo-Averroism in print, Strauss might be technically innocent of ignoring Aquinas's—not to mention Maritain's—argument that the cognitions of faith are higher than those of philosophy; but Strauss's position surely appears incomplete, just as a natural law position, because it again ignores context. Three contextual issues are crucial here: God's freely choosing to become man; the potential reasonableness of Christian belief in incarnational theology; and the consequence of that belief for the gnoseology of the natural law (this is not to mention the gnoseology of philosophy itself). In light of those issues, it is reasonable for a natural law philosopher to propose that the law can remain law, even as extrinsically perfected by grace. Strauss's categorizing the law, so understood, as only a vulgar reflection of natural right is not adequately nuanced, and, once again, the reason is inattention to historical context and development of law and of philosophy.

Put simply, Strauss ignores some components of the natural law position as it has actually evolved. In order to identify the natural law in its purity with Plato, one must imply that natural law philosophy has not evolved. Obviously that claim needs support. Thus, Strauss's natural law position is comparatively ill-grounded. We have already suggested that there is reason to suspect its adequacy on Platonic grounds alone.

---

[28] For a brief statement and critique, see our "Review of Deutsch and Soffer," forthcoming in *The Thomist*.

Robert E. Lauder

Creative Intuition in American Film: Maritain at the Movies

One of the more important tasks that Jacques Maritain set for himself was to apply the insights and principles of St. Thomas to contemporary problems. Believing that the vision of St. Thomas was sufficiently profound to lend itself to widespread and continual application, Maritain set his sights at commenting on and developing the doctrine of the Angelic Doctor. One area in which Maritain is judged to have made an original contribution is the philosophy of art. I am going to try to mimic Maritain's use of Thomas: just as Maritain applied the doctrine of St. Thomas to topics with which Thomas had not specifically dealt, I am going to extend Maritain's insights to an area about which the Frenchman did not write. Maritain's philosophy of art and especially his doctrine of creative intuition can be very helpful in looking at cinema. In this article I will limit myself to contemporary American cinema, to two films, each created by a cinematic genius and one other film that illustrates by contrast what Maritain thought about art.

Art can be considered as a virtue possessed by the artist or as a finished product.[1] Following Thomas, Maritain identifies the virtue of art as an intellectual virtue. It is a habit of the intellect by which the intellect knows how to make things. The habit is acquired through frequent acts. This habit of making can produce two types of product, two types of art. One has come to be called servile art; the other has come to be known as fine art.[2] Servile art is a product that is made for some practical purpose.

---

[1]Jacques Maritain, *Art and Scholasticism and Other Essays*, trans. J. F. Scanlon (New York: Charles Scribner's Sons, 1935), 9-11.
[2]*Ibid.*, 18, 32-35.

An automobile is a servile work of art, as are knives and forks. The artist who knows how to make servile works of art knows how to produce things that have a practical use. Fine art does not have any use. It is its own reason for being. The motto over the world-famous Metro Goldwyn Mayer Lion states the nature of fine art succinctly: *ars gratia artis* (art for art's sake). We do not use a Michelangelo statue as a doorstop or a Picasso as a kind of paper weight. Beauty has no practical use. However, this is not to say that fine art does not affect us. It can affect us profoundly. It can touch the deepest reaches of our souls. In a metaphysics such as St. Thomas's and Maritain's, why this should be is not difficult to understand. All beings are imitations of God. Each being is one, good, true, and beautiful to the extent that it is. In creating a fine work of art the artist is imitating the freedom of God in creating persons: neither the divine artist nor the human artist is making realities that are to be functional or used. The fine artist can make something beautiful. With typical directness Maritain writes:

> St. Thomas, who was as simple as he was wise, defined the beautiful as what gives pleasure on sight, *id quod visum placet*. The four words say all that is necessary: a vision, that is to say an intuitive *knowledge* and a *joy*. The beautiful is what gives joy, not all joy, but joy in knowledge; not the joy peculiar to the act of knowing, but a joy superabounding and overflowing from such an act because of the object known. If a thing exalts and delights the soul by the bare fact of its being given to the intuition of the soul, it is good to apprehend, it is beautiful. Beauty is essentially the object of intelligence, for what *knows* in the full meaning of the word is the mind, which alone is open to the infinity of being.[3]

Discussing beauty Maritain goes on to point out that beauty delights the mind because beauty reveals a certain proportion of things to the mind. He notes that the three characteristics that St. Thomas assigns to beauty are "integrity, because the mind likes being; proportion because the mind likes order and unity, lastly and above all brightness or clarity,

---

[3]*Ibid.*, 23.

because the mind likes light and intelligibility."[4] The fine artist has a marvelous vocation: to make the beautiful.

Just as any virtue, the virtue of art can be strengthened by frequent acts of making. A person might produce a work of art without having the virtue of art, and so the work of art would not be very good. Also, a person might have the virtue of art and might no longer be able to make any works of art. I am thinking of examples of an artist experiencing physical problems such as a painter losing his sight or a sculptor suffering from arthritis. Such artists would still have the virtue, they would still know intellectually how to produce a work, but they would no longer be able to execute what they know should be done.

In discussing works of fine art I find it helpful to use analogously the notions of matter and form from Aristotle's hylomorphic theory. These notions can illuminate the two key ingredients that go to make up a work of art. The matter is the particular type of material that the artist is using, for example, canvas and oil for painting, rock for sculpture, wood for carving, words for stories and novels. A person who has the virtue of art knows how to use a particular type of matter in order to produce some work. The other component, which is analogous to form in the hylomorphic theory, is what Maritain calls the *creative intuition*. By this he means a profound experience of reality. This experience has strong emotional overtones, but it is not merely an emotional experience. It is an insight, but it is not only intellectual; and it is certainly not conceptual. Maritain writes of it:

> ...the part of intuitive reason becomes absolutely predominant. Then, as our further analyses will show, we are confronted with an intuition of emotive origin, and we enter the nocturnal empire of a primeval activity of the intellect which, far beyond concepts and logic, exercises itself in vital connection with imagination and emotion. We have quit logical reason, and even conceptual reason, yet we have to do more than ever with intuitive reason...[5]

---

[4]*Ibid.*, 24.

[5]Jacques Maritain, *Creative Intuition in Art and Poetry* (New York: Meridian Books, 1955), 55. In applying Maritain's theory to film I am extending what Maritain calls poetic intuition to the intuition of any creative artist, such as a filmmaker.

This type of experience is had by many of us, but what distinguishes it for the artist is the creative component. When the artist has one of these experiences he or she has to incarnate it somehow into an external work. When the artist has such an intuition he or she is driven to *speak* it in a work of art.[6] For the artist this is the only way that the intuition can be spoken with any degree of adequacy. If the intuition could be articulated verbally, then there would be no need to produce a work of art. Because the intuition can only be incarnated in an external work, the artist might experience a kind of restlessness until the intuition is put into an external form. I suspect that one reason why artists seem to hate to be interviewed is that they find it very difficult to talk about their creative intuitions. I can recall artists such as Graham Greene or Alfred Hitchcock who almost seemed to put the interviewer off and in effect said to any questions they were asked: "If you wish to know, go look at the work. If there is an answer to what you wish to know, it is there in the work." I can think of no exception. As a matter of fact, this response is one of the best descriptions I have seen of a creative intuition. In an interview author/director Ingmar Bergman said:

> A film for me begins with something very vague—a chance remark or a bit of conversation, a hazy but agreeable event unrelated to any particular situation. It can be a few bars of music, a shaft of light across the street. Sometimes in my work at the theater I have envisioned actors made up for yet unplayed roles.
> These are split-second impressions that disappear as quickly as they come, yet leave behind a mood—like pleasant dreams. They constitute a mental state, not an actual story, but one abounding in fertile associations and images. Most of all, it is a brightly colored thread sticking out of the dark sack of the unconscious. If I begin to wind up this thread, and do it carefully, a complete film will emerge.[7]

For Maritain the entire work is contained in germ in the creative intuition.

---

[6]*Ibid.*, 98.
[7]Ingmar Bergman, *Four Screenplays of Ingmar Bergman*, trans. Lars Melmstrom and David Kushner (New York: Simon and Schuster, 1960), xv.

Everything is already there, contained in poetic intuition, everything is given, all the vitality, all the insight, all the strength of creativity which is now in act, like a dart filled with a power of intellectual direction; and in a certain sense (intensively—whatever part adventitious chance may have in the development) the totality of the work to be engendered was already present in advance, whether this totality is now virtually given in the first line of a poem, as a gift from the preconscious life of the soul, or virtually concentrated in the spiritual germ of a novel or drama.[8]

When there is a successful wedding between a profound creative intuition and the proper use of the matter, we have a great work of art; and great works of art are important revelations to us. Maritain writes that the creative intuition tends toward:

the humble revelation, virtually contained in a small lucid cloud of inescapable intuition, both of the Self of the poet and of some particular flash of reality in the God-made universe; a particular flash of reality bursting forth in its unforgettable individuality, but infinite in its meanings and echoing capacity...[9]

There can be works of art that display a certain skill or facility on the part of the artist with the matter used. However if the creative intuition is missing then the work of art suffers; if an artist has a profound creative intuition but has not developed his skill with the material he is using, then the work of art suffers.[10] The great artists are able to experience reality deeply and to incarnate their intuitions in matter. When we encounter the work of art it is the creative intuition of the artist that we should be encountering. It seems impossible to overemphasize the importance of creative intuition in Maritain's view of art. He wrote:

What I should like to stress is the fact that in creative intuition we have the primary rule to which, in the case of the fine arts, the whole fidelity, obedience and heedfulness of the artist must be

---

[8]Jacques Maritain, *Creative Intuition in Art and Poetry*, 98-99.
[9]*Ibid.*, 84.
[10]*Ibid.*, 99.

committed. I also should like to stress the fact that between this primary, primordial, primitive rule and all the other rules of making, however indispensable they may be, there exists an essential difference, so to speak infinite, as between heaven and earth. All other rules are of earth, they deal with particular ways of operation in the making of the work. But this primary rule is a heavenly rule, because it deals with the very conception, in the bosom of the spirit, of the work to be engendered in beauty. If creative intuition is lacking, a work can be perfectly made, and it is nothing, the artist has nothing to say. If creative intuition is present, and passes to some extent, into the work, the work exists and speaks to us, even if it is imperfectly made and proceeds from a man.[11]

Some creative intuitions are so deep and so beautifully enfleshed that we can encounter them again and again. I can recall vividly the first time I saw Da Vinci's *Mona Lisa*. I arrived at the Louvre at about four o'clock and had an appointment with someone in another section of Paris in about half an hour. I knew that I was pressed for time but wanted at least to get a look at the supposedly great masterpiece. My first reaction was that I wondered why this was supposed to be a great painting, but, little by little, the painting seduced me. Finally, after trying to leave the room several times, I wound up late for my appointment--because I could not stop looking at the lady with the haunting smile. The great works of art move us into the mystery of being.

With film we have a special problem. Whose creative intuition is at the heart of a film? There is not one artist who creates a film, but hundreds. There are producers, actors, musicians, lighting crew, make-up, set designers, screenplay writers and more. Any one of these people might have a creative intuition in relation to the making of a particular film and contribute enormously to the artistic success of a film. However, in this article, I am going to settle on the view that, if we are looking for one artist to whom the film might be attributed, it is the director. More than anyone else it is the director's film because he is the artist who must weave together the contributions of all the other artists. The director must allow his creative intuition to guide him throughout the making of

---

[11]*Ibid.*, 45.

the film. In effect, this will mean that the director must draw together the creative intuitions of all the other artists who are contributing to the film into a complete work of art. In the actual making of the filmwhat this will involve might range from a pre-shooting discussion with the author of the screenplay and the cinematographer to direct-ing some of the actors or actresses during the shooting to change their performances slightly or significantly. The director might have to supervise the camera man, make-up artists and music conductor. It would seem that the details of making a single film are endless and all of them the director wants to influence by his creative intuition. The two American film directors whom I would like to use to illustrate Maritain's theory are Orson Welles and Woody Allen, both of whom I consider extraordinary cinematic artists. Their personal contributions to their films are especially strong because they not only direct their films but they also are the authors of the screenplays and frequently appear in their own films.

I will use one film of Welles, *Citizen Kane*, and one film of Allen, *Crimes and Misdemeanors*, to illustrate Maritain's theory of creative intuition and one other film, *The Sea of Love*, to illustrate the absence of creative intuition in a film. *Citizen Kane*, which Welles co-authored with Herman Mankiewicz, might be the finest film ever made. It is an extraordinarily visual film. Welles learned the various uses of the camera one weekend from cinematographer Gregg Toland, and then, in his film, Welles used just about every camera device that had been employed by movie directors prior to 1941. In illustrating how Welles successfully wedded matter and form, the use of the camera with his creative intuition, I will refer to the brilliant uses of a few camera devices which distinguish *Citizen Kane* from almost all films which preceded it and most films which followed.

In his exceptionally good book, *What Is Cinema*? André Bazin, some-times referred to as the Aristotle of the cinema, argues persuasively that with *Citizen Kane* film came of age. Prior to talking films, the montage was often used to affect an audience's reaction to a film. Directors knew that by juxtaposing certain images they could profoundly influence the way an audience viewed a film. The most obvious example is the one done by a Russian director. In three different parts of a film the director inserted the same shot of an actor's face. By what preceded and followed the actor's face the impression was given that the actor was emoting dif-ferently in each of the three parts of the film when actually it was the same shot each time. Montage illustrated that one and one can equal more than two.[12] With the coming of sound pictures filmmakers made less use of montage so taken up were they with sound. The ability to use deep focus, the including within a shot figures close to the camera along with figures some distance from the camera was possible for some time prior to 1941, but it took the genius of Welles to use deep focus to capture the ambiguity of the main character. Bazin says that *Citizen Kane* illustrates that it has become possible for the director to write on film.[13] I will just point out a few of the visual devices Welles uses in *Citizen Kane* to write on film. The magic of Welles's camera fosters the revelation that a creative intuition can convey. In *Citizen Kane* the marriage between technique and intuition, between cinematic signs and philosophy of human nature, is nearly perfect. The film opens and ends with a series of visual metaphors. The opening metaphors include a series of dissolving shots: a sign ("No Trespassing") a wire fence on which the sign is fastened, heavy iron gates, a row of iron bars at the top of the fence, an iron emblem ("K") at the top of the iron bars, a gigantic, uninviting stark mansion. At the start of *Citizen Kane* these shots do not seem to mean much, but when they are repeated at the end of the film, and a puff of smoke is seen climbing from the chimney of the mansion, they are seen to be revelations of the personality and life of Charles Kane. The dead man's unloving and unloved personal existence is symbolized by all the metaphors including the smoke from the burning of the sled, *Rosebud*, which throughout the film has been the clue to the mystery of Charles Kane. That mystery is underlined throughout the film by deep focus shots of Kane in crucially important situations, shots which suggest the complexity and ambiguity of Charles Kane.

So with *Citizen Kane* we have a cinematic masterpiece that illustrates an artist completely at home with his material, confidently and successfully incarnating his creative intuition. Can we articulate the creative intuition? No. We experience it in the film. We might say that it is connected with an insight into the importance of being loved and loving, the danger of not recognizing anything more important than self. So I would suggest that the creative intuition at the heart of the film is related to a moral insight into human nature.

---

[12]André Bazin, *What Is Cinema?* Vol. I, essays selected and trans. Hugh Gray (Berkeley: University of California Press, 1967), 23-40.
   [13]*Ibid*.

Woody Allen's film, *Crimes and Misdemeanors*, though not as visually startling or dazzling as *Citizen Kane*, is an extraordinary film. Critic Richard Blake has suggested that some day Allen may be judged the greatest filmmaker of all time.[14] In *Crimes and Misdemeanors* Allen depicts two groups of people in what appear to be stories that have little overlays. One story seems terribly serious, the other quite amusing. Allen succeeds in weaving them together and posing some profound philosophical questions through the development of the film. With *Crimes and Misdemeanors* we are viewing an artist at the peak of his powers. Allen's creative intuition into what he dramatizes as the absurdity of reality is exceptionally powerful. I suggest that *Crimes and Misdemeanors* is Camus with comedy.

The Sea of Love, a contemporary murder mystery, which in the fall of 1989 grossed huge sums of money at the box office, is the antithesis of what Maritain has discussed. If there ever were a creative intuition at the heart of *The Sea of Love*, it was drowned in eroticism. The film is a good example of excessive violence and gratuitous sex. In spite of the sexual gymnastics in the film, *The Sea of Love* paradoxically trivializes sex.

Citizen Kane and *Crimes and Misdemeanors* have integrity, proportion and brightness or clarity. All great cinematic works do. When we view them we can appreciate the intuitions of their creators. The artist looks at things and reveals them to us. In fact the great artist may even reveal more to us than he consciously intends or realizes. Maritain is correct: "The artist, whether he knows it or not, is consulting God when he looks at things."[15]

---

[14]Richard Blake, "When, Out of the Past," *America*, March 21, 1987.
[15]Jacques Maritain, *Art and Scholasticism*, 64.

Ralph Nelson

Maritain's Account of the Social Sciences

From *The Degrees of Knowledge* to*The Peasant of the Garonne,* Jacques Maritain made frequent references to the social sciences, their definition, their subdivisions, and their relations to philosophy. However, he never treated the social sciences as a whole in a treatise; and, consequently, they are often mentioned in circumstances where they are not the principal interest. In investigating Maritain's reflections on the social sciences, particularly in his moral treatises, I was at first convinced that he had developed a single, consistent account of them. Later I became convinced that, in fact, there were two different accounts not easily reconcilable. Thus, rather than a fairly coherent survey, we are faced with a dilemma. My aim is to identify that dilemma and to attempt to see whether there is an escape from it.

An initial difficulty is encountered in *The Degrees of Knowledge.* There are several passages in which Maritain refers to the "moral sciences" (*les sciences morales*). In the first instance, he says:

> Moreover, we shall consider only theoretical sciences and leave aside the moral sciences which, concerned as they are with the practical side, and proceeding by way of synthesis to the very concrete determinations of action, belong to quite a different chapter of epistemology.[1]

---

[1]Jacques Maritain, *Distinguish to Unite: Or, the Degrees of Knowledge* (New York: Charles Scribner's Sons), 1959, 34-35. I have replaced "speculative" with "theoretical" for the sake of uniformity.

Maritain does, indeed, consider moral sciences in the seventh appendix to the book, about "The Proper Mode of Moral Philosophy,"[2] and he does this precisely by looking at the way of synthesis. He canvasses the question of the status of moral knowledge relying, in part at least, on the writings of the great Thomistic commentators, Cajetan and John of Saint Thomas.The first use of the term "moral science," then, refers to the Thomistic tradition in moral philosophy. In a subsequent passage there is a statement which seems to distinguish *between* philosophy and the moral sciences,[3] but somewhat further on, in a clearer way, he asserts that "a striking renewal of themes proper to the moral philosophy of Thomas Aquinas is evidenced in the moral and legal sciences of which we have not spoken in this essay."[4]

It is my contention that Maritain means "social sciences" when he speaks of moral sciences in this context. André Lalande has noted that the older name for the human or social sciences in France was moral sciences.[5] Indeed, this was the case in English; for when John Stuart Mill published *A System of Logic* in 1843, and many editions later in 1872, his main concern was with the logic of the moral, that is social, sciences. An additional piece of evidence to support this interpretation of Maritain is to be found in the vocabulary of Raymond Aron's *La Sociologie Allemande Contemporaine* (translated simply as *German Sociology*). Writing a few years after the appearance of *The Degrees of Knowledge*, Aron refers to moral sciences in his chapter on Max Weber.[6]

So the term moral science is used by Maritain both to refer to the Thomistic tradition in moral philosophy and to the modern social sciences. We must address the problem of how these two kinds of *science* are related.

From the instances cited, all the indications are that Maritain be-

---

[2]*Ibid.*, 456.

[3]*Ibid.*, 45-46.

[4]*Ibid.*, 66.

[5]André Lalande, *Vocabulaire Technique et Critique de la Philosophie* (Paris: Presses Universitaires de France, 1962, 958).

[6]"*L'originalité des sciences morales tient avant tout à la satisfaction particulière qu'y trouve la curiosité de l'esprit grâce à la 'compréhension.'*" *La Sociologie Allemande Contemporaine* (Paris: Presses Universitaires de France, 1966), 91. The first edition appeared in 1935.

lieved that the character of the social sciences depends on settling the larger issue concerning the character of the study of nature itself. It is imperative, then, first to examine what, if any, connections exist between philosophy and science when the study of nature is at stake.

Let us assume that, once the modern sciences of nature are established, there are generally three ways in which the philosophy of nature will be understood. First, there is the view, now identified with positivism, that the discovery of science, notably physics, has completely eliminated the old philosophy of nature. There are sciences of nature; there is no philosophy of nature. If philosophical concerns are relevant, this is so only in meta-scientific inquiries about the logic and methodology of the sciences. In a once common formulation, philosophy was called the logic of the sciences. In any case, philosophy no longer had any content of its own. Secondly, taking as its starting point scientifically established data, a philosophy of nature is developed, not as a parallel kind of inquiry, but as an extension of the sciences of nature. This seems to be the significance of Bergson's approach in *Creative Evolution*. The work is essentially a philosophy of nature.[7] Thirdly, there is the view that the discovery of the sciences of nature has not eliminated the validity of the philosophy of nature, as understood in the Aristotelian tradition, even though Aristotelian "science" has definitely been replaced.[8] Thus there is a dual knowledge of nature asserted, but it remains to examine how that duality is to be understood. Maritain offers a conception of the two kinds of knowledge as distinct, though complementary. Suffice it to say that his conception did not necessarily meet with acceptance in Thomistic circles.[9]

---

[7]See Henri Gouhier, "*Le Bergsonisme dans l'Histoire de la Philosophie Française*," *Revue des Travaux de L'Academie des Sciences Morales et Politiques*, Fourth Series, 1959, First Semester, 189-191. Maritain says: "With regard to Bergson it should be added that his direct objective was perhaps more in the order of the philosophy of nature than of metaphysics." *Science and Wisdom* (London: Geoffrey Bles, 1954), 48, n. 1. The book was based on three lectures given in 1934.

[8]See Yves R. Simon, "Maritain's Philosophy of the Sciences," in Jacques Maritain, *Philosophy of Nature* (New York: Philosophical Library, 1951).

[9]F.G. Connolly, *Science versus Philosophy* (New York: Philosophical Library, 1957).

Though the study is out of date, it does give some valuable information of nature in the 1950s. Stated in the simplest terms, Maritain maintains that there are two kinds of analysis of nature which together constitute the generic study of nature. They are empiriological analysis and onto-logical analysis. The two differ in their basic focus.While empiriological analysis is a focus on what Maritain calls "the observable and measurable as such,"[10] and, accordingly, is subdivided into empirio-schematic and empirio-metric inquiry, the ontological analysis of nature is focused upon intelligible being. Furthermore, there is a sharp difference between the two as to the resolution of their concepts: empiriological analysis de-pends upon the "permanent possibility of sensible verification and meas-urement," while ontological analysis resolves its concepts in intelligible being, essences.[11] Perhaps the contrast between the two can best be summed up as follows: the empiriological analysis of nature is a theoreti-cal discipline bearing on phenomena and their laws, utilizing mental constructs (*entia rationis*), employing causal explanation in terms of proximate or apparent causes--though clearly excluding teleology--and resolving its concepts in the sensible through verification, or, if we accept Karl Popper's rectification, through falsification. On the other hand, the ontological analysis of nature is a theoretical discipline, bearing on corporeal substances, ordinarily not having recourse to mental con-structs, employing causal explanation in the broad Aristotelian sense, and resolving its concepts in intelligible being--that is, the intelligible essence. Empiriological analysis cannot completely sever all connection with being, but its "'ontological index'...is indeed very week."[12]

Having distinguished the two kinds of analysis, and noting that even when they use the same language, it is often with a different meaning, Maritain then argues that they are complementary studies. Modern physics is not only an empiriometric kind of inquiry, but in Maritain's judgment corresponds to the old idea of *scientia media*, being physical as to its content, but mathematical in form, or, in other words, a mathemati-cal reading of physical reality. Biology is primarily an empirioschematic inquiry since the degree to which its finding are subjected to quantifica-tion is relatively limited.

---

[10]Jacques Maritain, *Philosophy of Nature*, 75.
[11]*Ibid.*, 75-6.
[12]Jacques Maritain, *The Degrees of Knowledge*, 194.

Now that Maritain's view on the two kinds of analysis has been sketched, we move on to his views on the relationship between the study of nature and the social sciences. Here there are really two sets of disciplines to be considered. As to the first set--the triad of psychology, sociology, and anthropology--Maritain has maintained that they should be seen as components of the empiriological analysis of nature, that is, they are fundamentally theoretical disciplines. At least that is one account of them. In contrast to this triad, which is Maritain's, there is another triad--composed of history, economics, and politics--supposedly social disciplines as well. Now although the study of history is extremely important in Maritain's educational philosophy, he has consistently argued that history is not a science. The definitive statement of his views on this subject is to be found in *On the Philosophy of History*.[13] So we shall concentrate on economics and politics for either they are considered to be social sciences or aspire to that status. Nowhere does Maritain appear to consider them as theoretical disciplines, nor indeed does he recognize them as autonomous disciplines--that is, standing on their own apart from moral philosophy.

The main problem in this paper concerns the assertion, at least in some of Maritain's writings, that the first triad is linked to the empiriological sciences of nature or, more simply, that they are sciences in the empiriological sense, and the assertion, in other writings, that two of them--sociology and anthropology--are subordinated to moral philosophy.

The first of the social sciences treated after the exposition of the duality of the study of nature is experimental psychology. It is first because the ontological analysis of psychology was approached after the philosophy of nature and life had been developed by Aristotle. I mean that there is a parallel relationship, between experimental and philosophical psychology. For Aristotle, of course, the study of the human psyche (*Peri psyche* or *De Anima*) was a theoretical discipline. So much is this so that the important analysis of voluntariness, after the confusing treatment of the topic in Plato's *Laws*, is to be found in the *Rhetoric* because it pertains to moral, legal, or political psychology--that is, to practical

---

[13]Jacques Maritain, *On the Philosophy of History* (New York: Charles Scribner's Sons, 1957), 2-3.

philosophy. In my opinion Maritain's main contribution to philosophical psychology is to be found in *Creative Intuition in Art and Poetry*.[14]

Maritain, strongly critical of Bergson's philosophy, did not always do justice to the latter's contribution to this kind of inquiry. As to the corresponding empiriological kind of analysis, experimental psychology, Maritain's argues against behaviorism that introspection has a part to play. Characteristically he stakes out a middle position between those who make introspection the sole avenue of knowledge, and those, including phenomenologists, who flatly reject it.[15] There is no doubt that he was particularly attentive to Freud's contribution to that new discipline once known as physiological-psychology. His essay on Freud is a careful attempt to sort out Freud's positive findings from his errors. Maritain was sensitive to the danger of the philosophical contamination of the social sciences, and he pointed out that Freud had succumbed to the influence of philosophical materialism in his psychology.[16]

Maritain also acknowledged Jean Piaget's work in child psychology, but did not thoroughly examine his contribution to the field as he has done with Freud. Had he done so, while accentuating the positive aspects, he might have noted the objectionable features of a theory which rejects philosophical psychology and shows the traces of French idealist philosophy in its epistemology. A thorough examination could hardly ignore Piaget's constant denigration of Aristotelian modes of thought. While recognizing the contributions of such major figures as Freud and Piaget, Maritain did not comment at length on the theoretical

---

[14]Jacques Maritain, *Creative Intuition in Art and Poetry* (Princeton: Princeton University Press, 1953), Chapters 3 and 4.

[15]Placing Thomas Hobbes at the one extreme because of his reliance on introspection in the *Leviathan*, I would take Maurice Merleau-Ponty as a representative of the other position in his *Phenomenology of Perception*.

[16]Maritain warns generally about this kind of contamination when he speaks of "the most deplorable metaphysical shackles" in *The Degrees of Knowledge*, 46. In Freud's case the "valuable ideas of a psychologist ... are obscured by a radical empiricism and an aberrant metaphysics." "Freudianism and Psychoanalysis," *Scholasticism and Politics* (Garden City: NY, Doubleday and Company, 1960), 140. Maritain also believed that Freud had confused empiriological and philosophical psychology.

disarray in empiriological psychology.[17] In fact, the essay on Freud was the only extensive scrutiny of the subject.

Just as psychology the second of the social sciences in this first set, sociology, is a theoretical, empiriological kind of analysis. There is no doubt that Maritain was quite well acquainted with the French school of sociology (for example, Comte, Durkheim and Lévy-Bruhl) and less so with German sociology, particularly Max Weber, whose ideas have greatly influenced epistemological discussions of social knowledge in the United States. Of course, Maritain has examined in great detail the thought of August Comte. Although Maritain obviously rejects Comte's famous law of the three stages and his positivistic conception of knowledge, he does accept the validity of the division of sociology into social statics and social dynamics. Comte had first called the new study social physics. He recognized the profundity of Comte's view that positive sociology could not ignore the ethical and religious dimensions of human life, as Emile Littre attempted to do when he broke with Comte over the subjective synthesis. It is remarkable as well that Maritain supports the idea that sociological inquiry should seek to formulate laws, an idea not endorsed by some sociologists. The works of Durkheim and Lévy-Bruhl are mentioned primarily for their views on the relationship between sociology and morality.[18] Whatever data sociology might offer to an adequately considered moral philosophy, it could not replace it. He is particularly critical of Lévy-Bruhl's thesis in this regard.[19]

Closely allied to sociology is the third theoretical, empiriological discipline--anthropology. More often than not there are references in Maritain to two branches of that study: ethnography and ethnology, the study of culture and the comparative study of cultures, rather than to the whole of anthropology.

Maritain offers both a critical comment and a constructive proposal when he looks at some aspects of French research in anthropology. He is

---

[17]For an examination of this disarray, see Yves R. Simon, "*Connaissance de l'Ame,*" *Gants du Ciel,* (Montreal: Fides, 1944). For a translation of this essay see "Knowledge of the Soul," *The Thomist,* LIV, 2 (1990): 269-91.

[18]See Maritain's preface to the third edition of Simon Deploige's *Le conflit de la morale et de la sociologie* (1923) in *Oeuvres Complètes,* II, 1282-4.

[19]Jacques Maritain, *Moral Philosophy* (New York: Charles Scribner's Sons, 1964), 265 and 345.

critical of Lévy-Bruhl's famous distinction between the primitive mentality and the civilized mentality, and the evolutionary explanation of the progression from one to the other. Maritain rejects the notion that here are two mentalities, or souls, as Lévy-Bruhl sometimes said, rather than two different states; but he came up with a constructive proposal, for if the two mentalities theory is discarded, along with the questionable use made of it, he proposed his own law concerning the passage from the *magical* state to the *rational* state of the human being in the history of culture.[20] The use of the term law has been elaborated in Maritain's philosophy of history.

To sum up the first stage of the argument, we find that Maritain treats the three disciplines of experimental psychology, sociology, and anthropology as instances of theoretical, empiriological analysis; or, to be more exact, there are a number of places where he does so. For there is an antithesis to the theoretical thesis which might be called a practical antithesis. This means that there are other instances where Maritain appears to deny these disciplines theoretical status--hence autonomy-- insisting that if they are practical disciplines, they are subordinate to moral philosophy. Take the first instance where his antithesis has been expressed. In *Science and Wisdom*, sociology and anthropology are described as sciences of experimental information connected to moral philosophy. They are "not autonomous sciences" since they fall under "the domain of practical knowledge"; in fact, they are not in actuality sciences at all.[21]

When Maritain examines the various disciplines from the viewpoint of their appropriate place in an educational curriculum based on philosophical principles, especially in *Education at the Crossroads*, there is, once again, the clear statement that sociology and anthropology are "intrinsically subordinated to ethics and natural law."[22] What is noteworthy in this context is that Maritain refers approvingly to a book by John U. Nef

---

[20]Jacques Maritain, "Sign and Symbol," *Ransoming the Time* (New York: Gordian Press, 1972), 227-39. He refers to the law again in *On the Philosophy of History* and says that Lévy-Bruhl indicated his agreement with the "states" thesis (97).

[21]Maritain, *Science and Wisdom*,171.

[22]Jacques Maritain, *Education at the Crossroads* (New Haven: Yale University Press, 1943), 80.

in which that author speaks of "analytical and theoretical fields" including psychology, sociology, and anthropology.[23] The reader is puzzled to say the least. On the one hand, these are theoretical, empiriological sciences which would seem to be autonomous, yet, on the other hand, the same disciplines, no longer considered to be either theoretical or autonomous, are subordinated to moral philosophy. If this contradiction is only apparent, it is not easy to see in what manner the two aspects can be reconciled.

Let us now turn to the second set of social studies which are examined by Maritain—economics and politics (Nothing has been said of geography. Whether it is to be classed as a natural science or a field straddling the natural and social sciences is not, to my knowledge, discussed by Maritain). Allusions to economics as a field of research are rare in Maritain's writings. He alludes to economics in the plural according to French usage; there are economic sciences or different subfields of economics in our usage. Little if anything is said about the nature of the discipline or its scope. Nor does Maritain deal with its development from the earlier emphasis on value, at one level of analysis, to the present emphasis—Marxists aside—on utility. Nor does he have anything to say about Keynesian ideas. The only thing we do know is that economics is subordinated to moral philosophy.

The issue of the status of political science has been principally examined in the essay on Machiavellianism. For Maritain, Machiavelli represents the attempt to render political knowledge autonomous, that is, to cut its connection with moral knowledge. Machiavellianism, then, represents "a profound split, an incurable division between politics and morality."[24] Furthermore, it is a kind of technical knowledge, not pure theory, that the Florentine promotes or, as Maritain prefers to say, a technical, as opposed to a moral, rationalization of political life. Whenever the question of the autonomy of political knowledge arises, Maritain tends to view in it the perspective of the option between a politics without ethics and a politics subordinated to moral philosophy. Political knowledge is never regarded as a form of theoretical knowledge. The current state of political studies is not surveyed. For instance, if we were to listen

---

[23]*Ibid.*, 81.
[24]Jacques Maritain, "The End of Machiavellianism," *The Range of Reason* (New York: Charles Scribner's Sons, 1958), 137.

to its claims to be a theoretical, empiriological science, in Maritain's sense, we would observe an empirioschematic treatment of political phenomena in comparative politics and developmental politics, where historical understanding and causal analysis are significant. We would observe an empiriometric treatment in which quantitative analysis is employed in regard to opinions, voting, and content analysis. We would note that the latter approach gives rise to a certain self-assurance in its practitioners, that may come with the possession of precise information. If we were to listen to the claims, Maritain thinks we would still have to reject them for if political science produces information, it is not science in the proper sense;[25] and it is certainly not autonomous. To deny theoretical status, then, is, *a fortiori*, to deny autonomy. There is no political science which is separate from moral philosophy. Very simply, Maritain has made the Thomistic division of moral or practical philosophy into *monastica*, *oeconomica*, and *politica* his own. Economics, obviously, includes the new political economy as well as the old household management.

There is no philosophical position without its difficulties. Surely much more needs to be said about the kind of knowledge and information attained through modern economic analysis and empirical political science, or studies if one prefers. That Maritain's treatment of these two fields is inadequate must be granted; but at least his remarks about economics and politics are consistent.

At this stage a comparison between Maritain and Leo Strauss is useful. Strauss made a very systematic study of a supposedly autonomous theoretical political science and was well known for his critical and, some would say, devastating attack on empirical political science.[26]

Strauss argued that both the divorce between facts and values on one hand, and that between means and ends on the other, are untenable and, if so, only a kind of political knowledge (and he means political philosophy) which combines consideration of facts and values as well as relates means to ends--let us say efficiency and purpose--is defensible. Up to this point, Maritain would seem to be in agreement with Strauss; but Strauss not only rejects the claims of empirical political science, but the claims of

---

[25]Maritain, *Science and Wisdom*,180, n. 1.

[26]Leo Strauss's strongest attack is found in "An Epilogue" in *Essays on the Scientific Study of Politics*, ed. Herbert J. Storing (New York: Holt, Rinehart, and Winston, 1962), 305-27.

sociology as well; and here some elaboration is necessary.

To the extent that Maritain characterizes sociology as a theoretical discipline within the science of nature, its autonomy is not placed in doubt. Nor does he perceive any adverse consequences in attributing autonomy to sociology. Autonomy is denied to a Machiavellian political technology since political knowledge is practical, not technical, knowledge, and thus must be subsumed under practical philosophy--moral philosophy in a broad sense. To the extent that Maritain considers sociology, as well as political knowledge, to be a practical discipline, it, too, is subordinated to moral philosophy. If this were his final position, there would be no significant difference between Strauss and Maritain in regard to the social sciences. The principal difference is that Strauss always denies that sociology is theoretical knowledge, and Maritain only does this on occasion.

Finally, to return to the main issue of this paper. Does Maritain offer us one account of the social sciences or two? I have argued that there are two accounts when it concerns sociology and anthropology. If these two, and psychology as well, fall under the sciences of nature, they are theoretical modes of knowledge and autonomous. If, on the other hand, they are practical modes of knowledge, then they are subordinated to moral philosophy and are not autonomous disciplines. I contend that they are alleged to be theoretical in *Quatre Essais, Neuf Leçons, Moral Philosophy*, and *The Peasant of the Garonne*. On the other hand, the antithetical view, that they are practical not theoretical, is articulated in *Science and Wisdom* and *Education at the Crossroads*. I contend, then, that not only are there two different accounts of the status of these disciplines, but that the accounts are inconsistent and incompatible. If, inevitably, a choice is required between the two accounts, I would argue for the position, stated in *Nine Lectures on the Primary Notions of Moral Philosophy*, that sociology and anthropology are autonomous, theoretical, empiriological sciences which furnish valuable data to the moral philosopher. They are not, as a result of this, parts of, or subordinated to, moral philosophy. The choice is defended not on the basis of a weight of evidence argument. After all, we are not in a court of law. No, the argument for the choice rests on the fact that Maritain seems to have given more reflection to the bonds between the social sciences and moral philosophy in this treatise than he had ever done before. Regardless of the reasoned choice one makes, I conclude that Maritain leaves us in this situation because the dilemma discerned in his treatment of the social sciences cannot be escaped.

William J. Boyle

Maritain and the
Future of Reason

One of the most significant determinants of the future of civilization will be the future of human reason. The initial *prise de conscience*, so to speak, of this distinctively human power and the subsequent articulation of its potentialities was the crowning achievement of classical Greece. Thinkers from Thales to Aristotle and beyond found in it a capacity to explore in an objective and systematic manner the structure of the universe from its lowest to its highest levels. So significant was this capacity in their eyes that an Aristotle could find in its possession the specifically defining characteristic of man.

As the Greek rational achievement in its fullest and most mature accomplishments came into contact with Christian revelation, an elaborate and enormous effort on the part of numerous Christian thinkers eventually forged a positive relationship between reason and revelation. The integrity of both was preserved and human reason was found to be a powerful tool for understanding Christian revelation and for guiding moral life in this world.

In modern times, however, human reason has entered onto stormy seas. Many conflicting conceptions of its nature, its capacities and its role have arisen. Western civilization has been exposed to a plethora of claims in its regard, many exaggerated (for example, Cartesian, idealistic, and enlightenment aspirations) and many minimalistic (for example, empiricist, positivist, Kantian, and analytical approaches).

At the contemporary moment the crisis of reason continues in unabated fashion. Heideggerian, existentialist, hermeneutical, deconstructionist, and sociological conceptions of reason exercise considerable influence in the intellectual and public arenas. Certain of these, especially, grow in strength.

In this climate the thought of Jacques Maritain on the nature, range, and limits of reason can be a beacon of light for many. In the face of various distorted and dangerous notions, his conception of reason retains the positive advances of Greek and medieval thought, and offers as well original thinking of his own refining the classical understanding at various points. His disengagement and exploration of the intellectual supraconscious, his efforts in the face of modern empirical science to delineate precisely the degrees of knowledge and even his treatment of the practical reason and its limitations in, for instance, *On the Church of Christ* exemplify his creativity in this regard.[1]

In this paper whose concern is with Maritain and the future of human reason, it will obviously not be possible to explore the issue in an expansive manner. Instead, what I intend to do is to examine briefly the present state of reason as manifested in John Caputo's recent book *Radical Hermeneutics*. As Caputo's own position as expressed in this book is, despite its differences, positively related in a number of respects to certain recent and contemporary continental thinkers, such as Martin Heidegger and Jacques Derrida, it is envisioned that this paper will be somewhat more broadly informative as well.

First of all, though, some further reference to Maritain. Having derived his fundamental notions of human reason from the Greek and medieval world, in particular from the work of St. Thomas, Maritain devoted a lifetime rationally to exploring the structure of reality in its multiple dimensions. This exploration unfolded in a number of books devoted to an extremely careful, precise and deeply insightful examination of various aspects of reality. Numerous works in areas such as metaphysics, natural theology, the philosophy of nature, moral philosophy, political philosophy, the philosophies of art, of beauty, of history, of education, etc. flowed from his pen throughout some sixty years of publication. Such a project presupposed Greek and medieval confidence in and understanding of the nature and scope of human reason and in

---

[1]Notice, for instance, this comment of Maritain: "In explaining (*Summa theologiae*, II-II, 11, 3) why the heretics must be put to death, St Thomas showed that the great speculatives, when they pronounce on the concrete, run the risk of being led astray by the regime of civilization and the mentality of the time." Jacques Maritain, *On the Church of Christ* (Notre Dame: University of Notre Dame Press, 1973), 283, n. 20.

particular in its ability slowly and systematically to apprehend the contours of reality.

In *Radical Hermeneutics* John Caputo has offered many of us not completely familiar with some of the most recent directions in contemporary philosophical inquiry a helpful tool for enrichening our awareness of what is actually going on. And to those committed to something approximating Maritain's project, the view provided by Caputo in this work is rather disturbing. Caputo concludes his book with three chapters entitled: "Toward a Postmetaphysical Rationality," "Toward an Ethics of Dissemination" and "Openness to the Mystery." From these chapter titles it can correctly be gathered that Caputo's work deals to some significant extent with the themes of metaphysics, ethics and philosophical theology, to all of which Maritain himself devoted considerable attention.

What becomes clear through reading Caputo's work, though, is that both he and a number of well known philosophic thinkers are providing the contemporary world with notions of human reason considerably restricted in comparison with the kind of reason provided us by classic Western thought as encapsulated in the works of a Plato, an Aristotle, a St. Thomas, and a Maritain. Reason is no longer considered capable of making the kinds of judgments or establishing the kinds of conclusions in metaphysics, moral philosophy or philosophical theology that such thinkers considered possible.

The very title of the first chapter previously referred to, "Toward a Postmetaphysical Rationality," seems to indicate that reason is somehow being stripped of its potentiality for metaphysical thinking. This appearance turns out, in fact, to be the case. Caputo writes:

> Radical hermeneutics is a lesson in humility; it comes away chastened from its struggle with the flux....It understands the power of the flux to wash away the best-laid schemes of metaphysics. It takes the constructs of metaphysics to be temporary cloud formations which, from the distance, create the appearance of shape and substance but which pass through our fingers upon contact. *Eidos, ousia, esse, res cogitans* and the rest are so many meteorological

illusions, inducing our belief in their permanence and brilliant form yet given to constant dissipation and reformation.[2]

For Maritain such a statement would appear only possible on the basis of what, in a term taken from Bernard Lonergan, could be called a "profound philosophical oversight." Something foundational has not been seen, has been overlooked, the absence of which seeing entails the correlative absence of an interior intellectual *habitus* upon which the careful and painstaking growth of the science of metaphysics can be grounded. As is well known, Maritain affirmed that metaphysical progress was based upon an intuition, a certain profound experiential contact with the fact that things exist, that they stand outside nothingness, in a word that they have being;[3] and this powerful awareness put the individual in contact with the object of the science of metaphysics in a manner that made possible its development. Without contact with its object, a science whose domain pertains to that object is not possible. Small wonder, then, that for Maritain great thinkers such as Immanuel Kant and Edmund Husserl, insightful as they were in certain respects, were, nevertheless, not philosophers in the deepest sense of the term—namely, metaphysicians.[4]

Yet according to Caputo, as quoted above, metaphysical concepts are "constructs," and "temporary cloud formations passing through our fingers." What does this mean? It certainly indicates that metaphysical concepts do not endure forever. They come and go, but what does this mean? Does it mean that they emerge and pass away because mankind's hold on truth is precarious and as a consequence the flow of history eventually snatches truth from our grip, perhaps to be recovered again at some future point in time? Or does it mean that such concepts come and go because their validity is not of a trans-temporal kind? In such a perspective these concepts could be seen as possessing a kind of truth and validity similar to certain instances of practical truth. For instance, no

---

[2]John Caputo, *Radical Hermeneutics*, (Bloomington: Indiana University Press, 1987), 258.

[3]Cf. Jacques Maritain, *A Preface to Metaphysics:: Seven Lectures on Being*, (New York: Books for Libraries, Reprint, 1962), 48-64.

[4]See Jacques Maritain, *The Peasant of the Garonne* (New York: Holt, Rinehart and Winston, 1968), 98-111.

one would wish to deny that certain political structures valid at one point in time are not appropriate at another. Heidegger's viewpoint seems to be similar to this latter possibility. For he appears to have eventually maintained that the diverse metaphysical conceptions of different periods of history, as they give way one to another through time, possess their own validity in such a way that as Caputo writes "there is no privileged meaning or 'truth' of Being...no sending enjoys any rights over any other";[5] and as Heidegger himself said "Not only do we lack any criterion which would permit us to evaluate the perfection of an epoch of metaphysics as compared with any other epoch, the right to this kind of evaluation does not exist. Plato's thinking is no more perfect than Parmenides. Hegel's philosophy is no more perfect than Kant's. Each epoch of philosophy has its own necessity."[6] Heidegger here seems to be acknowledging a kind of validity for diverse metaphysical systems, but clearly any validity they possess is not of a trans-temporal, not of a universal kind. Such a view of things would appear, of course, to Thomists in general and certainly to Maritain in particular to imply a radical misunderstanding of the nature of metaphysics. The principles of metaphysics are not ones whose meaningfulness and truth changes from one epoch to another. Such can, as already indicated, be the case with various forms of practical truth wherein prudential judgment can determine that what is fitting and appropriate in one set of circumstances is not so in another. Speculative truth of a metaphysical kind would for Thomists be judged immune from alteration through time.

Caputo, though, seems to be saying even more. He does not want a metaphysics for this time. Instead, he is concerned with a postmetaphysical rationality. For, as we have seen, his claim is that *Eidos, ousia, esse, res cogitans* and the rest are so many meteorological illusions.[7] An illusion, of course, is an appearance that does not have any reality standing behind it. According to this, then, metaphysical terms, for Caputo, do not stand for anything real. The radicalness of such a position is reaffirmed by such further statements as the claim that the function of radical hermeneutics is

---

[5]John Caputo, 180.
[6]*Ibid.*
[7]*Ibid.*, 258.

to keep the games in play, to keep us on the alert that we draw forms
in the sand, we read clouds in the sky, but we do not capture deep
essences or find the *arche*. If there is anything that we learn in radical
hermeneutics it is that we never get the better of the flux.[8]

Caputo is asserting, then, that human reason is never able to reach
fundamental, unchanging metaphysical principle of the kind that Maritain endeavored so carefully to elucidate in such works as *The Degrees of
Knowledge, Existence and the Existent*, and *Seven Lectures on Being*.

Maritain's position on these matters is clear. Following St. Thomas,
Maritain understood metaphysics to be a science of first causes, of first
principles. In regard to the knowledge of the absolutely first cause of all
being, this knowledge was understood to be analogical, not univocal,
and not comprehensive of its object in any sense of the term. Such
knowledge points beyond itself towards an object that in itself transcends human conceptual apprehension. Still, though He is transcendent, analogy makes possible some certain knowledge of God. Such
knowledge of first principle in any absolute sense is, however, excluded
according to these other thinkers. Heidegger's *Being beyond beings* is
never to be reached. There is "no privileged sense of Being and hence no
privileged epoch either. There is just a-letheia, the incessant giving and
taking of presence over the epochs, the incessant repetition, or playing
out again and again, of one metaphysical scheme after another";[9] and for
Derrida there is "no history of Being, no metaphysics...only the free play
of differences";[10] and for Caputo, bereft of ultimate principles, we are
offered membership in "a *community of mortals* bound together by their
common fears and lack of metaphysical grounds, sharing a common fate
at the hands of the flux, sent by a *Geshick* which will not disclose its name,
which does not have a name."[11]

What about Caputo's chapter on ethics? What kind of ethics emerges
from his attitude towards the unattainability of fundamental, unalterable metaphysical principle? What arises is a conception of the function
of ethics that is quite different from the kind of moral philosophy

---

[8]*Ibid.*
[9]*Ibid.*, 181.
[10]*Ibid.*, 170.
[11]*Ibid.*, 159.

envisaged by Maritain. As is relatively well known, Maritain entertained a position regarding moral philosophy that was controversial in Thomistic circles. The question at issue had to do with the relationship between moral philosophy and moral theology. Rather than holding as did a large number of Thomistic thinkers that moral philosophy was a science completely autonomous and independent in its own right, though admittedly inadequate to the actual structure of reality as known through Christian revelation, Maritain argued that the principles of moral philosophy were subalternated to the principles of moral theology.[12] However his position is to be precisely interpreted on this point, it is certain that for Maritain human reason is able to attain through its own resources a knowledge of certain stable moral principles possessing unalterable validity for a universal science of ethics.

But with Caputo things are quite different. The inability of reason to apprehend stable, universal principle leads for him towards what he calls an ethics of dissemination. Such an ethics arises from the collapse of metaphysical ethics, which collapses with the fall of metaphysics. Heidegger, Caputo indicates, ascertained that there is no truth of Being or unitary meaning to Being. Instead there are many meanings or truths to Being;[13] but if there is no privileged truth to Being, then there is no privileged ethics or moral philosophy. We are left instead with the realization that, as Caputo writes, "there is no primordial ethos but only the manifold senses of ethos, the array of historical differences";[14] but what does such a situation entail for the possibility today of guiding human action in these complex times? Where can we turn if moral philosophy is subject to the same dissolution as metaphysical systems? To this Caputo writes: "My argument will be that action today takes its point of departure not from fixed points of reference and steady principles (as in a metaphysical ethics) but precisely from the dissemination of principles and primordial epochs. It is precisely from the breakdown of standpoints and resting points of all sorts that we begin to act."[15] Such

---

[12]See Jacques Maritain, "*De la Philosophie Chrétienne,*" *Jacques et Raïssa Maritain, Oeurves Complètes*, V (Fribourg: Editions Universitaires, 1982), 302-316.

[13]John Caputo, 238.

[14]*Ibid.*

[15]*Ibid.*

a viewpoint leads Caputo to conclude that we should not act from the vantage point of those who have all the answers, of those who are completely secure in the rightness of their course. We should act rather with a heightened sense of our own fallibility.

In his final chapter, "Openness to the Mystery," Caputo speaks of God, of faith, of religion, and of various related themes. To one who has come to understand and accept the traditional Catholic concept of faith what he has to say about faith appears flawed. He writes:

> Religion is...*authentic* only as long as it *owns up* to the contingency of its symbols...we do not know who we are, not if we are honest, or whether or not we believe in God: that is the point of departure of any genuine faith....The believer is not someone who has been visited on high by a supervenient grace but someone who, like the rest of us, does what he can to construe the darkness, to follow the sequence of shadows across the cave, to cope with the flux.[16]

Clearly, though, Catholic faith is not something that "owns up to the contingency of its symbols," nor would it accept that we do not know who we are. In regards to the latter, for example, faith enables us to understand that we are children of God, persons made in his image and likeness; and the believer is someone who does, in fact, believe that he has been visited from on high by grace, at least in the form of an offer. He believes this because he understands that we are called to share in a higher life, in God's very own life and joy and that such sharing requires a principle greater than those principles intrinsic to our nature, namely grace; and the believer is one to be sure who does what he can to cope with the flux; but he is also one who knows through faith of realities beyond the flux.

In regard to this chapter, however, it is not primarily of such matters that I wish to speak. Instead, I want to consider the theme of philosophical theology. Early in the chapter, I began to wonder whether somehow I had been seriously misunderstanding Caputo up to that point. One can begin to get the impression there that what he is saying is more in accord with St. Thomas and with Maritain than at first appeared; and, at this point, the validity of some of my judgments regarding what he was

---

[16]*Ibid.*, 281.

actually saying began to come into question in my mind. Had I really been able to sufficiently pin down his meaning? What, in fact, did he really mean? Did he really mean what he seemed to mean? Were many of his words really saying what they obviously seemed to be saying? Or, in radical hermeneutical terms was something *now emerging into presence that would thrust what I thought was there back into the flux*? Was Caputo less radical than he had earlier seemed? Further reading and analysis, however, re-established prior evaluations and led to the conclusion that earlier judgments made regarding his meaning were relatively adequate.

In this last chapter Caputo begins to speak of a difference between our concepts and what is beyond our concepts. Meister Eckhart is brought forth as exemplifying someone who appreciated this difference and knew not to take our concepts too seriously. For Eckhart knew a point of the soul where contact with God revealed the futility of human concepts, revealed them, in fact, to be nonsense.[17] Apart from calling human concepts nonsense, Caputo's distinction between what our concepts can capture and the domain transcending our concepts is thoroughly Thomistic and Maritainian; and so at this point we can, as I mentioned above, begin to wonder whether Caputo is as much an enemy of traditional conceptuality as he earlier seemed. Is his position one that in his own terms merely involves shielding God or the Godhead from the glaring light of metaphysical conceptuality? Such a viewpoint would be more in line with classical Thomism, and more satisfactory for a Thomist. Yet it would not be not completely satisfactory. For a Thomist would vigorously deny that metaphysical conceptuality attempts to place God in a glaring light; but let that pass. "Radical hermeneutics," Caputo writes, "arises only at the point of breakdown and loss of meaning, the withdrawal and dissemination of meaning, in short, the thunderstorm";[18] and he adds that radical hermeneutics involves "coming to deal with this loss of meaning by confronting the meaning of the loss, of the withdrawal, of the *lethe* itself."[19] It entails "the particular way one has found of remaining open to the mystery and venturing out into the flux."[20]

Are Caputo and radical hermeneutics, then, relatively traditional

---

[17]*Ibid.*, 268-69.
[18]*Ibid.*, 271.
[19]*Ibid.*
[20]*Ibid.*

after all--just a vigorous effort to point out in a clear manner the limitations of our concepts, and to caution us against believing that we get a firm grip upon God through them? Do then some of his earlier statements about meteorological illusions and transitory concepts have to be interpreted as expressions of this effort? To this one must finally conclude in the negative. For in the end, what is beyond our concepts turns out for Caputo not necessarily to be God. In the end we are warned that we can never be absolutely sure what is beyond our concepts. Caputo indicates that in regards to this beyond or this abyss, as he occasionally calls it, our conceptual schemes can never give us assured knowledge. He writes: "What is calling to us from that abyss? Whose voice is it? Or is it no voice at all but the rumble of the cosmos in its endless transformations...."[21] Later he writes: "I do not think that we know whether we believe in God or not, not if we face the cold truth";[22] and towards the end we find him saying:

> All this talk about the abyss and dark nights is not supposed to be a midnight metaphysics, or a *theologia negativa*, but a way of awakening to the flux and hence of staying in play with oneself.... And what is playing in the play? Is it God? the soul? the world?...*Dilige, et quod vis fac.*[23]

In other words, this final chapter is speaking of openness to the mystery which might be God, but which might not be God; and whatever it is, one thing seems sure and that is that for Caputo we can never be certain of knowing what it is. We have then in Caputo's final chapter no traditional philosophical theology. Such an endeavor seems for Caputo to be impossible. Maritain would, I am sure, be quite critical of all this, though as with so many others whom he criticized in the interests of truth, he would also be interested and intrigued by such developments. He would also, I am certain, consider human reason to have been seriously shortchanged by Caputo's analysis; and he would finally without doubt have concluded that to the extent to which such thinking expands its influence the future of civilization will be impoverished.

---

[21]*Ibid.*, 286.
[22]*Ibid.*, 288.
[23]*Ibid.*, 293.

Part V
Unnatural Humanisms
and Post-Civilized Minds

Robert Royal

Human Nature and Unnatural Humanisms

We have arrived at a new moment, or perhaps a new crisis, in the old discussion about humanism. All intellectual metaphors limp, and the one we shall begin with has probably also been overused; but it would not be too far off the mark to say that many of our most influential philosophers have shifted from conducting a kind of orderly Newtonian reflection on man to producing a kind of discontinuous post-Einsteinian dispersion of discourse into scattered fragments and evanescent traces (the appropriateness of this semi-barbaric rhetoric will become clearer below). In spite of the seeming hopelessness of the attempt, it is worth our while to try to make some sense of these scattered fragments and traces, first by identifying the structure of thought that lies behind their production; second, by sorting them into some intelligible categories--an anatomy of contemporary humanisms--and finally, by suggesting some ways to move beyond the impasse presented by postmodern "humanism."

Let us be clear about how what we will call postmodern humanism differs from the old modern variety. The old humanism, Newtonian humanism if you will, moved through largely regular and predictable orbits. In the period before and just after the Second World War, for example, a Catholic like Jacques Maritain and an agnostic like Albert Camus began their speculations on humanism by trying to avoid the false extremes of totalitarian communities (Communism and Fascism) on the one hand, and a radical bourgeois individualism on the other.

In addition, they both rejected the false opposition of theism and humanism. Camus's first sentence in *L'Homme Révolté*, "There are crimes of passion and crimes of logic," also reflects an honest analysis of the experience of the first half of the twentieth century, in which logical constructions of one kind or another resulted in unprecedented slaugh-

167

ters.[1] Organized atheist humanism could never again assume easy superiority to organized religion--in fact, humanism's excesses have proved to be far worse than religion's. Both Camus and Maritain sought a humanism based primarily on a common-sense, nonideological view of human nature and human community that did not rule out God.

The odd thing—and here is the crux of the new moment in thinking about humanism—is that in the last few decades Marxism, individualism, and the very idea of human nature have become very weak forces in public discourse, whatever residual appeal each has in particular circles. Modern philosophical and literary currents display a wide spectrum of alternatives to classical humanism; but the strongest contemporary currents draw on a common and pervasive force that denies the very possibility of human nature and shall be our principal focus here: the deconstruction movement.

The difficulties of understanding deconstruction are notorious. The language of many deconstructionists is all but impenetrable. The deconstructive method seems to undercut systematically any formulation of its own basic concepts. In fact, both the very notion of an origin or a basis, and every relationship of concepts to such points of departure, are precisely what deconstruction deconstructs. A joke about these difficulties gets the feeling of most readers exactly right. Question: "What do you get from a *mafioso* who is a deconstructionist?" Answer: "An offer you cannot understand."

Unfortunately, it is imperative that *we* do understand if not everything about deconstruction, at least its general implications and influence in contemporary intellectual life. If Maritain—or Camus—were alive today, they would recognize the centrality of this movement to the understanding of our whole culture, starting with what might seem an absurd question: Is the assertion that we can know something about the order of things and can communicate that knowledge Fascist? Does the very concept of transcendent meaning immediately impose on and ultimately threaten human liberty? These are not merely academic questions, because while the deconstruction movement flourishes primarily on the campuses—in France, America, and elsewhere—it has wide-ranging implications for the world outside.[2]

---

[1] Albert Camus, *The Rebel* (New York: Vintage Books, 1956), 3.
[2] For example, in the essay "Violence and Metaphysics" (where the

Take for example, the following statement of an intellectual program by one of the leading expositors of deconstruction:

> Let us give up 'literature' for *writing* [that is, *écriture* in the deconstructionist sense]. In doing so, we forego 'meaning,' the 'final signified,' the 'author,' 'law,' 'science,' and ultimately 'God.' We accept the freeplay of the world and of signs without truth and without origin. We go beyond humanistic man.[3]

That last phrase, "go beyond humanistic man," is ominous and significant. Paradoxically, it is in the *Humanities* departments of the universities that this anti- or metahumanism is being disseminated. The task is nothing less than a grand revision or reversal of Western metaphysics through an attack on language. The same author quotes Martin Heidegger approvingly about the difficulty of overthrowing traditional metaphysics:

> That difficulty lies in language. Our Western languages are languages of metaphysical thinking, each in its own way. It must remain an open question whether the nature of Western languages is in itself marked with the exclusive brand of metaphysics, and thus marked permanently by onto-theo-logic, or whether these languages offer other possibilities of utterance—and that means at the same time of a telling silence.[4]

---

two terms are viewed as virtually synonymous), Jacques Derrida puts the deconstructionist indictment in its most comprehensive form. For him the Greek *logos* and all similar concepts that serve as a foundation for meaning are "an oppression certainly comparable to none other in the world, an ontological or transcendental oppression, but also the origin or alibi of all oppression in the world." Thus all traditional religious, philospohical, and scientific views of the world point inevitably, says Derrida, toward Nazism. See Derrida's *Writing and Différance*, trans. Alan Bass (Chicago: University of Chicago Press, 1978), 83.

[3]Vincent B. Leitch, *Deconstructive Criticism: An Advanced Introduction* (New York: Columbia University Press, 1986), 104-05.

[4]*Ibid.*, 68.

Why such a process needs to be carried out is telling, too: "As functions, God, Author, Phallus, Being, Center all play a similar role: they reduce the flight of the sign and close the space of interpretation in a determination of stable meaning or truth."[5] Roughly speaking, the deconstructionist abhors God, Author, Phallus, Being, Center, stable meaning, and truth for the same reason that a theist abhors strict materialism: each seems to fix human life into a straitjacket with no room for freedom. The deconstructionist alternative is a free, if empty, play of "the world and of signs without truth and without origin."

In light of this metahumanism, many traditional quarrels pale. No longer is the threat an attempt to reduce man to an animal in a tribe as in Fascism. Nor is Marxist humanism through collectivist tyranny the problem. You cannot even call this vision anthropocentric because it eventually deconstructs the substantial *anthropos* as much as anything. This is not a classical skepticism either. Skepticism at least had the good sense to leave the skeptic intact. After meeting deconstructionists, the Biblical Fundamentalist who abhors *secular humanism* should embrace an old Classical Rationalist--say Voltaire--like a beloved long-lost brother. At least both of them believe that a human nature exists and that human beings exercise the power of reason, whatever ultimate role they assign to reason. By comparison, the new *metahumanist*, if that is what he is, belongs to an entirely different mental species.

All of this is important because deconstructive assaults on Western thought will energize many combatants in the *Kulturkampf* of the next few years, whatever the academic fortunes of specific fashions like deconstruction. Marxism, secular humanism, and other Newtonian humanisms will continue to exert some influence; but the drive to desubstantialize the world has deep currents in our culture and will find other modes of expression even if the dominant modes of today fade. Deconstruction traces its origins from Martin Heidegger through his student, Jacques Derrida. William Barrett has rightly observed that while much can be said immediately against a desubstantializing philosophy like that of Heidegger, we should realize that Heidegger

cannot be dismissed; that desolate and empty picture of being he gives us may be just that sense of being that is at work in our whole

---

[5]*Ibid.*, 54.

culture, and we are in his debt for having brought it to the surface. To get beyond him we shall have to live through that sense of being in order to reach the other side.[6]

I. Humanism in Sartre and Heidegger

As a first step towards reaching that other side, let us look briefly at two crucial figures in the development of modern humanism—Heidegger and Jean Paul Sartre. Though Sartre's work is based on his reading of Heidegger, we will begin with Sartre because he developed an explicitly existential humanism that Heidegger later repudiated on significant grounds.

Existentialism, at least by that name, has already become a rather stale philosophical movement, but the basic views elaborated by Sartre in a text such as his 1946 lecture, *L'Existentialisme est un Humanisme*[7] continue in circulation under other guises. In existentialist forms of humanism, "we must begin from the subjective," says Sartre. Following, he thinks, Heidegger, Sartre declares that existence precedes essence, and, therefore, "Man is nothing else but that which he makes of himself. That is the first principle of existentialism." Many have taken this as a license for caprice and avant-garde self-indulgence, says Sartre; but, he warns sternly, in reality this is "the least scandalous and the most austere" of teachings. It places the responsibility for his life—and the lives of others—precisely on each individual's shoulders. We are responsible for the principles we choose and the passions we allow to guide us. Freedom and responsibility are total.

At first glance, this seems to resemble the radical individualism of the earlier individualism/totalitarianism opposition, but Sartre denies that his thoroughgoing subjectivity is bourgeois. For him, "God is dead," and he quite correctly points out that this has consequences, among them Dostoyevsky's "everything is permitted." This saying is not a justification of everything, argues Sartre, merely the clear-sighted recognition that

---

[6]William Barrett, *Death of the Soul: From Descartes to the Computer* (Garden City, New York: Doubleday, 1986), 140.

[7]For a convenient translation of this lecture see Walter Kaufmann's *Existentialism from Dostoyevsky to Sartre* (New York: Meridian Books, 1967), 287-311.

there is nothing outside of man by which to judge choices. In fact, even if God existed, he says, *we* would have to choose to understand how he wants us to act. For Sartre subjectivity, in the Cartesian sense, is inescapable.

There is one way out of this apparent solitude, however, in that we must recognize other people as constitutive of our own selves and freedom. The argument here takes a strange twist and should be followed carefully. Sartre has already laid down as a bedrock rule that "in reality and for the existentialist, there is no love apart from the deeds of love; no potentiality of love other than that which is manifested in loving; there is no genius other than that which is expressed in works of art." Yet who is to decide whether any of these conditions have been fulfilled in fact? If it is the actor himself, he may be self-deceived. Oddly, Sartre puts the judgment of whether these things have actually occurred into the hands of others. His existentialist

> recognizes that he cannot be anything (in the sense that one says one is spiritual, or that one is wicked and jealous) unless others recognize him as such. I cannot obtain any truth whatsoever about myself, except through the mediation of another. The other is indispensable to my existence, and equally so to any knowledge I can have of myself. Under these conditions, the intimate discovery of myself is at the same time a revelation of the other as a freedom which confronts mine, and which cannot think or will without doing so either for or against me. Thus, at once, we find ourselves in a world which is, let us say, that of *inter-subjectivity*. It is in this world that man has to decide what he is and what others are.[8]

In such a world, there can be no fixed human nature, although *conditions* repeat themselves often enough that human choices in those conditions will be broadly understandable. The old philosophies of human nature made man a fixed end, says Sartre, and even in secularized forms like Comte's, they inevitably lead to Fascism in their imposition of a conceptual frame over man. Man is always to be made: "Man is all the

---

[8]This resort to inter-subjectivity may permit Sartre to believe that he has escaped becoming a kind of bourgeois *salaud* only concerned about himself; but, as Derrida astutely perceived, existential subjectivity led

time outside of himself: it is in projecting and losing himself beyond himself that he makes man to exist; and, on the other hand, it is by pursuing transcendent [i.e., outside himself, not metaphysical] ends that he himself is able to exist."

II. Heidegger's Reaction

To those only vaguely acquainted with Martin Heidegger, all this may seem to echo with the master's voice; but Heidegger read Sartre's lecture and was horrified. In his reply, *Letter on Humanism* (1947), Heidegger will have nothing to do with this rootless freedom.[9] His idea of human being (*Dasein* may be translated by those two words among others) situates it squarely within an all-encompassing Being. This is not the place to go into a full investigation of Heidegger's objections to Sartre, but several of the points he makes will be useful in sketching the contours of contemporary anti-humanisms.

Heidegger immediately marks out the difference between Sartre and himself on the matter of existence preceding essence. He admits to having said that the essence of man is his *ek-sistence,* but he does not use these terms in the way of traditional metaphysics. For Heidegger

> Metaphysics closes itself to the simple essential fact that man essentially occurs only in his essence, where he is claimed by Being. Only from that claim has he found that wherein his essence dwells. Only from this dwelling *has* he *language* as the home that preserves the ecstatic for his essence. Such standing in the light of Being I call the ek-sistence of man. This way of Being is proper only to man. Ek-sistence so understood is not only the ground of the possibility of reason, *ratio*, but it is also that in which the essence of man preserves the source that determines him.

---

naturallly not so much to inter-subjectivity as to inter-rogation--that is, the mutual questioning of one another that ultimately deconstructs every position, not by refuting it, but by showing that, on existential principle, it never had substantial reality in the first place.

[9]For a good English translation of this text see Martin Heidegger, *Basic Writings*, ed. David Farrell Krell (New York: Harper and Row, 1977), 193-242.

As many commentators point out, in passages such as these, Being, despite all protestations by Heidegger, appears like nothing so much as the traditional ground that created the world--that is, God. Heidegger is careful to note differences between his concepts of Being and existence and those of the medievals, Hegel, and Nietzsche (as Heidegger construed him), but he shares with these thinkers a firm sense that man is defined by something absolute, outside of himself, however obscure this Heideggerian Being may be in comparison with the traditional metaphysics of presence. Heidegger thinks of Being as "mysterious, the simple nearness of an unobtrusive governance....What is essential is not man but Being." In the open space of the self-giving of Being, man takes on his proper and profound dignity instead of the inauthentic and superficial dignities foisted on him by traditional humanism.[10]

For all of his life Heidegger saw this deeper humanism as requiring quiet thought and an organic rootedness in nature, nation, and place. Consequently, he was susceptible to the elements in National Socialism roughly congruent with his own thinking. Though Heidegger made some attempt to explain the complexity of his attitude toward Nazism, his behavior and some of his remarks during World War II were quite simply bad; and even decades later he always avoided a full repudiation of National Socialism. Nor did he ever express horror or even regret over the Holocaust. Many critics saw his political blindness as deriving from philosophical errors.[11] No one took up this theme more vehemently than one of Heidegger's students, the father of deconstruction, Jacques Derrida.

---

[10]In spite of the philosophical majesty of this formulation, Heidegger felt compelled to present this Being-being humanism in terms of the peculiarly modern thrill of the abyss. Leo Strauss once characterized existentialism as "a race in which he wins who offers the smallest security and the greatest terror," and predicted Heidegger would win the race. See Strauss, *Liberalism Ancient and Modern* (New York: Basic Books, 1968), 256.

[11]For the best accounts of this controversy see Victor Farias, *Heidegger and Nazism* (Philadelphia: Temple University Press, 1969).

III. The Deconstructive Turn

Derrida comes from an Algerian Jewish family and is justifiably sensitive to Heidegger's involvement with the Nazis, but he did not merely denounce the specific political faults he found in Heidegger. Though Derrida acknowledges that without Heidegger his own work would have been impossible, he saw in Heidegger's very assertion of a *proper dignity* of the human being the root of his weakness for Nazism. In the last few years, Derrida has carried this critique to larger and larger circles, until in a recent interview he stated "I believe in the necessity of showing—without limit, if possible--the profound attachment of Heidegger's texts (writings and deeds) to the possibility and reality of *all* nazisms."[12]

This remark, perhaps better than that of any other major contemporary thinker, formulates the predicament in which we find ourselves at the end of the twentieth century: is it possible to have *any* theory of human nature that does not become an intolerable chain on human freedom? In short, do all metaphysics and humanisms inevitably lead to what we may call for shorthand totalitarianism? Do systematic views entail totalizing politics?

Heidegger himself had thought he was breaking with all false *metaphysical* systems. To simplify greatly from Heidegger's complex and often murky writing, he sought to deliver humanistic thought from what he regarded as two false strains in the tradition: Platonic transcendence and scientific immanence. Each of these, in his view, had led man to *forget Being* by directing attention to some lesser realm. Heidegger thought that by opening ourselves to Being, a process in some ways similar to mystical contemplation (though Heidegger tried to distinguish his thinking from all previous *onto-theologic* thought), we could retrieve a *dignity proper to man.*

All this seems to the good. False idealism and reductive scientism are the two traditional dangers to an authentic humanism.

For Derrida, though, this was Heidegger's crucial error. In spite of all Heidegger's attempts to get free from Western metaphysical limitations,

---

[12]Quoted in Thomas Sheehan's article,"Heidegger and the Nazis," in *The New York Review of Books*, June 16, 1988, 47. The original remarks by Derrida appeared in *Le Nouvel Observateur*, November 6-12, 1987, 173.

said Derrida, he had fallen here precisely into one of those dangerous traps that he sought to avoid. In Heidegger man is a being composed of both absence and presence; he is never simply *there*, because *Dasein* can only be understood fully in light of—mostly absent, for us—Being.[13] Against the classical *metaphysical* systems, Derrida argues that there is no *proper* dignity to man because there is no human nature that may be properly described. The only way in which we may describe human nature is in human language; and human language, by *its* nature, is a compound of the sign and something else, a kind of non-distinct shadow that simultaneously gives rise to verbal meaning and subverts it. Both the speaker and the human nature being spoken about are situated within this network of language and, therefore, themselves are deconstructed by the nature of the linguistic sign. It is not simply that language raises doubts about an existing reality. Derrida's linguistic analysis argues that this would make deconstruction a fall from presence. In Derrida there was never any presence there to begin with. The origin is a non-origin, and deconstruction is merely the recognition of this predicament.

To understand what Derrida means by this requires us to look at his theory more fully.[14] In many of the principal texts of Derrida's most fruitful period,[15] an opposition of a sort is set up between the classic age

---

[13]In a further development of Heidegger, Derrida also disputed the role of Being as a kind of guarantor of meaning and beings--a role, Derrida correctly perceived, analogous to God's in classic metaphysics. For Derrida's essay responding to the Sartre-Heidegger humanism debate, see his "The Ends of Man," *The Margins of Philosophy*, trans. Alan Bass (Chicago: University of Chicago Press, 1982), 109-36.

[14]Though the analysis that follows seeks to bring clarity of concept and language to an almost always confusing subject, as it advances into the *arcana* of deconstruction, it inevitably begins to reproduce some of its style. Deconstruction labors against the most natural pathways of Western langauges, and any attempt to explain deconstruction finds itself involved in this linguistic turmoil. The reader who finds himself stranded in orbit by this explication might prefer to try re-entry by skipping to **Part VI (Political Humanisms of Deconstruction)** of this essay.

[15]The most important titles from this very fecund period (around 1968) include at least the following: *La Voix et le Phenomene, De la Grammatologie, Marges de la Philosophie,* and *L'Ecriture et la Différance*.

of Western metaphysics and something that is *after* or *outside* or *on the margins* of that epoch. In some ways Derridas thinking here repeats Heidegger's well-known attempt to get behind or beyond Western metaphysics; but for Derrida, Heidegger himself is part of the very epoch he hoped to escape. In *Of Grammatology* and elsewhere, Derrida often says that we can now begin to glimpse the "closure [*clôture*] of the metaphysical epoch."

The very idea of the "closure of an epoch" is, in deconstructive terms, problematic because to speak of such a concept carries with it obvious ties to a *metaphysical* discourse. The "closure of an epoch" seems to posit a conceptually stable, simply *past* presence that may be referred to with confidence, a variation on the classic *in illo tempore*. Strictly speaking, deconstruction does not permit belief in such a historical reality because there is *always already* [*toujours déjà*] at work, in the concept and in the attempt to demarcate the period, a kind of writing that produces discourse distinct from a subject that was never simply *there* in the first place. Any text from that period would be equally inaccessible, strictly speaking, because any text produced *about* the earlier text exists as irreducibly different.[16]

"Closure" in Derrida does not mean the *end* of the metaphysical epoch. Probably the best place to examine this distinction is in the *Exergue* to *Of Grammatology*. There Derrida lays out the difficulties of his *science of writing*, [that is, grammatology] explicitly in term of its relationship to the closure of the metaphysical epoch:

> such a science of writing runs the risk of never being established as such and with that name. Of never being able to define the unity of its project or its object. Of not being able either to write its discourse on method or to describe the limits of its field. For essential reasons: the unity of all that allows itself to be attempted today through the most diverse concepts of science and writing, is, in principle, more or less covertly yet always, determined by an historico- metaphysical epoch of which we merely glimpse the closure. I do not say the end.

---

[16]One of the Yale school of *boa deconstructors*, Harold Bloom, has formulated this as "All reading is misreading." Other deconstructionisit slogans make the same point: "All texts are pretexts," and "All interpretations are interpretations of interpretations." See below for the deconstructive meanings of the term "*différance*."

Grammatology, then, finds itself obliged to use a language that is hostile at its very core to what grammatology seeks to establish, perhaps makes that meaning impossible to express fully.

> The idea of science and the idea of writing—therefore also of the science of writing — is meaningful for us only in terms of an origin and within a world to which a certain concept of the sign (later I shall call it *the* concept of the sign) and a certain concept of the relation ship between speech and writing have already been assigned. A most determined relationship, in spite of its privileges, its necessity, and the field of vision that it has controlled for a few millennia, especially in the West, to the point of being now able to produce its own dislocation and itself proclaim its limits.

The science of writing that Derrida has in mind must carry out a double operation. Not only must it distinguish itself from the previous metaphysical systems, it must not become a *metaphysical* system in its own right. Even Heidegger, in Derrida's view, had failed at this operation because his reflections on Being became yet another continuation of the Socratic-Platonic metaphysical project in that it sought a final understanding, a kind of *logos*, as well as a *telos* in the openness of human beings to Being. Instead of trying to go *outside* the metaphysical tradition, Derrida transposes his efforts into a different dimension:

> The movements of deconstruction do not destroy structures from the outside. They are not possible and effective, nor can they take accurate aim, except by inhabiting those structures. Inhabiting them in a certain way, because one always inhabits, and all the more when one does not suspect it.

Derrida repeatedly chooses the word "closure" to mark this approach to that epoch.

> The age of the sign is essentially theological. Perhaps it will never end. Its historical closure is, however, outlined....Within the closure, by an oblique and always perilous movement, constantly risking falling back within what is being deconstructed, it is necessary to surround the critical concepts with a careful and thorough discourse....designate the crevice through which the unnameable glimmer beyond the closure may be glimpsed....For a proper under-

standing of the gesture that we are sketching here, one must understand the expressions 'epoch,' 'closure of an epoch,' 'historical genealogy' in a new way; and must first remove them from all relativism."

IV. Escaping the End of History?

The *new way* may perhaps be best understood in contrast to how a Hegel would have understood the terms listed above. For Hegel, previous philosophical work represented a movement of Absolute Spirit towards self-consciousness in Subjective Spirit. Though past events and philosophical systems can have a double perspective—both as simple events in themselves and as steps in a self-defining cosmic process— what Hegel sought was precisely closure in the sense of a final unity or *end*. The end of history does not mean the end of the world, but an achievement of the Spirit that ever after unites the various processes of reality. In Hegel, there can be no outside that is not absorbed by the dialectic, nor are there "crevices" in the system. Whatever may be glimpsed on the "outside" *must* be capable of integration into Hegel's all-embracing dialectical realization of the Idea.

Deconstruction, however, by its very nature discerns a radical otherness, even in the metaphysical epoch. That epoch is not simply what it presents itself as; it reflects the unsystemizable absence/presence characteristic of everything. Nothing is, for us, simply *there*. For Derrida, everything shows the operation of *différance*, the central term in deconstruction, a term that Derrida once described as "not a concept, and not even a word." "*Différance*" with an 'a' does not exist in French any more than in English. Derrida has coined the word for two purposes. First, he denies that there is any simple presence to the sign we call a word. Much of his rebarbative book *Of Grammatology* [17] seeks to show the falseness of the assumption that spoken language is a simple presence of which written language is a derivative. *Différance* is spelled the way it is because it is a word than can only be properly appreciated when written. It forces us, therefore, to recognize that all language, says Derrida, is a form of *writing*, in the sense that it is a human product rather than a simple, *natural* presence. Even the product should not be regarded as transpar-

---

[17]Trans. Gayatri Chakravorty Spivak (Baltimore, MD: Johns Hopkins University Press, 1976).

ent; rather, all language becomes an endless *dissemination*, a production of texts about texts spurred by other texts, *ad infinitum*.

Différance is a kind of non-foundational basis for all signs. Derrida nowhere gives a straightforward definition of it--such a definition would be false to *différance*--but we might simplify his complexifications and say there are two large components to *différance*, one spatial and one temporal.

Every linguistic sign, like every object in the world, is *different* in that it is spatially separated from other objects. A word, for example, is initially recognizable because it is different from all the other words in a language. Nevertheless, a word or object is not *simply* present as a distinct space. All the other words in the language, or all the other objects in the world, are implicit in the very recognition of difference. We cannot, therefore, know this thing as simply, in itself, *there*.

Similarly--and here we come to the second main sense in *différance*-- a word or object is different in that it *defers* finality. In a concrete sense, human language is a way of going on, of not arriving at a final, and therefore dead, appropriation of reality. Deferring the end of thought provides the interspace where human life, as uncertain meaning, goes on.

Even this absence/presence, though glimpsable, cannot be reduced to a system, is not a kingdom of the *trace* [18] or of *différance*, a kingdom that might usurp the governance of presence and unity. In its very nature, the *writing* [*écriture*] that results from *différance* disseminates itself without end, producing texts productive of other texts with no possible return to a point of origin.

This is an important point because otherwise the metaphysical epoch becomes an origin in the very sense that Derrida seeks to deconstruct in other systems. It would play a role in Derrida similar to the role played, for example, by *nature* in Rousseau, or Being in Heidegger. *Différance* would be a simple fall from originary unity, a breaking of the *metaphysical* molds, understandable in terms of unity; but that is precisely what Derrida everywhere seeks to prevent.

---

[18]In deconstruction the *trace* replaces the *data* of metaphysical systems; a *trace*, as the name implies, is as evanescent, and insubstantial, as the trace left by a sub-atomic particle in a cloud chamber. It is more the result of the passage of something unknown than a substantial existence.

In spite of his intentions, however, there are enormous difficulties in denying all originating functions to the *metaphysical epoch*. This becomes most evident when we look at how the concept of *trace* relates to the question of a metaphysical epoch. The movement of thought in Derrida here is, and must be, double. On the one hand, he must look back upon the metaphysical epoch in a way that does not simply make it part of another metaphysical system, does not allow a new system to absorb what is intended to be by nature resistant to all systemization. As he puts it, "To see to it that the beyond does not return to the within is to recognize in the contortion the necessity of a pathway [*parcours*]. That pathway must leave a path in the text." In concrete terms for the subject being addressed here, this means that the very writing about the existence and closure of the metaphysical epoch must contain within it an element that simultaneously shows that no such simple entity preceded the current thinking about it. Paradoxically, the period being looked at must disappear *in a certain way* from the discourse while still persisting. It is only in the self-reflection of writing that Derrida recognizes the *trace* that gives rise to the concept of a metaphysical age in the first place: "The trace is not only the disappearance of the origin—within the discourse that we sustain and according to the path that we follow it means that the origin did not even disappear, that it was never constituted except reciprocally by a nonorigin, the trace, which thus becomes the origin of the origin."

However much contrary to common sense notions, this even obliterates the pastness of the past:

> [I]f the trace refers to an absolute past, it is because it obliges us to think a past that can no longer be understood in the form of a modified presence, as a present-past, the absolute past that is re tained in the trace no longer rigorously merits the name 'past.' Another name to erase, especially since the strange movement of the trace proclaims as much as it recalls: *différance* defers-differs.

The problem, says Derrida, is similar to the *delayed effect* of Freudian theory in which the presentness of the past and the pastness of the present in the psyche are confounded to such an extent that it calls into question the very terms commonly used such as "time," "now," "anterior present," "delay," and so forth.

Perhaps the most convenient way to understand this relationship between the deconstructed concept of a metaphysical epoch and the *after* represented by the play of writing and difference is to use Derrida's term *brisure* ["hinge"], which denotes both a breaking and a connection. The very idea of a *metaphysical epoch* depends, for its existence, on a position that differs from it. This position cannot be wholly without relation to the metaphysical epoch, because that would allow no way to understand, or at least grasp, the *previous epoch*. The *brisure* between these two epochs is both a connection that preserves the inside/outside distinction and a form of writing that invades the words *metaphysical epoch, soliciting* (in the deconstruction sense of *stirring up*) the certainties within that epoch but also calling into question the very nature of what is referred to by those two words.

The contrast with Hegel—or even Heidegger—here could not be more stark. However much Hegel believed that his own philosophy represented the final culmination of previous efforts, his system does not alter the nature of earlier thinking, merely its place in the universe of thought.

Nietzsche's destruction of origins takes a further step, says Derrida, and Heidegger's attempt to step outside metaphysics is indispensable.[19]

---

[19]We usually assume that Derrida is a more faithful reader of Nietzsche than was Heidegger. Yet in light of examining the *closure of the metaphysical epoch*, it is instructive to try to imagine how the *Eternal Return* could be conceptualized or regarded as real from the standpoint of the "free play of *différance*." Some residual metaphysic of nature continues in Nietzsche that Derrida would try to overlook. How, for example, can we *know* about the Eternal Return unless we have reached a point similar to the end of history? Or how, for that matter, can we arrive at a recognition of the free play of signs without some similar standpoint at the end of history? See, for example, the paragraph at the end of Derrida's highly influential "Structure, Sign, and Play in the Discourse of the Social Sciences," which asserts a *metaphysical* view of the world as surely as any traditional system did, "Turned towards the lost or impossible presence of the absent origin, this structuralist thematic of broken immediacy is, therefore, the saddened, negative, nostalgic, guilty, Rousseauistic side of the thinking of play whose other side would be the Nietzschean affirmation, that is, the joyous affirmation of the play of the world and of the innocence of becoming, the affirmation of the world of signs without fault, without truth, and without origin which is offered to an active interpretation. This affirmation then determines the noncenter otherwise

For Derrida the erasure of simple being must invade even simple *historical* categorization. Even the use of the term "invade" here, though appropriate from one point of view, is inappropriate from Derrida's. For Derrida, there is no simple, secure preserve to be *in-vaded*; the assault from the *outside* is already *within* the closure. Since the metaphysical conception of this history has *always already* been destabilized by elements Derrida reveals, the invasion is really nothing more than a recognition.

V. A Non-Linearist History

All of these aspects of Derrida's thinking about the *closure* of an epoch contribute to a view of history in which the past is also present and the present absent. Derrida explains that this does not reduce everything to uniformity:

> This pluri-dimensionality does not paralyze history within simultaneity, it corresponds to another level of historical experience, and one may just as well consider, conversely, linear thought as a reduction of history....Simultaneity coordinates two absolute presents, two points or instants of presence, and it remains a linearist concept.

---

than as loss of the center, and it plays without security. For there is a sure play: that which is limited to the substitution of given and existing, present, pieces. In absolute chance affirmation also surrenders itself to genetic indetermination, to the seminal adventure of the trace" (in *Writing and Différance*, trans. Alan Bass[Chicago: University of Chicago Press, 1978], 292). Derrida has second thoughts about the innocence of the Nietzschean affirmation in *The Ear of the Other*, trans. Peggy Kamuf and Avital Ronnell (New York: Schocken Press, 1985), since the Nazis found plenty of ways to adapt Nietzsche for their purposes; but, even here, we may remark how the genetic indetermination is in danger, if that is the right way of putting it, of becoming a kind of metaphysic all its own. The Eternal Return is Nietzsche's sorrowful (see Zarathustra's slowness in affirming the realization) recognition of some pattern in the otherwise *baseless* play of the world, pure play alone could never give rise to the reality or the concept of Eternal Return.

Likewise, the major figures in the history of thought come under this pluri-dimensionality. Derrida describes as frivolous the belief that *Descartes, Leibniz, Rousseau, Hegel*, are simple identities or causes any more than are abstractions such as the *French Eighteenth Century*: "The indicative value that I attribute to them is first the name of a problem." This attitude, which undercuts the reading of major Western texts of the past, performs a similar operation on contemporary texts.

Clearly, this not only undercuts common-sense views of historicity, but those of a historicist like Hegel as well. At the extreme, Hegel would have assimilated history to the history of philosophy; but in Derrida, such a philosophical appropriation is impossible because the very history of philosophy is part of the metaphysical age in which several systems had transparent, simply present, meanings. This history of philosophy is *supplemented* by what grammatology brings to its deciphering: it brings *writing* to the reading of that history.

> Hegel's formula must be taken literally: history is nothing but the history of philosophy; absolute knowledge is fulfilled. What exceeds this closure is *nothing*: neither presence of being, nor meaning, neither history nor philosophy; but another thing that has no name, which announces itself within the thought of this closure and guides our writing here.

This *nothing* that guides the writing insures that the origin is never simple but is always already *supplemented*, or possessed by an obscure shadow. All commentary on that supplement is merely the supplement of a supplement, never a return to absolute origins. Seeking to deconstruct the metaphysical epoch does not arrive at a different *understanding* of that epoch in the sense of a new *reading*; it can only be, for Derrida, a *writing* on a text that was already supplemented by writing.

Though this *nothing* hardly seems worth all the fuss deconstruction has caused, no less formidable a critic than George Steiner has warned:

> *On its own terms and planes of argument*, terms by no means trivial if only in respect of their bracing acceptance of ephemerality and self

dissolution, the challenge of deconstruction does seem to me irrefutable."[20]

Part IX of this essay will explore other terms and planes by which to refute deconstruction; but, first, let us look at its practical implications.

VI. Political Humanisms of Deconstruction

Deconstruction is not merely a question of metaphysics and epistemology. Its practitioners often aim at a worldly program as well, which seeks to displace the classical forms of humanism. Deconstructionists have coined terms such as *phallogocentrism* (Derrida's invention) to get several villains simultaneously into one concept. It is no accident that the highly esoteric program of deconstruction comes down to earth with a program to abolish God, Author, Phallus, Being, and Centers. Each of these aims has clear political counterparts in secularism, multi-culturalism, feminism, relativism, and Third World ideologies. As anyone who has spent time on a university campus recently can attest, the exoticism of deconstructive theory and the homeliness of radical *praxis* seem to sense a kindred spirit in one another.

All of these forms of deconstructive politics also co-exist peacefully with one another and with neo-Marxisms that one scholar classifies as *critical* neo-Marxisms as opposed to scientific Marxism.[21] The former take an *open* approach to social questions. The latter have resulted in Stalinist regimes such as the Soviet Union. The distinguishing factor in what shall be called here deconstructive political movements is that, like the philosophical base of deconstruction, the revolution is not so much in favor of some alternative as it is in the thorough subverting of every substantial center of social authority.

Though at first sight a freewheeling system such as deconstruction appears to have little to do with the ponderous and tyrannical modes of thought we associate with Marxism, Derrida has described himself an

---

[20]George Steiner, *Real Presences* (Chicago: University of Chicago Press, 1989), 132.

[21]See Michael Ryan, *Marxism and Deconstruction: A Critical Articulation* (Baltimore, MD: Johns Hopkins University, 1982), xiv.

open Marxist because he recognizes a kindred spirit in the idea of perpetual revolution:

> I would reaffirm that there is some possible articulation between an open Marxism and what I am interested in....Marxism presents itself, has presented itself from the beginning with Marx, as an open theory, which was continually to transform itself.[22]

From this neo-Marxist perspective, the Western tradition with its metaphysical center and various ways of discriminating value is viewed as an ideology of oppression: "...metaphysics is the infrastructure of ideology, and until that infrastructure is deracinated, ideology will reappear, against the best intentions of revolutionary activists."[23] Metaphysics claims to provide some absolute point of knowledge from which to judge the historical, but this view is mistaken:

> The only absoluteness that can be claimed for truth and knowledge is that which characterizes the description of the historical world at a specific moment in the process of material transformation. It is the absoluteness of a relation between two points in two chains which are inseparably interwoven—a linguistic-conceptual chain and the historical world. It is not of the paradigmatic order of an ideal truth, which transcends the seriality of empirical history it describes. Both marxism [sic] and deconstruction suggest that this sort of truth is a fiction.[24]

How we can *know* that such a truth is a fiction without a concept that belongs to the metaphysical order of truth is a paradox our author does not perceive. He concludes instead: "The most absolute truth would be that which least pretends to absoluteness and instead attends to its own historicity. Fashion would simply be another name for science."

Why does this vision of language, the world, and human nature recommend itself? Fragmentary, meaningless, rootless existence seems

---

[22]*Ibid.*, xv.

[23]Michael Ryan, *Marxism and Deconstruction: A Critical Articulation*, 117.

[24]*Ibid.*, 214.

precisely the evil fate many modern thinkers hope to avoid. As was often the case in the past with Marxism, however, deconstruction provides a temporary community united to destroy some perceived oppression. It enables both vigorous criticism and a sense of solidarity. These are potent attractions; as Jacques Maritain observes at the very beginning of *Integral Humanism*, one of the great modern hungers is search for a heroic humanism. Deconstruction provides various intellectual occasions for *la lutte continue*. The aim is radical liberation with the return to meaning indefinitely postponed.[25]

What more often occupies the attention of deconstructors, however, are more palpable political targets. These targets will probably become more and more important in Western cultural debates as a compensation, if the Soviet Union and other Marxist states continue their ideological decline.

VII. The End of History Debate

In 1989 Francis Fukuyama published a now-famous article entitled "The End of History" that tries to describe what the world will be like after

---

[25]Liberation, of a sort, there must be, but it comes at quite a high price. The best formulation of this predicament is the novelist Walker Percy's description of *the lost self*:

"With the passing of the cosmological myths and the fading of Christianity as the guarantor of the identity of the self, the self becomes dislocated...is both cut loose and imprisoned by its own freedom, yet imprisoned by a curious and paradoxical bondage like a Chinese handcuff, so that the very attempt to free itself, e.g., by even more refined techniques for the pursuit of happiness, only tighten the bondage and distance the self even farther from the very world it wishes to inhabit as its homeland." (*Lost in the Cosmos* [New York: Farrar, Strauss, and Giroux 1983], 12).

It is important to recognize how deconstruction takes this process to an extreme. In the past people sought release from external constraint in revolution or from internal neurosis in psychology. The deconstructive vision seeks to do both of those things and to free the self from the limitations of being a self. A kind of radical freedom becomes possible, but only at the cost of radical self-annihilation.

the demise of the ideological struggles of the twentieth century. Fukuyama's thesis is that the close of the twentieth century points "not to an 'end of ideology' or a convergence between capitalism and socialism, as earlier predicted, but to an unabashed victory of economic and political liberalism."[26]

Fukuyama argues, further, that this marks not merely "the passing of a particular period of postwar history, but the *end of history as such*" (emphasis added). The phrase "the end of history," of course, comes from Hegel, where it means a definitive shift to a final and recognized form of society. As Fukuyama sees it,

> ...at the end of history it is not necessary that all societies become successful liberal societies, merely that they end their ideological pretensions of representing different and higher forms of human society.

Fukuyama concludes with a somber picture of what the world will be like in which history has ended:

> ...the worldwide ideological struggle that called forth daring, courage, imagination, and idealism, will be replaced by economic calculation, the endless solving of technical problems, environmental concerns, and the satisfaction of sophisticated consumer demands. In the post-historical period there will be neither art nor philosophy, just the perpetual caretaking of the museum of human history....Perhaps this very prospect of centuries of boredom will serve to get history started once again.

It is difficult to believe that history, in any sense, is about to end. Even Fukuyama has hinted that his article was meant to be more provocative than prophetic, but the widespread reaction to his argument shows how widespread is the feeling that we are at a new moment in world history. For our present subject, however, it is useful to look at some of the forces Fukuyama thinks might replace the old ideological struggle, all of which

---

[26]Francis Fukuyama, "The End of History," *The National Interest*, Summer, 1989, 3.

are Hegelian *contradictions* within liberalism: religion, nationalism, ethnicity, feminism, and environmentalism.

The curious fact about each of these forces—with the notable exception of religion—is that they have all been flowering in the shade of Marxism for some years now. Even religion has gotten some reception in radical circles in the form of liberation theology. More to the point, these forces lead to movements that offer themselves as substitute heroic humanisms.

Someone might object that deconstruction does not logically entail political radicalism, and that their linkage is rather a cultural accident. Perhaps; but such movements are closely connected with Barrett's identification of our culture's *sense of being.* There is no logical reason why deconstructive politics should not, say, support the right to life of the fetus against a feminism pushed to the extreme of demanding the slaughter of innocents; but the whole spirit of such politics lines up against the child. It is difficult to imagine a pro-life deconstruction, though it would be a challenge to several of the most potent *centers of authority* in our culture—the universities, the media, radical individualism, and the feminist movement itself.

Though the old Marxist, Fascist, and bourgeois individualist ideologies are discredited, they each have one or more analogues in the new *humanist* movements that stem from the Hegelian contradictions within liberalism. These movements are vague and characteristically know more about what they want to destroy than about what they hope to create. Let us look briefly at some of these issues individually to see what sort of human and humanistic vision each covertly or openly presents.

First, nationalism. Nationalism in its extreme forms is discredited in First World nations. The Fascism of Italy, Spain, Japan, and other countries failed militarily and left a strong intellectual presumption against that kind of nationalist model. Even the rise of nationalism in the Soviet Union has elicited strong fears. In the Third World, however, aggressive nationalism is condoned and even encouraged in various quarters. As unbelievable as the conjunction may seem, Western intellectuals have been known to make excuses for anti-Western regimes like those in Iran, Iraq, and Libya. These pundits really intend a double outcome from encouraging these nationalisms: the creation of alternative models for society and the decentering (to use a deconstructionist term) of global power, especially when that means destruction of power in the West. The old Marxist-Leninist rhetoric about developing countries is largely dead except in places like Cuba, but the virulent mixture of totalitarian control and a vague anti-Western socialism can persist under cover of an otherwise respectable desire for national self-identity.

A related movement that has already shown strength in this country as well as elsewhere is *ethnicity*. In Africa and the Middle East, but also in Latin America and lately in Eastern Europe, a potentially dangerous combination of nationalism and ethnicity has sprung up. In some instances, the nationalism still has vague Leninist anti-imperial overtones. This leads to a mixing of what Maritain called the totalitarianism of the *social or racial community* with the totalitarianism of the *political state*. In the original French edition of the *Twilight of Civilization*, Maritain observes these two totalitarianisms *"peut-être même un jour arriveront-elles se fondre et se compénéterer, pour le grand malheur des hommes"* ("perhaps even one day they will come to melt into one another, to interpenetrate, to the great sorrow of the human race").[27]

For us Americans, ethnicity has positive value. All of us can trace our families' arrival to some other, longer-standing culture. Ethnicity is a real component of all of our lives and many of its manifestations are not only benign but positive enrichments of our national heritage. The *ideology* of ethnicity, however, is another story. Some African-Americans, for example, have begun to define their very being by their blackness. Everything else must be calibrated according to that standard. Perhaps, strictly speaking, this should be called *racialism*, but the principle is the same. Human value and the pattern of what constitutes an authentic human life —that is, humanism—are defined according to near tribal standards. These give rise to a kind of *Volksgeist* that could be harmless enough in itself. In many of its forms, however, it is a radical de-centering, fine as a refuge from the neutrality of the common culture, but less than ideal as a balanced vision of humanity. Authentic ethnicity would entail recognition that for the very same reason that one group takes pride in itself, others should be respected in their own ethnic identification.

If nationalism and ethnicity continue in some ways the Fascist impulse under more respectable forms, what of the other Newtonian humanism? Can we find any contemporary analogs to *scientific* social-

---

[27]Inexplicably, this sentence does not appear in the English translation. Perhaps the defeat of Nazism eliminated Maritain's most immediate fear.

ism, that is, Communism? After all, perhaps the greatest appeal of Communism to intellectuals was that it provided a rational explanation, a theory by which to understand individual human life and human history.

My candidate to replace scientific socialism may seem odd, but it aspires to be scientific and in most of its manifestations is quirkily socialist: the environmentalist movement.

Now, only a fool or a lunatic could be opposed to wanting to preserve the healthiness and beauty of the world; but it is precisely *a world* and not *an environment* that human beings live in. The very language of the movement is significant. An animal, strictly speaking, inhabits an environment; it responds in easily predictable ways to specific stimuli. Even highly evolved primates show predictable behavior in response to an environment. The spirit behind a certain kind of environmentalism—an ideological environmentalism—seems to want to limit or abolish everything in human behavior it finds *unnatural*; hence its totalitarian temptations. Its typical targets are business, free economic systems, and human population growth.

Environmentalism proper also seeks to mangle the fully human. By what he is, a human being does not exist in a network of stimulus and response. A person acts in a near infinity of ways that no mere stimulus-response theory can explain. Nature is not, for us, a mother, but a kind of older cousin, a fellow creature to be listened to up to a point but left behind in many ways as we engage in quintessentially human acts.

The environmental movement proper seems to have lost sight of this irreducible being of man in the world. It assumes, instead, that human beings can be restricted to some given natural environment that is an ideal.

The point of all this for our reflections on humanism is that lurking behind their environmental concerns, at least in some quarters, are Marxist or neo-Marxist determinisms that hate human freedom and industry. As more overt expressions of this hatred become less feasible, we are likely to see far subtler intellectual and political battles over man and environment.

VIII. Feminism and Deconstruction

The connection between deconstruction and feminism, and their common spirit, has already been noted. In itself, feminism may be a legitimate demand for justice at home and in society; but in deconstruct-

ing certain oppressions associated with *the Phallus*, when an entire
society is taxed with blindness for its failure to see the connections
between missiles and penis envy, is bullied into rewriting Scripture, and
is written off *tout court* because men and women do not show equal
performance in all sectors of society, despite natural limits, we are in the
presence of a revolutionary impulse run wild rather than a practicable
humanism.

The impulses behind nationalism, ethnicity, feminism, or environmentalism are not to be dismissed wholesale. Rather, we should distinguish between the legitimate, limited forms and the radically deconstructive forms of each. In *The Rebel*, Camus put this opposition as one
between *revolt* against a specific injustice and *revolution*, entailing a
murderous annihilation of everything that stands in the way of what
presents itself as a desire for absolute justice.

Each of these movements reflects a basic confusion about the nature
of human beings. Any humanism worthy of the name in the contemporary world must be more richly articulated than the humanisms of the
past. If there is a common fault of the humanisms of the early part of this
century, it is that they focus on too few elements of real human life,
usually the individual or the person on the one hand and the state on the
other. Maritain's *Integral Humanism*, for example, insufficiently emphasizes various other social factors like family and community, and even
physical factors like region and climate. By the time he came to write
Reflections on America, though, he remarked that he had become aware of
the various social and political structures that help America to be both
personnaliste et communautaire.

In fact, anything less falsifies the picture of true human life considerably. Full human beings have family ties, however tenuous these may
be in some cases. Ideological ethnicity seeks to assert the value of those
ties. It also, along with nationalisms, seeks to preserve the smaller
communities--Edmund Burke's *small platoons*--that also help situate human persons in the world. Humanism must deal with the difficult and
crucial question of how the freedom of persons is to be balanced against
the common good; but that does not exhaust the question by far: in fact,
as every credible school of psychology attests and as recent studies of
poverty and welfare have shown, family and community influences are
generally more important to authentic development of a person than is the
state. The state can protect and foster this development in smaller
groupings, or it may harm that human matrix in ways that are all too
familiar; but the real site of human development and flourishing is in

those more intimate settings. How else could we account for some of the most remarkable human beings of our time—Alexander Solzhenitsyn, Natan Scharansky, Maximilian Kolbe, and others--who grew to greatness in prison camp communities of solidarity in the teeth of some of the most bloodthirsty states in human history?

Furthermore, the old opposition of types of states, as Fukuyama says, is probably over. Democracies based on constitutions guaranteeing the dignity of human persons, an incipient natural law grounding, are likely to appear in many places in the near future. Hungary has gone peacefully from the Marxist to the democratic camp, for example. Poland has undergone unprecedented changes, and East Germany and West Germany are coming to terms on reunification. The news from the homeland of international socialism, the Soviet Union, is hard to believe from day to day. Chinese Marxism seems to be destined to face domestic opposition. Of course, a shakeup of the Soviet Union, or an economic downturn in the West, could arrest or slow this process, but the intellectual and historical conclusions to be drawn about Marxist systems are now clear. We should be on our guard, therefore, that we not accept Marxism incrementally under the banner of one or more kindred movements when the human race has rejected it as a totality.

IX. Toward A Reconstruction

Let us return to deconstructive theory, however, to see how we may reconstruct a more fully human intellectual and political order in our current circumstances. Some deconstructionists admit the need of deconstructing deconstruction lest it, too, become merely another oppressive Center of meaning. Centers there will be, regardless of the desire to do without them, simply because the dynamic character of human life demands more than the dispersion of energies. George Santayana put this well over fifty years ago in *The Genteel Tradition at Bay*:

> A universal culture always tolerant, always fluid, smiling on every thing exotic and on everything new, sins against the principle of life itself. We exist by distinction, by integration round a specific nucleus according to a particular pattern.

The appeal of deconstructive revolution is precisely its momentary integration of forces against some particular targets. The question for those of us who are not deconstructors is whether there is not some wider, more substantial center of meaning to give this vigor to life.

A rather traditional deconstructing of deconstruction might begin with a different approach to the idea of language. Far from being a free play of signs, language situates us in several overlapping communities. The French critic Roland Barthes had an intuition of this, which he expressed by saying that all language is "quite simply Fascist"; but perhaps there are less sinister ways to conceptualize this fact.

As we now know, an isolated Cartesian *ego* does not exist. No subject of which we can conceive could have the linguistic and conceptual skills to assert *Cogito ergo sum* without already belonging to a family and language community of a particular sort. Similarly, the deconstructive free play of signs can be understood to depend upon a community of a certain sort for its beginnings--paradoxically the free communities of the West.

Language theory is the basis of this whole movement, and in some ways deconstruction does us a service in showing that language is not merely a mechanical *adaequatio* of a string of words to an object. Deconstruction's profound insight is that in purely mechanical terms there exists a gap between word and object. A word is a thing, a sign if you will, but also a thing; and the link, if it exists, between word and object is mysterious. Early in this century, the French linguist Ferdinand Saussure proposed a scientific correspondence theory that repeated several *adaequatio* arguments, but both Saussure and his followers found the very gap deconstructionists emphasize hard to explain. The word and all language, in a sense, posit an *absence* of the object, and a whole system of absences may be made to arise from that intuition. Derrida even speaks of a metaphysics of absence.

Any adequate reply to deconstruction must confront this language problem. There are resources in realist thinking that might help here, particularly a renewed and expanded theory of intentionality that would underscore the difficulties of all sorts to which the free play of signs immediately gives rise; but even more importantly, an elaboration of a theory of knowledge as the "immaterial union of the knower with the known"[28] could dispel several dangerous errors. That union will scan-

---

[28]See, for example, Marc F. Griesbach's enlightening remarks in his "Presidential Address: Restoring Philosophical Realism in Today's Intellectual World," *1983 Proceedings of the American Catholic Philosophical Association.*

dalize any number of schools of contemporary philosophy, but it is the kind of mystery that clarifies and vivifies as opposed to the mystifications of a movement like deconstruction that lead to more and more obscure dead ends.[29]

Furthermore, as the American critic M. H. Abrams has pointed out, a deconstructive reading of a text is not so radically agnostic as Derrida would have us believe: "Deconstruction can only subvert the meanings of a text that has always already been construed." The old-style, *metaphysical* reading Abrams designates as reading1 and the deconstructive reading, added to the first reading, he calls reading2. In Derrida, as Abrams well recognizes, reading1 is *always already* an interpretation; but it is precisely the general agreement about this reading1, however pluralistic our approach to the text may be, that Abrams finds casts doubt on the deconstructive opening. How is it that we can identify what most people presume to have been Rousseau's intention, for example, and can communicate to one another with a fair degree of completeness and certainty, that reading of the text, whatever doubts we may later introduce?

To take a notorious example, in *Of Grammatology* Derrida examines Rousseau's use of the term "nature" in the "Essay on the Origin of Language." Derrida has little trouble in showing that Rousseau's "nature" is an incoherent concept that is always providing occasion for supplementarity when pure "nature" becomes inadequate to the tasks to which Rousseau wishes to put it. Abrams observes:

> Derrida designates his reading1—the determinate construal of the *legibility* of passages of Rousseau—as no more than a strategic phase, which though indispensable, remains *provisional* to a further *critical* or deconstructive reading. One of Derrida's moves in this critical reading is to identify strata, or *strands* in Rousseau's text which, when read determinately, turn out to be mutually contradictory. A number of earlier commentators, of course, have found

---

[29]George Steiner has observed: "The chain of signs is infinite. It is one's perception of the nature and status of that infinity, either transcendent or, in the severest yet also most playful sense, meaningless, which will determine one's exercise of understanding and of judgment" (Steiner, *Real Presences*, 59).

Rousseau's linguistic and social theories to be incoherent or contradictory, but have regarded this feature as a logical fault or as
assimilable to an overall direction of his thinking. Derrida, however,
regards such self-contradictions not as logical mistakes which
Rousseau could have avoided, but as inescapable features not only
in Rousseau's texts but in all Western texts, since all rely on fixed
logocentric ground yet are purely conventional and differential in
their economy.[30]

We might push this insight still further. Derrida seeks to prevent
deconstruction from being reabsorbed by a scientific system by positing
an uncanny absence standing outside of the Western metaphysical
discourse, a *no-thing* irreducible to the language of presence. Yet as in all
such attempt at heterology, the mere notice of the wholly Other in
language gives language some way to appropriate what appears to be its
own outside. In the *metaphysical age*, for example, apophatic theologies
arose to describe the contours of what God was not. Some of the
Kabbalists, too, posited a pure Truth that could not be sullied by the
impure approaches of human thought. These examples make the charac-
terization of the metaphysical age as an age of presence and certitude
historically doubtful (both Heidegger and Derrida may simply have
erred in this respect).

Derrida is in part aware of these earlier strategies and tries to go
beyond even them; but it is not at all clear that the mere negation of that
negative theology protects deconstruction from becoming yet another
metaphysic. Even without falling into a new version of the Hegelian
dialectic, such a vision inevitably begins to make what was outside of
language part of the inside. How else can we account for the fact that we
understand what Derrida has written in the several books that appeared
around 1968 and that made seminal contributions to our understanding
of the *post-structuralist* situation? We may not consider the inevitable
capture of his sense by language a fault, as he might, but neither are we
entirely convinced that deconstruction has found a way past "metaphysical" language.

There is also a *historical* problem with Derrida. We may agree with

---

[30]M.H. Abrams, *Doing Things with Texts: Essays on Literary Theory*
(New York: Columbia University Press, 1989), 148.

Nietzsche and Derrida that the *past* is always already a set of interpretations, yet that realization does not free us from certain limits on historical assertions. Derrida has often claimed that his work does not intend to subvert the objective work of the *sciences* within their own sphere. He intends only to operate on the margins of the text, upon the things taken for granted. It is difficult to see, however, how deconstructive *sollicitation* does not upset the meaning of all signs. What archi-principle, itself resistant to deconstructive readings, would limit such *sollicitation*? To take a concrete example, Nietzsche's *Birth of Tragedy* and several of his writings on history are brilliant interpretations worthy of careful reading by every generation of scholars interested in the issues he addresses; but we know with as much certainty as human beings can know that Nietzsche's account of the evolution of tragedy in ancient Greece is founded on demonstrably false historical premises—in the sense of simple sequences of events. Do the ascertainable facts limit the correctness of the reading? Of course, they do, as Derrida admits; but what then of the belief that all texts are already interpretations? Some interpretations must retain at least limited authority and an *a priori* trust that makes them something more than *mere* interpretation for us to be able to carry out critical historical analyses.[31]

What can be written can take on enough determinate sense that we may argue to a large extent about its meaning. The meaning of "closure" in *Of Grammatology* is clear enough that we can judge its truth value compared with that of the *end of history* in Hegel. In the final analysis, *closure* and *end* suggest systems of thought, even if those systems have very different characteristics. The metaphysical epoch, and Hegel as part of it, seem to have a gravitational pull that Derrida's centrifugal forces, for all their brilliance, cannot fully overcome.

Furthermore, we should emphasize the historical role of traditional

---

[31]Perhaps it was the realization of the difficulties of consistency in writing the deconstructive essay that led Derrida, after the burst of creativity around 1968, to bring out works more avowedly creative than analytic. *The Postcard, Glas,* and other texts over the last decade or so seem to try to embody the belief that the free play of signs, outside of determinate analytical meanings, is the only proper way of *writing*, once we have discovered the true nature of the sign.

humanistic beliefs in restraining totalitarian oppression. Deconstruction is right to apply to Nietzsche, Hegel, and Heidegger the test of "by their fruits you shall know them." Yet we should look at other forms of humanism, too, in this light.

The different ways that Jews were treated in Germany and Italy after the state had in each case passed official anti-Semitic decrees is here instructive. Most German Jews were rounded up and died; most Italian Jews were hidden by families and individuals of no greater ethical stature than their German counterparts. The Italians, however, simply would not do certain things even if the state insisted. Do we really want to deconstruct these human decencies?

You may argue that these families and communities should be deconstructed because their centers of meaning are in various ways oppressive; but viewed in another light, they are precisely the kinds of forces that, at times, best resist the economic and political pretensions of progressive systems.[32] There are political dangers lurking within deconstruction. M. H. Abrams asks:

> Which of the following alternatives is more apt to open a cultural vacuum that will be filled by power-hungry authoritarians who have no doubts about what they want nor scruples about how to get it: A systematic and sustained enterprise to deconstruct the grounds of all truths or values asserted by our culture-bearing texts, and to subvert even our confidence that we can communicate determinately with one another? Or a reformulated version of the central

---

[32]One of my differences of emphasis with Michael Novak's latest book, *Free Persons and the Common Good* (Lanham, MD: Madison Books, 1989) is that, in trying to defend a society of free persons against a tribal view of a unitary common good, his language occasionally is too sweeping. He writes, for example, of premodern attachments to family and clan: "naturally the human race experiences a profound nostalgia for such tribal solidarities. Adolf Hitler traded upon these solidarities, as have all modern collectivists" (84). True enough, but something akin to a good form of tribal solidarity also inhibited the execution of Jews under Italian Fascism. Novak knows the importance of these small platoons as well as anyone, but his language does not always reflect it.

Romantic hope that, by a revolution of mind and heart, man may yet achieve unity with himself, community with his fellow men, and reconciliation with a nature in which, because it can be humanized, he can feel at home?[33]

Realizations such as these open up the way to talk about the importance of the habits we call virtues. In deconstructive views, stable behaviors reflect petrifications of a free flow; but there are certain forms of stability, encouraged primarily in family and community settings, that have inestimable value both in the personal and in the largest spheres of human life.

A perceptive French response to deconstruction has come from two thinkers seeking to take into account both Derrida's concerns and the impasse to which his speculations lead. In *French Philosophy of the Sixties: An Essay on Antihumanism*,[34] Luc Ferry and Alain Renaut pit themselves against all the major names in French poststructuralism. The common error of these theorists, say Ferry and Renaut, was to identify humanism with metaphysics. Conceding the dangers posed by what they regard as all such complete explanations of human natures, Ferry and Renaut argue the need for the creation of a *non-metaphysical humanism*. This last would defend human rights and might even seek to justify *"liberté, égalité, et fraternité,"* though obviously on different philosophical grounds than did the thinkers of the Enlightenment.

In the current climate of thought, even this modest form of humanism is a welcome development; but we might ask Ferry and Renaut just what a non-metaphysical humanism could be if it has a definite content? If human rights, however defined, are to be considered as in some fashion a reflection of human nature, this nature must have some, at least partly identifiable, form, leaving the door open to metaphysics again. To be clear about this, if there is some specifiable human nature, "a dignity proper to man," in Heidegger's words, we may choose not to use theistic or classically metaphysical terms to define it; but that some irreducible,

---

[33]M.H. Abrams, *Doing Things with Texts: Essays in Criticism and Critical Theory* (New York: W.W. Norton, 1989), 268.

[34]Trans. Mary Schnackenberg Cattani (Boston:University of Massachusetts Press, 1990).

metaphysically modest, yet metaphysically anchored human nature is being posited is inescapable; and once we resort to this hypothesis, we might as well give up the pretence of avoiding metaphysics and face the problem squarely: what is the best and most accurate metaphysical description of human nature and humanism?

Ultimately, we arrive at the old issues of humanism: what form will the state take? Fascism, Communism, and bourgeois individualism have long been discredited intellectually, and history has shown the intellectual analyses were correct. If Fukuyama is correct, liberal democratic regimes will be our future, and the primary political questions of the future will be to enhance liberty within democratic order. Deconstructive critiques, however, go beyond mere correction of errors to call in question the very legitimacy of all ordered structure. This is the nub of the question that must be faced by any serious reflection on humanism today: Can we justify *any* regime?

This already long essay is perhaps the preamble to a longer analysis, and we can only point out here the direction an answer to this question might take. As G. K. Chesterton once remarked about America:

> The melting pot must not melt. The original shape can be traced on the lines of Jeffersonian democracy; and it will remain in that shape until it becomes shapeless. America invites all men to become citizens; but it implies the dogma that there is such a thing as citizenship.

In democracies like ours, where citizens are expected to take charge of their own government, not many of us will be seduced by the deconstructive movement. Quite a few of us, especially during our university years, might be harassed by various forms of deconstruction that would seek to deny the dogma of free citizenship or destabilize the defense of free institutions that check and limit one another. In some ways, an unchecked deconstruction is just as dangerous as an unchecked *duce*. Each ultimately demolishes the order that preserves liberty. We absolutely require dogmas such as the citizenship of free persons whose very resistance to all attempts to deconstruct them keep us free from the false freedoms that in their own way finally enslave.

Joseph J. Califano

Human Suffering and Our Post-Civilized Cultural Mind: A Maritainian Analysis

In *The Twilight of Civilization* Maritain warns us that the defeat of the pagan empires in World War II would not necessarily solve "the problems of freedom to be won, of civilization to be rescued and rebuilt."[1] For it seems that the secular counter humanism[2] (opposed to the humanism of the Incarnation)[3] which produced these empires and its principle of hatred for those who suffer[4] could outlive their military defeat. For the coming into existence of these empires in human history were merely eruptions of forces deeply entrenched in the sophisticated mind of twentieth century man. This was and still is the case since the same erroneous philosophy of man and life[5] at the core of secular humanism has thrived in our times; where the individual is "set up as a selfish god"[6] and man flings himself pathologically "into the abyss of animality."[7] Having banished God from the affairs of men and having rejected the possibility of receiving any wisdom from above; the secular humanist is driven by and consumed within a hatred for truth and wisdom. Therefore the secular

---

[1]Jacques Maritain, *The Twilight of Civilization*, trans. Lionel Landry (New York: Sheed and Ward, 1943), ix.

[2]*Ibid.*, 8.

[3]*Ibid.*, 13.

[4]*Ibid.*, 9. "When love and sanctity fail to transfigure the condition of mankind or to change slaves into sons of God, the law claims many victims. Nietzsche could not endure the sight of the lame and halt of Christianity: even more than Goethe, he revolted against the Cross."

[5]*Ibid.*, 62.

[6]*Ibid.*, 13.

[7]*Ibid.*, 19.

humanist seeks the impossible: a "communion in human animality"[8] and truth in the myth of anthropocentric self sufficiency.[9] In such a context the compassion of the good Samaritan is judged to be foolishness[10] by those who are ruled by the "dominion of hate."[11] Here the myths of "the homicidal errors of bourgeois individualism"[12] are given full reign over man's consciousness and produce a hideous malformation of man's moral conscience.

As a result of the tenacity of the above, in our present world humankind has been experiencing an evaporation of self-knowledge. This expanding lacuna in our knowledge of our very *being* has necessarily caused an evaporation of our consciousness of justice and the foundation upon which all genuine human relationships are based. This dissolution of our awareness of what we *are* can also be described as a journey to the end of the era of the civilized mind and the coming into existence of the cultured mind that is devoid of civilization. There has been a tremendous accumulation of *data* about man, but this fascination with *data* has clouded rather than enlightened man's understanding of himself.

Nothing manifests the characteristic roots of this post-civilized cultural mind more clearly than the attitude it produces towards pain and human suffering. There is the coincidence of a twofold shunning of reality manifested here: one, of the reality of human suffering; and, two, of the reality of human nature and our relationship to one another. Ultimately this is an occultization of the nature of man as a transobjective-subject among other trans-objective-subjects. What has resulted from this twofold shunning of reality is a *deconstructed world* where there are no existing human subjects who suffer or who undergo pain—a world devoid of truth, where arbitrary judgments and the dialectical art of rhetorical persuasion reign.

Human suffering or pain does not easily submit itself to a real definition. The etymological origin of the English word "pain" is rooted in Greek and Latin notions of pain as that which is suffered as retribution or punishment for an evil deed that was done—a just recompense. A view that has survived throughout the centuries in certain popular religious

---

[8]*Ibid.*, 21.
[9]*Ibid.*, 4 and 34.
[10]*Ibid.*, 39.
[11]*Ibid.*, 41.
[12]*Ibid.*, 58.

beliefs; such views have been applied to the horror of AIDS and other forms of human suffering. The worse perversion of religious sentiment that is found in the above is the conclusion that people who suffer are getting what they deserve from God, and, therefore, they should be shunned and abandoned. If such a view were entertained by an innocent person--for example, if a child were suffering from a painful chronic debilitating disease, this child might conclude that God did not love him/her and thereby devalue his/her own existence. Such a conclusion represents a terrorizing error in reasoning too perverse to comprehend.

It is very difficult to conceptualize principles for a genuine division of pain that would provide us with an adequate means of classifying pain. This is true whether we are looking at it from the point of view of medicine, the social sciences, or philosophy. Those who have tried to develop a taxonomy of pain have found that a natural division of pain which would avoid all artificial elements and overlapping categories is not attainable. This is the case because there are so many (at least nine if not more) different perspectives from which one can attempt to measure and classify pain.[13] For example, one can attempt to distinguish pain in terms of: its cause, its duration, its intensity, whether the cause of the pain is treatable or whether the pain is relievable without massive health trade-offs. There is also the issue of trying to understand the relationship between pain and dysfunction. Pain and human suffering can also be looked at from the point of view of the effects on: the individual, the family, the community, the state, and the world viewed as a global community, and the various moral issues related to all of the above.

The most recent comprehensive definition of pain from the point of view of medicine ("an unpleasant sensory and emotional experience associated with actual or potential tissue damage or described in terms of such damage"[14]) is of great value because it preserves the unity of the psychosomatic composite of the person while including psychosomatic illnesses which have the potential to damage tissue and avoiding the pseudo-division between physical pain and emotional pain.[15]

---

[13]"*Pain*," The Journal of the International Association for the Study of Pain, " Classification of Chronic Pain," description of chronic pain syndromes and the definitions of pain terms; supplement 3, 1986, S4-S5.

[14]Cf. Robert Feldman, *Understanding Psychology* (New York: McGraw Hill, 1987), 447 ff.

[15]*Pain*, S217.

When one attempts to make pain subject to divisions from the perspective of the cause of the pain, one can only develop somewhat overlapping categories--such as whether the cause of pain is a natural phenomenon (for example, a flood, an earthquake, or volcanic eruption); or whether the cause of the pain is a result of human social institutions, economic or political. In either case, pain comes into existence by reason of physical injury or from the deprivation of basic needs such as food, water, or air. The above categories can be distinguished from the clinical causes of pain--for example, pain due to infectious disease or a neoplasm.

The above-cited definition of pain also avoids the problem of attempting to identify whether the stimulus which is causing the pain is a normal or abnormal[16] stimulus--both of which can be identified as producing a pleasant or unpleasant experience. For example, normal sexual stimulation can be experienced as painful, as a result of injury to the spinal cord; and abnormal stimulation from certain types of electrical stimulation can be identified as pleasant. However, the fact that substance abuse can be viewed as pleasant requires further clarification.

In the case of the snorting of cocaine, the abuser identifies as pleasant a sensation by an abnormal stimulus that produces massive damage to the nasal tissue which will eventually lead to the collapse of the nose among other types of tissue damage to vital organs, including the central nervous system. This is interesting because it represents a masochistic confusion of pleasure and pain which, in many cases, is related to psychological disorders of several kinds--such as, a poor self-image, a lack self-worth, an abnormal desire for punishment and/or self-destruction.

Pain can be distinguished as to cause from the point of view of moral philosophy as to whether it is inflicted on the sufferer by another human agent. Pain created in this way can be divided into pain intentionally inflicted on another person or other persons (such as in the cases of torture or war[17]) or through negligence (such as an auto accident).

When one seeks to distinguish pain from the perspectives of duration, intensity, and from the point of view of a simultaneous experience of bodily dysfunctions, one discovers that the first leads to a distinction

---

[16]Thus "paraesthesia" is identified as an abnormal sensation which is not unpleasant; and "dysaesthesia" is identified as an abnormal sensation which is unpleasant.

[17]Cf. Joseph Califano, "Technology and Violence," *Divus Thomas* 8 (Piacenza: Collegio Alberoni, 1975).

between pain and acute pain(pain that lasts no more than three months) and chronic pain (pain that has a duration of more than three months). However, chronic pain should be further distinguished into chronic, permanent pain (a permanent reality for the remainder of one's life) and chronic, relievable or curable pain (or pain in which there is at least some hope of relief). Chronic, permanent pain should be divided into chronic, permanent, progressive pain where pain and dysfunction increase at various rates and chronic, permanent, benign pain where there appears to be no noticeable progression of either the pain or dysfunction. Tissue damage in such cases may be identified as a result of a normal aging process. Attempts to classify various intensities of pain present us with the difficulty of conceptualizing a spectrum from pain as a minimal awareness of discomfort to excruciating agony that takes one's breath away and causes muscle spasms. The latter I call *paralyzing pain,* and it usually causes tissue damage and/or atrophy of the muscles.

Physicians often try to describe pain in terms of pain thresholds, the least experience of pain that a person can recognize, and pain tolerance,[18] the greatest level of pain a person is prepared to tolerate. However, the definition of pain tolerance presents us with many problems. This is the case because a person who is experiencing permanent, chronic, intractable, progressive pain may be in a no-win situation where the pain he is prepared to tolerate is irrelevant in respect to the pain he has to tolerate. In the case of permanent, chronic, intractable, progressive pain, one is often faced with a situation in which the choice to relieve the pain involves a person in serious health trade-offs: for example, 1)the long term use of drugs to anesthetize the sensation of pain can lead to addiction, personality changes, and additional tissue damage to various vital organs; 2) by ignoring or suppressing the pain which signals that damage is being done to human tissue, one may be falling into deeper levels of mental and physical dysfunction. Therefore, the fear of further loss of function or addiction to pain-relieving drugs that may adversely affect the quality of one's life even further might cause a patient to endure agonizing pain rather than accept addiction and the mental oblivion that drug therapy offers and/or paralysis.

In such a circumstance pain presents the sufferer with a manifold reality difficult for many people to grasp: pain as a horrible sign that something is wrong; pain as a constant companion; pain as the signal of

---

[18]*Pain,* S220-S221.

progressive levels of dysfunction. One finds oneself in a situation where to endure the pain--to continue to function in spite of the pain--causes damage to tissue and, for example, the atrophy of muscles. The issue here is not a question of "no pain, no gain," but of pain and unavoidable loss no matter what one is willing to suffer. The attack on one's liberty of movement and action is so great that the battle to sustain a genuine sense of self-worth (the value of one's own existence) and hope in such a situation is quite overwhelming. In conjunction with the struggle to maintain an appreciation of the value of interpersonal relationships within the family for all concerned, this battle requires something the present world has found comfortable to ignore. Also, the difficulty of finding the right way to function in the context of the above is the greatest of all barriers to overcome. The greatest danger to the suffering person here is that out of frustration and anger the suffering person loses patience[19] and despairs and, thereby, makes matters worse by indulging in self-destructive behavior. For example, one can focus only on how unfair life is and wallow in self-pity. This preoccupation with what is absent in one's life can lead one to become bitter and disagreeable towards others or to hide in substance abuse. Thus one makes oneself and everyone around one miserable and negates one's own sense of self worth and the value of one's interpersonal relationships. The acquisition of the wisdom to accomplish this in the concrete situation takes it own time in coming for those who seek it. The prevalent cultured mind devoid of civilization discussed below will never provide it. Without a profound understanding of the spirituality of the human reality, the question in our decivilized culture, has become "Suicide and euthanasia--why not?"

Granted, we seem to be able to deal better with acute--that is, short-term--human suffering; for example, right after a hurricane or earthquake there seems to be genuine, intense, short term identification with those who are rendered homeless and are suffering in many ways. However, this identification quickly dissipates along with media coverage, even though the worst of these catastrophes are the chronic, intractable, progressive pain and post-traumatic syndromes that victims must live with for the rest of their lives. It is the shunning or phobia of chronic, intractable, progressive, paralyzing pain that is deserving of more serious consideration. Likewise we have become accustomed to the chronically homeless people all over this nation who live in parks and railroad

---

[19]Note that patience is the virtue which fortifies the irascible appetite against despair when confronted with evils other than death itself.

stations, many of whom really are very disturbed people and need some kind of institutionalized help.

Now let us look at pain from the point of the individual and the family; and here we are going to concentrate on chronic, intractable, progressive, paralyzing pain--the kind of pain which when first experienced causes in a person a desire physically to run away from one's own body (sometimes acted out) in order to escape the pain--until one realizes there is no place to run. For wherever one runs one must take one's pain along too. This kind of pain causes one to objectify one's body in a Cartesian manner which almost makes one forget the psychosomatic unity of the human person, in that one's own body can be viewed as something foreign, as an alien causing one harm. When the person has to accept the full realization that the situation is permanent, one feels an isolation that is difficult to verbalize--a foretaste of death fills one with the cold sensation of ashes. This feeling of isolation can cause one to doubt not only the value of one's own existence but also whether one is of value to anyone else--especially one's loved ones. The suffering person asks himself whether he has become a burden to everyone concerned (for our post civilized culture tells one that life is the domain only of the healthy).

All of the above is accompanied simultaneously by the disbelief that what is happening is real and irreversible and also by the absolute certainty that this is one's reality. One's body becomes redefined daily as those parts that work today. The amount of psychic energy that must be expended in the simplest task is inexpressible. The monotony of constant pain and the wearisomeness of the fact that it demands so much of one's life be consumed in dealing with the pain can become most depressing. Constant pain thus is very boring.

One finds that most people consciously shun the reality of the suffering person. This is noticeable by the fact that many avoid looking into the eyes of the person in pain, or they will look at the suffering person until the person who is suffering notices that they are looking, and then they will quickly look away. There is a defensive denial of the reality of pain that can be seen in too many contexts to explicate here. This can take the form of a healthy person cutting off a handicapped person to take a handicap parking space, or an insurance company making it almost impossible to get a prosthetic device or aid to mobility that is absolutely necessary; and those who balk at making a building in which the handicap lives or works handicap accessible (not to mention that doctors who are employed to save insurance companies money, will, for a fee, lie or deny the reality of a victim's sufferings without examining the victim).

There is a kind of victim phobia that has a somewhat universal character in our contemporary world--a kind of view that if I do not let the other person in pain enter into my consciousness, then I do not have to deal with him or her and I cannot be held responsible for not dealing with these realities. This view involves a withdrawal from pain and the reality of death which, in fact, is a withdrawal from the reality of life itself. Thus is born the theory of negative rights, or laissez-faire morality.[20] As long as I do not do anything directly to harm another person, human rights are preserved. Justice is preserved by doing nothing wrong and acts of omission are no longer acts related to justice. Love of another person as a person is excluded from my cognitive comportment, although desire for the other as a source of pleasure or comfort is quite acceptable. This is the foundation of the cultured mind devoid of civilization. This view has a pervasive influence in all levels our contemporary social organization, whether the family, the community, the state, or the world viewed as a global community. In such a context, one might throw money in an impersonal way at a problem in order to protect oneself from having the problem invade one's consciousness, but any involvement beyond this point is too risky for the contemporary cultured mind. This view in reality limits itself to admitting only the secondary and negative understanding of the first principle of moral reasoning--namely, to do no evil. However, the affirmation of the real first principle of morality is that one is to do good and avoid evil, with an emphasis on doing the good. For one could spend one's whole life sleeping and do no evil, but one would fail to live a human life, which requires the doing of the good in more than an egocentric fashion.

A positive understanding of the moral law is necessary not only for the elimination of much human suffering but also for the stability of a family, and we all know of instances in which families that lack the spiritual bond of benevolent love do not survive. For benevolent love is a reality that cannot be recognized as existing or be explained if we see man only as the highest kind of animal. Thus families fall apart when they are forced to face serious problems and they lack benevolent love--the

---

[20]Joseph Califano,"Modernization and Human Values,"*Jacques Maritain: The Man and His Metaphyics*, ed. John F.X. Knasas (Notre Dame: American Maritain Association, 1988); "Modernization and the Law of the Prise de Conscience,"*Freedom in the Modern World*, ed. Michael D. Torre (Notre Dame: American Maritain Association, 1989).

necessary means for their survival. There are numerous cases where the contemporary sophisticated, cultured mind is the prime mover in the way a family deals with a chronically ill family member. The ill member becomes an object to be discarded. Thus, just as cars or pet animals, people and human relationships are viewed as discardable objects.

There is also a transference of the evil of the affliction to the existence of the victims and potential victims who become evils to be destroyed. Since we only seek to destroy that which we hate as an evil, it must be recognized that euthanasia and abortion are examples of the above transference in which an actually suffering human being (such as someone chronically ill) and a potentially suffering human being (such as an unwanted child who might become an actual sufferer) are deemed to be evil, hateful objects to be destroyed. There is a negation of the existence of persons as subjects which enables many to identify them as hateful objects. This transference is not merely, as some would have it, to keep the victims at arm's length but a radical negation of the goodness of their existence in order to keep them hateful objects to be destroyed. If this were the right approach, then the way to solve domestic violence--the abuse of women--would be to kill all the wives who are possible victims of such actual violence.[21]

One might say that such a way of behaving depicts an irrational or insane approach to actual or potential suffering. However, contemporary psychotherapy would affirm the sanity of the contemporary decivilized cultured mind since the healthy person is identified as an autonomous, hedonistic, goalless person who is free of guilt and who sees his self realization in and through self gratification.[22] He is one who adapts well and is logical or at least consistent in his behavior, who is free of the

---

[21]There is an even more callous view of disinvolvement with others in the case where a woman views a child as an evil to be destroyed simply because she does not consider it a good time to have another person around for whom she might have to be responsible or love in some way. For she might have to give up an activity that she views as essential. Thus you hear statements that "I am not ready at this time to have a child"; or, as I once heard, "I cannot give up my tennis lessons to have a baby now." Thus human sexual acts that would cause a pregnancy are devoid of any human significance since the consequences if undesired are surgically quite correctable.

[22]Cf. B. Ashley and K.O. O'Rourke *Health Care Ethics*, (St. Louis, MO:

conflicts of deliberations about whether the end justifies the means, and who, therefore, acts and follows orders without reflection—a man devoid of any sense of justice.

Thomas Merton notes Adolf Eichmann was judged by psychiatrists to be perfectly sane in light of the criteria in our modern world devoid of all spiritual and, therefore, genuinely human values,[23] and Jean-François Steiner describes how Kurt Franz developed a perfectly rational and scientifically exact method of mass murder.[24] Such evaluations of rationality do not appear different from the contemporary abortionist saying, "I am logically consistent. Since abortion is legal, I do what I am paid for—that is, perform abortions—to solve people's problems. I leave all moral considerations up to the patient and society."

Through genuine knowledge and love persons transcend the confines of their material individuation,[25] discover the roots of their existential spirituality, and enter into communities—for example, the family—and discover an authentic, common good to share. The human soul exercises a spiritual self-possessing and self-giving activity rooted in the identity and difference in genuine acts of knowing and loving that enables persons to be open to other persons and God. Thus persons are wholes in themselves, and they are also a part of another whole—for example, the family. For love is always a singular act between persons as singular subjects which can be shared with the other as an individual. This is only possible because human beings are not completely bound to matter like animals. No man or woman does or should see himself as existing or suffering alone. A wife or husband and children—for example, of someone who is suffering with chronic, intractable, progressive paralyzing pain—suffers intensely also. As the person who suffers attempts to adapt to life and ever changing situations so also do all around him/her have to make such adjustments. However, the preservation of one's self-

---

The Catholic Hospital Association, 1978); also editions II and III.

[23]"A Devout Meditation in Memory of Adolf Eichmann," *Raids on the Unspeakable,* (New York: New Directions, 1966), 45-49.

[24]*Treblinka,* (New York: Simon & Schuster, Inc. 1967).

[25]Joseph Califano, "Maritain's Philosophy of the Person and the Individual," *Notes et Documents* 8 (Rome, August 1977). "Maritain's Democracy of the Human Person or Man as a Moral Agent," *Jacques Maritain: A Philosopher in the World,* ed. Jean-Louis Allard (Ottawa: University of Ottawa Press, 1985).

worth is only possible in the recognition by all of the non-material level of the spiritual identity of the human person and the benevolent love that is shared as a common good. Thus shared suffering in the context of shared love brings people closer together rather than tears them apart.

There are two principal ways in which we can view human beings. The first is that man is the highest kind of animal, an object among other objects, shut off from all other objects. The second is that man is a trans-objective-subject and all that this entails. The first is rooted in a pseudo-empirical and pseudo-scientific view of man where the intellect and the will are turned outward in a fixed comportment away from themselves and only towards the other things as objects; the emphasis here is on the other as other--the other as thing and thing as object. Here is a world devoid of dianoetic knowledge and devoid of subsistent subjects; a world devoid of persons. Any reflection upon oneself is viewed as spurious and illegitimate knowledge. All reflective knowledge of the activity of the intellect and the will that would bring one an awareness of the genuine spiritual realities of the human person are shunned because of the moral consequences that their admission would bring into one's consciousness. A recognition of these realities necessarily would result in such a radical transformation of one's perspective that the contemporary cultured will and intellect *a priori* refuse to accept or consider them. In this way, an occultization of the foundation of comprehending the intrinsic worth of a human being becomes a complete and necessary foundation for the cultured mind devoid of civilization. Once one accepts this perspective, all comprehension of human goods and the genuine common goods of human life are viewed as bastard children. The consequence is a people highly cultured in an artificial sense yet devoid of civilization; they have become separated from any genuine understanding of the human reality while they hold fast to the counterfeit notions of human beings and a human world.

All genuine understanding of the human reality begins with an awareness of the fact that man lives in a world of subjects and not a world of objects only. A person is a being who, although not perfectly, through dianoetic and ananoetic intellection, is able to grasp the *esse* and *essentia* of the subjects that coexist within and through judgment. Thus man is understood properly to be a trans-objective-subject among other trans-objective-subjects, a being who, through genuine knowledge of himself and other subjects, is capable of love.

Thus there are two truths that must be comprehended to discover a bona fide moral perspective in regard to human suffering. First, a bona fide ethics requires the metaphysical knowledge of the spiritual *esse* of the human person; and, second, this metaphysical knowledge must bring with it an intuition of the existence of other existing subjects as real and the metaphysical knowledge that oneness, goodness, truth, and beauty are identical to that *esse* as the act of an *essentia*. Thus the proof for God's existence from the gradation of pure perfection—such as life, intelligence, and the transcendentals cited above—is essential to sustaining our proper moral comportment.

The recent attempts to develop a kind of a rationalist ethics devoid of the certainty of these truths is an exercise in futility. Such efforts will of necessity have the short life proper to fads that fade as quickly as they appear and attract our attention. Ethics without the realization of the above can never identify the human goods to be sought after in an authentic moral life; for all authentic notions of justice which aim at determining what is due another are rooted in the recognition that the existence of the other is a good to be preserved. The right to life and all that the right to life contains is the first right, and all other rights presuppose it. One cannot exercise liberty, and so on, if one does not exist. The cultured minds devoid of civilization often takes refuge in the pseudo-dialectical question of how does one get an *ought* from an *is*? They do this often in the name of a material realism, a material realism which is not a realism at all because it excludes everything that is genuinely human, by reason of a self-inflicted blindness. Dialecticians produce numerous solipsistic, bizarre worlds of thought which terminate in only solipsistic silence. Hume was well aware that his philosophy was a nightmare. Hume's successors in solipsism such as Wittgenstein and Heidegger have fared no better. Whereas for the dialectician no amount of discussion is sufficient to attaining an answer, to the metaphysician who grasps the reality of things in an existential judgment no further discussion is necessary. What the dialecticians fail to see, because they have chosen not to see (and therefore they have chosen not to be in contact with reality) is that the *is* is the *ought*. From this existential fact the myth of egocentric autonomy is overcome and also a whole gamut of positive human rights are understood as flowing from this existential fact. Having separated what is identical, cultured minds devoid of civilization destroy the unity of man's being and the unity of man's moral thinking. They dwell in a world of counterfeit notions of man and reality. Just as the fabled Humpty Dumpty, man is pushed off the wall of reality and his being is fragmented; *and all the deconstructionists cannot get man back together again.*

All of the above makes one realize that acts of omission are also matters of justice. Thus the premoral experience of freedom of autonomy and its exercise is transformed into the conquest of our freedom. This transformation is the only authentic foundation for living a civilized life. Once man sought to be civilized; now man seeks merely to be free. Man seeks to be free in a *total* -- that is, indeterminate--sense, where freedom has no meaning. Man seeks to be free from the reality of himself and the reality of the other, whether the other is another human person or God.

Unless in the future democracies take seriously the warning of Maritain in the *The Twilight of Civilization* (with which I began this paper), we will be confronted with living in the darkest of ages. If we continue to reinforce the defensive denial on all levels of the realities of human suffering and the demands of justice, then we may never again see the renaissance of civilization. If democracies do not heed the warning of the above and return to the vital principle at the root of their existence "which is justice and love...in the rediscovery of God,"[26] then we will truly be a lost generation. Therefore, only in giving God His proper place in the affairs of men, with all that this requires, can the resurrection of a civilized way of life take place.

A Prayerful Postscript

As we have noted above, a person who loses patience in the context of chronic intractable progressive paralyzing pain risks everything positive in his life by actualizing a self-hatred. The result is that a person makes himself into a self-destructive mechanism mirroring what the secular humanist has judged the suffering person to be. This is a terrible self-deception which proves the worst lies are the ones we tell ourselves.

I am convinced that the only way one can sustain patience in the day in and day out struggle with constant pain and, also, avoid becoming swamped by the tidal waves of negative feelings and the potentially overwhelming states of depression which such feelings produce (which in turn produce self-destructive behavior) is through a daily life of genuine prayer. Secular humanism has nothing to offer the suffering person but nihilistic annihilation--a solipsistic nihilism rooted in the necessary dumbfounded silence of Wittgenstein, vacuous solipsism of Husserl, or the inescapable dread of Heidegger.

One can only pray for the grace to face and get through the present

---

[26]Jacques Maritain,*The Twilight of Civilization*, 63.

moment. No more can be asked for, nor can more be granted. In the final analysis, does one have any other constructive choice? When one is confronted concretely with the radical finitude of one's existence, one either finds God concretely or one is lost in abstract solipsistic nothingness.

The confined suffering person is called simultaneously to act at once on two planes,[27] the concrete unavoidably painful situation and the spiritual level. Through such a duality of action one does not escape from the concrete order of suffering nor does one becomes less conscious of the paralyzing enslavement of constant pain (angelism is not an option), but one is able to turn away from the solipsistic dwelling on pain to that which is other than one's self--ultimately, God.

John Howard Griffin confirms my own experience--namely, that the person who is seriously suffering eventually discovers that the self even in pain "is less interesting than other objects of contemplation,"[28] and one sees the beauty of other people even in every day activities. For me it was a day when I could barely move and my eighteen month old granddaughter insisted on playing with me by bringing things to me. Such a simple act of a child who is learning to share does not permit one to remain within oneself. Likewise, a wife who provides one with the physical care normally due a child and who does not permit one to give in or give up on oneself because she will not is a grace from God.

I believe once one is able to realize the above, one is able to see in a way that defies description ("for no fine reasoning could have the same effect"[29]) how God calls one to see the truth. "From this can spring a truth that confuses those who know little of suffering: the core of joy that lies at the heart of even the most intense suffering; the supreme activity of wisdom that does not need movement."[30]

One realizes how God asks the suffering person to look and see what I have created and how good it is. I believe, therefore, the suffering person, if only through a glass darkly, sees that God creates what he loves and loves what he creates and that no suffering is without meaning, if it places one in the presence of God.

---

[27]Cf. Raissa Maritain, *Raïssa's Journal* (Albany, NY: Magi Books, 1974), 241; and John Howard Griffin, "The Terrain of Physical Pain," *Creative Suffering*(Kansas City, MO: Pilgrim Press, 1970), 27.

[28]Griffin, Ibid.

[29]Raissa Maritain, *Raïssa's Journal*, 241.

[30]John Howard Griffin, "The Terrain of Physical Pain," 28.

John G. Trapani, Jr.

Maritain and Rifkin: Two Critiques

"The unleashed power of the atom has changed everything save our modes of thinking, and we thus drift toward unparalleled catastrophes."
Albert Einstein

Maritain delivered his compact, yet cogent, lecture, which in translation and book form bears the title *The Twilight of Civilization*, at the Marigny Theatre in Paris on February 8, 1939, a week short of seven months before Hitler's invasion of Poland and the beginning of World War II. It is a prophetic essay in its assessment of the political forces already at work in prewar Europe, shaping the future destiny of civilization. Employing his gift for understanding and interpreting the movement of historical events by tracing the influence exerted upon them by their attendant ideologies, Maritain's essay displays not only shrewd political savvy but also a great depth of philosophical insight.

In his essay, Maritain identifies the contrast between Communism and Fascism as a "totalitarianism of the social community" on the one hand, and a "totalitarianism of the political state and racial community" on the other hand.[1] The French philosopher understood, however, that these two political ideologies were in themselves symptomatic of two corresponding philosophical positions concerning human nature which were their causes; and although the twilight of Western civilization was being occasioned by the increasing power and influence of these two political ideologies, Maritain's lecture wisely focuses upon their under-

---

[1]Jacques Maritain, *The Twilight of Civilization*, trans. Lionel Landry (New York: Sheed and Ward, 1943), 17.

lying philosophical positions. For, regardless of whether we know or wish to acknowledge it or not, theoretical principles always have consequences in the practical order.

As a Christian philosopher, Maritain does not surprise us by his distinction among three types of humanism: the first two of which are entirely secular, while the third is contrastingly Christian. Maritain identifies the first as "Classical or Anthropocentric Humanism." It avers a human nature and reason that is turned-in and shut-up upon itself; it espouses a human self-sufficiency that is the source of its own solutions to whatever problems, public or private, social or political, may be encountered. It is a humanism which glorifies the notion of *Progress* and the promises of the Enlightenment, as it separates the human from, and denies it any connection or relation with, the Divine.[2]

The second form of humanism, unique to the twentieth century, Maritain refers to as "Counter-Humanism or Anti-Humanist Irrationalism." This form of humanism is the culmination of the historical evolution of classical Enlightenment humanism—it is characterized by the hollow emptiness of the existential void. About this evolution, Maritain writes:

> Well, all of this simply did not work: the unfolding of the story —of history—has shown it clearly enough. After having put aside God in order to become self-sufficient, man loses his soul; he seeks himself in vain, turning the universe upside down in his effort to find himself again. He finds only masks, and, behind those masks, death.[3]

The third form of humanism which Maritain identifies is Christian or Integral Humanism. In this version, human nature is not only causally rooted in the Divine in metaphysical dependence, but spiritually transformed and redeemed by grace through Jesus Christ.[4]

In *The Twilight of Civilization*, Maritain contends that, because the *bourgeois pharisaism*[5] of the nineteenth century was finally revealed for the

---

[2]*Ibid.*, 4-6.
[3]*Ibid.*, 6.
[4]*Ibid.*, 11-14.
[5]*Ibid.*, 6-11.

masquerade that it was, there followed an "irrationalist tidal wave,"[6] the effects of which were being witnessed by a Europe poised on the brink of madness. The truth of this observation was certainly obvious in the social/political arena, the ostensible subject of Maritain's essay. Astutely, however, Maritain uses his analysis of this new manifestation of *counter-humanism*[7] to explain the root causes of the evils immanent in both forms of those totalitarian storm-clouds then sweeping over Germany and the Soviet Union, and threatening the peace and security of Western Europe and, eventually, the entire world.

Maritain's analysis of the failure of classical, anthropocentric humanism in relation to the political realities of 1939 displays his uncanny metaphysical insight. His conclusion and lasting admonition is, in the end, quite simple: political systems grounded in any humanism that is not Christocentric are doomed, in any age and corner of the world, to the misfortunes of "materialism, atheism, anarchy bearing the mask of State-Despotism, and finally dictatorship...."[8] For this reason, his remarks concerning political governments and his critique of the aberrant forms of humanism which underlie them retain a timeless validity.

Yet attractive and seductive errors die slowly (if at all); and if as Americans in the fifties and sixties we waved the flag of freedom proudly, unthreatened by any immediate dangers to our national security, all the while blissfully unaware of the underlying Christian humanist philosophy that was the theoretical ground that sustained these liberties, I suspect that presently the evidence is compelling that our culture at that time also began to embrace yet another, though different, manifestation of classical, Enlightenment humanism. What began as a tentative, unarticulated pre-supposition soon became a new social creed, one that placed its faith in science and technology, confident that they would create a better world, enhance the quality of life, solve humanity's problems, and bring us to that *New Frontier* which President Kennedy both proclaimed and symbolized. The economic and industrial successes which had become such a part of postwar American society, coupled with the proliferation of technological advances and achievements were together instrumental in rekindling this anthropocentric-humanist be-

---

[6]*Ibid.*, 8.
[7]*Ibid.*, 8.
[8]*Ibid.*, 58.

lief in the salvific power of scientific knowledge and technological mastery.

Since that time, however, after half again as many years from the essay of Maritain's to which we pay tribute, we again hear the truth of his words: "Well, all this simply did not work." Health and environmental problems of colossal proportions continue to capture headlines with increasing frequency and seriousness. The disillusion of failed promises from atomic energy technology, the pollution of our soil, water and air, the hazards of pesticides, chemical additives and animal-antibiotic residues in our food and drinking supplies, the erosion of the ozone layer in the atmosphere, *Acid Rain*, and the foreboding threat of the *Greenhouse Effect* have all rained on science's parade of otherwise breathtaking achievements in medicine, space, computer technology, communications, and genetic engineering, to name but a few.

If the cliche that the idealism of the sixties gave way to a pragmatism of the seventies has been left incomplete concerning a prevailing conscience of the eighties, I suggest that the concurrence of the successes and failures of science and technology in the past three decades have culminated in not one but two divergent consciences for the eighties. On the one hand, we can observe a blissful agnosticism on the part of those who choose to enjoy the appearance of bounty and economic prosperity of the eighties while ignoring the warning signs of serious potential danger. On the other hand, we find a dedicated activism of those who, in various degrees of expression in word and deed, take the present ecological health-report seriously, and endeavor to raise the consciousness of both the general public and her elected representatives so that changes in public-policy decision-making might be made before it is too late.

It is against a background such as this that we can best appreciate the critique of science and technology made by Jeremy Rifkin in his book, *Declaration of a Heretic*.[9] Although he is not a professional philosopher, it is nonetheless instructive to observe that his critique of the scientific and technological foundations of Western culture reflect in the ecological order conclusions similar to those of Maritain in *The Twilight Of Civilization* concerning the political order.

Rifkin's motivation for developing his critique grows out of his as-

---

[9]Jeremy Rifkin, *Declaration of a Heretic* (New York: Routledge and Kegan Paul, 1985).

sessment of the present dangers which the two most significant scientific achievements of the twentieth century have created. In December of 1942, American physicists produced the first sustained nuclear reaction; a decade later, Watson and Crick unraveled the molecular structure of DNA and discovered the double helix. With these achievements, we entered the Atomic and Genetic Ages respectively, and we now face the uneasiness that comes from our appreciation of the assumed benefits and potential risks.

Rifkin contends that our uneasiness and confusion are generated by the fact that our culture holds *unqualified faith* in the ability of science and technology to create a problem- or trouble-free world, and that, in the face of its failure to do so, we tend as a culture to deny the fact that the present precarious position in which we find ourselves is actually a result of the very faith-system, namely a scientific world-view, which received our unquestioned trust and affirmation. Our malaise, Rifkin says in a fashion reminiscent of Maritain, "is rooted in our ideas about security and the nature of what it means to be a human being."[10]

The drive to overcome our basic experience of insecurity lies at the heart of the human quest for a knowledge that enables us to have the power to control our environment. This basic thrust, although a foundational characteristic of human nature as Rifkin sees it, is neither our nature's exclusive feature nor is it inexorably tied to only one necessary way of looking at the world. For our Western tradition, the prevailing epistemology has been the *scientific* approach, where science has come to be understood as a way of penetrating the secrets of reality in order to control the environment to our own best advantage, and ultimately using the power which is derived from it as a means of satisfying our innate desire for security. The roots of this notion of science are not to be found with Aristotle and the ancient Greeks, however. Rather, in tracing the sources of our contemporary ideas about science and our humanist faith in its promises, Rifkin, in a fashion again reminiscent of Maritain, prudently indicts the Enlightenment philosophers:

Today's orthodoxy is steeped in the catechism of the Enlightenment. The apostles of truth are no longer Peter, Paul, John, Mark and Luke. They are Bacon, Descartes, Newton, Locke and Darwin.[11]

---

[10]*Ibid.*, 26.
[11]*Ibid.*, 4.

Under the influence of Enlightenment humanism and its ideas concerning the nature and purpose of knowledge and the mechanical, empirical nature of the material world, Rifkin contends that the natural human drive to overcome our species's fundamental insecurity led to the Enlightenment formula concerning our relationship to the natural world: namely, that "Knowledge is Power, Power is Control, Control is Security." This formula continues to exert its unquestioned influence over the thinking of all of Western culture.

Just as Maritain identified the different forms of government as rooted in the different types of humanism, so too Rifkin observes that it is our thinking about human nature that underlies our ideas about overcoming our innate insecurity. "What becomes transparent in re-examining the ideas that comprise our existing world view," Rifkin writes, "is that it is our attitudes about 'human nature' that govern the approach we take to insuring our own security."[12] Once again, theoretical principles have their consequences in the practical order.

Rifkin's remarkable challenge to this prevailing scientific world-view is not to echo the oft heard call for a responsible use of technology or an ethical conscience for scientific research. His position is more radical. After detailing the serious threats and dangers posed by Atomic Energy technology and Recombinant DNA technology throughout the main sections of his book, Rifkin draws the perhaps startling conclusion (his *Declaration of Heresy*) that what needs to be changed is our very thinking about science itself which has deceived us into believing that an increase in scientific knowledge always means more power and that more power and an increase in technology and the efficiency of business ultimately translates into more progress and increased security and benefits for the human species and, indeed, the entire planet.

While acknowledging the enormity of the task of reorienting our culture's prevailing scientific way of looking at the world, Rifkin does mention four specific areas where he believes signs of an alternate consciousness have already begun to appear. Additionally, he names several twentieth century examples of people (Gandhi, Martin Luther King, Mother Teresa) who, in the witness of their lives, have embodied the very ideas he calls to our reflection. Moreover, through an extensive bibliography, the author also identifies a whole new "generation of scholars" who

---

[12]*Ibid.*, 28.

are working to "redefine our approach to knowledge, redirect our relationship to technology, reformulate our ideas about the nature of economic activity, and re-establish a new framework for achieving security."[13]

These are the four specific areas (knowledge, technology, economics, and power/security) for which Rifkin proposes alternative ways of thinking—alternatives worthy of serious consideration and reflection by professional philosophers. Specifically, Rifkin proposes that 1) for "Controlling Knowledge" we substitute "Empathic Knowledge"; 2) for "Controlling Technologies" we substitute "Empathetic Technologies"; 3) for an "Economics of Exploitation" we substitute an "Economics of Stewardship"; and 4) for the "Exercise of Power" we substitute the "Renunciation of Power" as the expression of true strength and as the means for attaining genuine and lasting security for the human family. Finally, in the place of the Enlightenment formula that "Knowledge is Power, Power is Control, Control is Security," Rifkin's alternative vision proposes that "Knowledge is Empathy, Empathy is Participation, and Participation is Security."

Naturally, these terminological *buzz-words* can not convey the richness of Rifkin's developed thought. For the present, however, the following summary should provide a sufficient indication of the spirit and vision that animates his ideas:

Changing world-views means changing basic assumptions about how we choose to organize ourselves and the world around us. Do we use the human mind to seek power over the forces of nature, or to empathize with the rest of the living kingdom? Do we use technology to maximize our advantage over the environment and each other, or to establish an equitable give-and-take relationship between all living things? Do we define economic activity in terms of growth and unlimited expansion, or in terms of borrowing and maintaining a proper regard for nature's ability to replenish itself? Do we define security as exercising greater control over our surroundings, or as participation in the larger communities of life that make up the ecosystems of the planet?[14]

However radical these ideas may seem, or however extraordinary and distant from common folk the people of his examples may be, Rifkin's

---

[13]*Ibid.*, 82.
[14]*Ibid.*, 98-99.

final conclusion certainly has appeal for us as Christian philosophers, not to mention as disciples of Jacques Maritain. For underlying the changes in our thinking about knowledge, technology, and economics is the more fundamental change in our thinking about power/security; a change, Rifkin tells us, which can only be successfully accomplished by careful reflection upon the true meaning of our Biblical and Divine command to have *dominion* over all of God's creation. Mistakenly, Rifkin contends, our culture has generally interpreted that mandate as a justification for the exercise of power, control and domination. Rather, Rifkin reminds us that we are called to view our role as one of steward and caretakers.

> A steward's role is to preserve, to restore and to heal....[Stewards] participate with and nurture other things.
> Their sense of security does not come from being in control, but rather from taking care of other beings.[15]

Nevertheless, reverential stewardship itself is only possible if we affirm a Christocentric humanism, or at least a humanism that affirms that not only is God the creator of the natural universe and that our dependence is in a personal God, but also that it is the causal participation in God's divinity which gives to all of creation its proportioned sanctity, and which places this gift under our sacred care. This is the *sine qua non* for the vision of stewardship; life must be "resacralized at every level of existence."[16] In this regard, at the foundational level of their respective critiques, Maritain and Rifkin share a common vision and spirit.

Regardless of whether we consider Maritain in the political order or Rifkin in the ecological order, the essence of their respective messages is the same: a view of life that is cut-off from its sacred rootedness in the Divine is destined not only to failure but also to serious, negative consequences. In the political order, the result is aberrant, totalitarian forms of government that bring war and untold human suffering; in the ecological order, the result is aberrant views of science and power which threaten the very delicate balance of nature's ecosystems and thus threaten the very survival of the planet itself.

The lesson of their respective critiques is also quite clear. The stakes

---

[15]*Ibid.*, 108.
[16]*Ibid.*

cannot be higher, and, as a consequence, their respective admonitions are worthy of serious heed. For Maritain, it is the dignity and sanctity of human life in the social/political order involving truth, values, freedom, and the preservation of human rights. For Rifkin, it is the dignity and sanctity of human life in the techno/ecological order involving the care and protection of the natural environment and the future of human and planetary survival.

Both are essential to the attainment of true human happiness and fulfillment. Only this time, particularly in the latter case as perhaps never before in history, there may be precious little margin for error, since, in the words of the Worldwatch Institute, "Good Planets Are Hard To Find."

Part VI
Civilization
at the Crossroads

Peter A. Redpath

Poetic Revenge
and
Modern Totalitarianism

"We are waging a war of civilization," observes Jacques Maritain in his essay "Education for the Good Life." "What we are fighting for," he states "is human dignity, justice, freedom, law, the eternal call which makes every human person worthy of respect and love, and the openness of the future to liberating and fraternal work. All these things," he continues, "are rooted in the moral and spiritual order."[1]

In another essay, *Education at the Crossroads*, he reiterates the same theme. "This war," he says, "is not waged for domination over man or over matter. It is waged for liberty and justice, for equal rights, for releasing the onward movement of human history toward a commonwealth of free peoples; we are repeatedly told that it is waged for Christian civilization. All these are mainly spiritual values. What are we fighting for," he asks, "if the only thing reason can do is to measure and manage matter?" Indeed, he argues:

> If we have no means of determining what freedom, justice, spirit, human personality, and human dignity consist of, and why they are worthy of our dying for them, then why are we fighting and dying only for words? If we and the youth who will be educated by the future democracies hold everything that is not able to be calculable or workable to be only a matter of myth, and believe only in a technocratic world, then we can indeed conquer Nazi Germany militarily and technically, but we ourselves shall have been con-

---

[1] Jacques Maritain, "Education for the Good Life," in *The Education of Man*, ed. Donald and Idella Gallagher (Garden City, NY: Doubleday and Co., 1962), 180.

227

quered morally by Nazi Germany. For the preface to Fascism and Nazism is a thorough disregard for the spiritual dignity of man, and the assumption that merely material or biological standards rule human life and morality. Thereafter, since man cannot do without some loving adoration, the monstrous adoration of the totalitarian Leviathan will have its day. Technology is good, as a means for the human spirit and for human ends. But technocracy, that is to say, technology so understood and so worshiped as to exclude any superior wisdom and any other understanding than that of calculable phenomena, leaves in human life nothing but relationships of force, or at best of pleasure, and necessarily ends up in a philosophy of domination. A technocratic society is but a totalitarian. But a technocratic society may be a democratic, provided this society is quickened by an inspiration which is supra-technological, and if it recognizes, with Bergson, that 'the body, now larger, calls for bigger soul,' and that 'the mechanical' summons up 'the mystical.'[2]

Maritain was of the opinion that the West was losing the war for civilization because of "a general skepticism about the moral and spiritual realities without which democracy is nothing but nonsense." As he saw it, "The great predicament of the democracies is the fact that they had lost intellectual faith in the truths that constitute their very soul and their very principles."[3] For these fundamental spiritual, moral, and metaphysical truths they had substituted bourgeois individualism--an anthropocentric concept of man and culture cut off to all forms of transcendence. "After having put God aside in order to become self-sufficient," Maritain claims, "man loses his soul; he seeks himself in vain, turning the universe upside down in his effort to find himself again. He finds only masks, and, behind these masks, death."[4]

For Maritain, then, at the source of the twilight of civilization lies a self-sufficient and anthropocentric humanism--"a humanism that fell short of the mark";[5] and the remedy for this situation, as he sees it, is a new

---

[2]Maritain, *Education at the Crossroads*, 114.

[3]Maritain, "Education for the Good Life," 181.

[4]Jacques Maritain, *The Twilight of Civilization*, trans. Lionel Landry (New York: Sheed and Ward, 1943), 6.

[5]*Ibid.*, 8.

humanism open to spiritual and transcendent realities and supported by liberal education:

> If mankind overcomes the terrible threats of slavery and dehumanization which it faces today, it will thirst for a new humanism, and be eager to rediscover the integrity of man, and to avoid the cleavages from which the age suffered so much. To correspond to this integral humanism there should be an integral education....
>
> Bourgeois individualism is done for. What will assume full importance for the man of tomorrow are the vital connections of man with society, that is, not only the social environment but also common work and common good. The problem is to replace the individualism of the bourgeois era not by totalitarianism of sheer collectivism of the beehive but by a personalistic and communal civilization, grounded on human rights and satisfying the social aspirations and needs of man.[6]

The problem of replacing bourgeois individualism and avoiding totalitarianism by means of an integral humanism, then, is, in Maritain's eyes, a problem of education. For him, however, education is a function of philosophy. Furthermore, he thinks "liberal education cannot complete its task without the knowledge of the specific realm and the concerns of theological wisdom."[7] As he sees it, also, this is particularly so in the case of education in Western culture and civilization. Hence he says:

> ...theological problems and controversies have penetrated the whole development of Western culture and civilization, and are still at work in its depths, in such a way that the one who would ignore them would be fundamentally unable to grasp his own time and the meaning of its internal conflicts. Thus impaired, he would be like a barbarous and disarmed child walking amidst queer and incomprehensible trees, fountains, statues, gardens, ruins, and buildings still under construction. The intellectual and political history of the sixteenth, seventeenth, and eighteenth centuries, the Reformation and the Counter Reformation, the internal state of British society

---

[6]Maritain, *Education at the Crossroads*, 88-89.
[7]*Ibid.*, 74.

after the revolution in England, the achievements of the Pilgrim Fathers, the Rights of Man, and the further events in world history have their starting point in the great disputes on nature and grace of our classical age....Modern philosophy itself, from Descartes to Hegel, remains enigmatic without that, for in actual fact philosophy has burdened itself all through modern times with problems and anxieties taken over from theology, so that the cultural advent of a philosophy purely philosophical is still to be waited for. In the cultural life of the Middle Ages philosophy was subservient to theology or rather wrapped up in it; in that of modern times it is but secularized theology. Thus the considerations I have laid down regarding philosophy are still truer of theology. Nobody can do without theology, at least a concealed and unconscious theology, and the best way of avoiding the inconveniences of an insinuated theology is to deal with theology that is consciously aware of itself.[8]

If such be the case--if, that is, the replacement of anthropocentric, bourgeois humanism, and the avoidance of totalitarianism require an integrated liberal education, and if such an education is impossible without an understanding of philosophy and theology; if, in fact, education is a function of philosophy, and, as Maritain asserts, of philosophy of man--then the achievement of a truly integrated liberal education, and its attendant truly communal society, becomes impossible without shattering once and for all the confusion which abounds in philosophy and theology in our age and which has roots in the philosophy of subjectivity created by the *Father of Modern Misosophy*, René Descartes.

Yet such a shattering presupposes that one have clearly in view just what is the nature of this philosophy of subjectivity which lies at the root of modern and contemporary bourgeois individualism, its totalitarian replacements, and (since philosophy is the source of formal education[9]) of the educational system which fosters these warped views of human nature. What, then, is the nature of this so-called *philosophy*?

According to Maritain, this philosophy is no philosophy at all. Philosophy in modern times, he tells us, is "secularized theology"; but

---

[8]*Ibid.*, 73-74.
[9]Jacques Maritain, "Philosophy and Education," *The Education of Man*," ed. Donald and Idella Gallagher, 40.

what is secularized theology? Certainly it is not supernaturally revealed theology; if it were Maritain would not have called it "secularized." Furthermore, it is not, properly speaking, philosophy. For, in addition to what he has already said, in *The Peasant of the Garonne* Maritain states quite emphatically that a philosopher cannot be a subjective idealist of the modern sort. "All these men," he asserts,

> begin with thought alone, and there they remain, whether they deny the reality of things and of the world (Descartes still believed in it, but on account of a wave of the magic wand by the God of the *cogito*), or whether, in some way or another, they resorb this reality into thought. What does this mean? They impugn from the outset the very fact on which thought gets firmness and consistency, and with out which it is a mere dream--I mean the reality to be known and understood, which is here, seen, touched, seized by the senses, and with which an intellect belongs to a man, not to an angel, has directly to deal: the reality *about which and starting with which* a philosopher is born to question himself: if he misses the start he is nothing. They impugn the absolutely basic foundation of philosophic research. They are not philosophers.[10]

Begging his readers not to take his statements as the whims of a crazy old man, and admitting the exceptional intelligence, importance, worth, and even genius, of many modern thinkers in the lineage of Descartes, Maritain, nonetheless, stated he had never "spoken more seriously" than when he challenged "with might and main, and with the certainty of being right" the right of subjective idealists to call themselves philosophers. Maritain called such people "ideosophers" and their doctrine "ideosophy."[11]

What, however, is *ideosophy*? Clearly it is important to have a precise understanding of the nature of this doctrine in order to get a precise understanding of the root causes not only of contemporary bourgeois individualism but also of modern totalitarianism in all its forms. What, then, is *ideosophy*? Is it philosophical knowledge? Is it religious knowledge of some sort? Is it a kind of art?

---

[10]*Ibid.*, 101-02.

[11]Jacques Maritain, *The Peasant of the Garonne*, trans. Michael Cuddihy (New York: Holt, Rinehart and Winston, 1968), 100.

In order to answer the question about the precise nature of ideosophy, it seems to me that one might be greatly assisted by a rather startling assertion made by Dr. Mortimer J. Adler in his excellent text, *Reforming Education: The Opening of the American Mind*. On page six of this work Adler observes:

> I have never thought that Plato was right in his assessment of the poets. His characterization of them was right, but not his judgment of their influence. They are storytellers; they are men of imagination rather than of thought; they certainly cannot be relied upon to give youth sound moral and political instruction; but they are not important as compared with other educational influences, much less so in our day than in earlier times.[12]

What is startling about Adler's remark is how off the mark it seems to be with respect to the educational and political influence which poets have had both in ancient times and in the modern period. In ancient Greece they were the chief educators of the people, and among the people most responsible for the death of Socrates; and in the modern age, if one understands the term "poetry" more or less in the same broad sense in which it was undrestood by an ancient Greek of the time of Plato and Socrates,[13] these individuals seem to me still to maintain positions of major educational and political influence.

In order to understand why I make the latter claim, however, one needs to recall some things about the origins of the discipline we call "philosophy," and just what was the nature of the age-old battle between philosophers and poets in ancient Greece which is reported by Plato in Book X of his masterpiece, the *Republic*.[14]

Before the coining of the term "philosopher"--reportedly by Pythago-

---

[12]Mortimer J. Adler, "This Prewar Generation," *Reforming Education: The Opening of the American Mind* (New York: Macmillan, 1988).

[13]Of course, if one understands the term "poet" to mean what it commonly does in twentieth century American English, then Dr. Adler's assessment of Plato *would be* on the mark. To attribute such an understanding of this term to Plato, however, is without justification.

[14]Plato, *Republic*, X, 607A-608C.

ras--philosophers were called *sophoi*-- that is, wise men. This label was used to classify not only men such as Socrates but also men such as Homer, Hesiod, Themistocles, Simonides, Daedalus, Aesop, and any other man the Greeks considered to be possessed of extraordinary knowledge. At first, the term was used to identify people who were possessed of extraordinary practical knowledge, and who were commonly thought by the Greeks to possess their extraordinary abilility through inspiration from goddesses whom the Greeks called "Muses." Hence the *sophoi* were also called musicians, and the subject of their expertise was named "music."[15]

Because these people provided the ancient Greeks with those technical skills whereby they were empowered to free themselves from ignorance and the toil of manual labor--because, that is, they provided them with the means to achieve the leisure needed for higher intellectual and moral pursuits--Aristotle called these individuals the greatest of benefactors,[16] and the ancient Greeks as a whole treated them with special respect and considered them to be superior human beings.[17]

Since the source of the special knowledge possessed by Greek *sophoi* was thought to come from the gods, the originating principles and causes of ancient Greek sophistic knowledge were inextricably joined to Greek religion; and since, among the Greek men of wisdom, it was the poets who, as sons of gods,[18] transmitted to the Greek people the message of the

---

[15]See Plato's treatment of the education of the guardians beginning with Republic II, 376E and continuing through Book III; for additional support of this interpretation of the ancient Greek understanding of the terms "music," "poetry," and "sophist" see: Joseph Owens, *A History of Ancient Western Philosophy*, 155-57, 268; Werner Jaeger, *The Theology of the Ancient Greek Philosophers*, 1-17 (especially, 9-10), and *Paideia: The Ideals of Greek Culture*, 2nd ed. (Oxford: Oxford University Press, 1965), 36-43; C.M. Bowra, *The Greek Experience* (New York: New American Library, Mentor Book, 1957), 134-54; *The Worlds of the Early Greek Philosophers*, ed. J.B. Wilbur and H.J. Allen (Buffalo: Prometheus Books, 1979), 6 and 241.

[16]Aristotle, *Metaphysics*, A, 1, 981b13-35.

[17]See Plato's ironic and critical descriptions of those possessed of sophistical knowledge, especially the poets, in the *Meno*, 99A-100C; see also *Ion*, 530A-D, and *Republic*, 365A-366A.

[18]Plato, *Republic*, 366B.

special election of the Hellenes by the gods, the poets occupied first place among the Greek *sophoi* in the area of professional honor. They were the most highly respected of ancient Greek *sophoi*--at least until philosophers came on the scene.

Philosophers arose from the class of Greek musicians--specifically from the class of Greek poets. Similar to other *sophoi* who had come before them, they sought to apprehend the super-visible realities at work in the sense world in order that they might become wise as the gods are wise. In a manner different from the other *sophoi*, however, the ancient Greek philosophers sought to derive their inspiration about the gods totally from activities which they could causally connect to sense events. They derived their rules of reasoning not from supernatural inspiration but from añ ordinary human one--namely, from generalizations naturally initiated from happenings in the sense world.

This approach taken by the ancient philosophers caused a revolution in ancient Greek education, and it shattered the poetic distinction (which, in the *Phaedo*, Socrates says the poets were always "dinning into the ears" of the ancient Greeks)[19] between sense knowledge, which was imprecise, and inspiration, which was wisdom channeled directly from the gods. The philosophical approach to learning, in other words, was a direct challenge to the educational monopoly held by the ancient Greek poets, and through them, to the other Greek *sophoi*. By opening up learning to the natural powers of all human beings the ancient Greek philosophers were undermining the authority and monopolistic power of the established professional educators of Hellas.

Viewed from the perspective of these professionals, there could be only one cause for this challenge to their authority--alien inspiration coming from alien gods.[20] Consequently they considered it their civic

---

[19]Plato, *Phaedo*, 65B.

[20]Since the poets and other non-philosophical *sophoi* of Socrates's era had reduced all knowledge to two categories--namely, ordinary sense knowledge and inspiration by the gods (that is, extraordinary knowledge)--and since they had reduced all artistic and scientific knowledge to *inspired knowing*, they logically concluded that the source of Socrates's peculiar knowing powers was divine inspiration; and since Socrates was critical of their own brand of knowing--and, indeed, used his own special knowledge as a weapon against their *arts*--they similarly concluded that

duty to short-circuit the influence of the new *lovers of learning*[21] both by behind-the-scenes smearing of their reputations and through formal political moves--such as the trial and death of Socrates.[22]

Even a cursory glance at the development of ancient Greek philosophy reveals the extent to which this new method of learning was essentially dependent upon the origins of philosophical knowledge in sensation.[23] The uniqueness of the ancient philosophical method, in fact, was

---

the gods or spirits who were the source of Socrates's inspiration were *alien* or *new*.

[21] *Phaedo*, 82C-84C.

[22] It should be recalled that the chief prosecutors of Socrates at his trial were representatives of non-philosophical groups of *sophoi*--that is, artists of various sorts (poets, orators, statesmen, craftsmen), and that Socrates claimed to have been especially appointed by the god Apollo (indeed, similar to Hercules, he was give his own Labours to perform) to test the knowledge of people who had a reputation for being wise. Socrates, in short, was claiming to be a super-hero sent by the god to expose the bogus knowledge of the charlatans of his own time who were claiming to be legitimate educators. See Plato's *Apology*, 20E-23C.

[23] None of the ancient Greek philosophers--including Parmenides, Plato, and Plotinus--proceeded from ideas to sensation. They always did the reverse. As Joseph Owens states: "Parmenides...correctly appeared to Aristotle and the Greek doxographers as a physicist in the ancient sense, a philosopher of nature" (*A History of Ancient Western Philosophy*,70); see Aristotle's comments about the origins of ancient philosophy, *Metaphysics*, A 3, 983b8-993a28; G.S. Kirk and J.E. Raven, *The Pre-Socratic Philosophers* (Cambridge: Cambridge University Press, 1966), 270, note that the incorporeal was unknown to Parmenides and that "no vocabulary therefore existed to describe it"; regarding the first of the ancient philosophers they state: "What gave these the title of philosopher was their abandonment of mytho-poetic froms of thought, of personification and anthropomorphic theistic exlalnations, and their attempt to explain the seen world in terms of seen constituents," 72; see also: Werner Jaeger, *The Theology of the Early Greek Philosophers*, 103. It should be noted that Aristotle supports the view that no conception of a separate realm of immaterial beings existed before Plato (*Metaphysics*, M 3, 1078b30-32), and he says that the Platonists were seeking the causes for physical things (*Metaphysics*, A 8,

precisely due to its ability to derive rules of reasoning from a purely natural intellectual consideration of activity taking place in the sense world, rather than from subjective inspiration channeled directly to the human intellect from the gods. What gave birth to philosophy, that is, was precisely the rejection by philosophers of the subjective method of mental inspiration intrinsic to the wisdom of the poets--the very same method which was enshrined by the *Father of Modern Misosophy* as the only legitimate approach which could be taken to achieve genuinely scientific learning. Clearly this method of learning is nothing more than a return to the method of ancient mythological poetry.

According to Descartes, it was precisely because they began their philosophical reasoning with knowledge derived from sensation that the ancient philosophers were precluded from ever achieving true philosophy. Hence, for him, there exists an inverse proportion between a person's study of ancient philosophy and that person's ability to learn a true one.[24]

For Descartes human wisdom is perfect knowledge of all that man can know.[25] To achieve such knowledge one must begin with a perfectly known principle; for "all the conclusions deduced from a principle that is not evident cannot themselves be evident."[26]

990b1-5). Also, in the dialogues of Plato Socrates continually reasons from physical realities to forms (see, for example, the procedure he uses with Menon's slave in the *Meno*, 82B-86B; the way he proves the existence of different parts of the soul using a universal principle of motion in the Republic, IV, 436A-441; and the sense origins for his arguments for the nature of temperance (*Charmides*), of piety (*Eutyphro*), of friendship (*Lysis*), and of the art of reciting (*Ion*). One must first see the images on the cave world before apprehending the light of the Good (*Republic*, VII, 514B-517A). Regarding Plotinus it should be noted that he begins his reasoning from sense beauty and ascends to the One; he does not start his reasoning from a conceptual grasp of the One and proceed to reason to the reality of sense beauty (see *Enneads*, I).

[24]René Descartes, "Letter Preface," *Principles of Philosophy*, in *Descartes: Discourse on Method and Other Writings*, trans. Arthur Wollaston (Baltimore: Penguin Books, 1960), 178-80.

[25]*Ibid*., 173-74.

[26]*Ibid*., 178.

According to him, such principles can never be derived from sense knowledge. For sense knowledge lacks the evidence demanded of truth. It is far too obscure to be the starting point of perfect human knowledge. Perfect knowledge must start with perfect thought. Philosophy, in short, is the knowledge of truth through its first cause—that is, through the clear and distinct idea of absolute perfection, or God.[27]

This is so true (in a non-Cartesian sense of "true") that Descartes claims the idea of God "contains in itself more objective reality than any other," there being "none that is more true in itself, and less open to suspicion that it is false";[28] he contends he has within him in some way the notion of God "anterior...to the notion of the finite, that is to say to the idea of myself";[29] and he states, further, he does not think it is possible for the human mind to know any other idea with more clarity and certainty because the idea he has of God is "at once the truest, the clearest, and the most distinct, of all the ideas I have in my mind."[30]

In short, for Descartes, the idea of God is the natural light of human reason, against the background of which he deduces all his other objective ideas. God, indeed, is recognized by Descartes to be the author of every clear and distinct idea;[31] and he says he recognizes very clearly "that the certitude and truth of all knowledge depends upon the knowledge of God alone so that, before I knew Him, I knew nothing perfectly."[32] Having this knowledge, he states, he has the means of acquiring a perfect knowledge of an infinity of things, not only relative to him but also concerning physical nature, "in so far as it may be made the object of mathematical enquiry and proof."[33]

Because of the utter dependence of philosophical knowledge upon the idea of God, Descartes considers metaphysics to be the first of philosophical disciplines in the order of learning. After this comes physics and all the other sciences which, for him, grow out of physics--which consist

[27]*Ibid.*, 176, 179.

[28]René Descartes, *Meditations,* in *Descartes: Discourse on Method and Other Writings,* "Third Meditition," 128.

[29]*Ibid.*, 127.

[30]*Ibid.*, 31.

[31]*Ibid.*, 150-51.

[32]*Ibid.*, 151.

[33]*Ibid.*, 151.

principally of medicine, mechanics, and ethics. The proper order of human reasoning is, therefore, not from the world to God but from God to the world.[34]

Clearly, given such a bizarre understanding of the nature and method of philosophical investigation, can there be any serious doubt about the poetic and mythological nature of Descartes's teachings? Descartes the philosopher is really Descartes the fiction-monger. His writings are not philosophical; they are poetic myth; and his approach to philosophy is not that of a philosopher but that of a creative artist.

The order of reasoning followed by the ancient philosophers was not just one way of doing philosophy among other ways; the philosophy of objective realism is the only way of doing philosophy. Hence Descartes's critique of ancient philosophy is not a philosophical critique; it is a poetic one. Indeed, the philosophy of Descartes is not philosophy at all. The thinking of Descartes owes its line of historical, intellectual descent not to philosophy but to *secularized Christian theology*. For what it is is a synthesis of the meditative method of the medieval mystics and the ontological argument of St. Anselm constructed, among other reasons, to eliminate the influence of pagan Greek thought from Christian theology. It is precisely the meditative doubt about the reality of the philosophical world of the ancient Greeks, the world of natures, apprehended with the aid of the senses, from physical beings, which distinguishes the thought of this man. Descartes was no philosopher; he was an anti-philosopher.

Modern philosophy, as a Cartesian creation, therefore, is not an age in which practical science dominates over theoretical science. Rather, it is an age in which unbridled artistic creativity (creativity based upon uprooted, realistically blind, and subjective inspiration) is the measure of all truths--those of practical and theoretical science included.

At the root of Descartes's meditative method, in other words, is not natural reason enlightened by the world, but unmoored inspiration of the will--what, today, is commonly referred to as *freedom of expression*. It is the will, one should recall, which Descartes says principally tells him that he bears "the image and resemblance of God."[35] It is through the strength of the will's attachment to the idea of God, which idea God has

---

[34]Descartes, "Letter-Preface," *Principles of Philosophy*, 182-85.
[35]Descartes, *Meditations*, Fourth Meditation, 138.

put into Descartes's mind, that Descartes apprehends all clear and distinct ideas. It is the will that affirms and denies, and it is the will that meditates. It is by freely choosing to see things only through the idea of Godthat one comes into contact with the objective world. Clear and distinct ideas must be true for Descartes, however, because, once seen, one cannot choose to judge them otherwise; and one cannot choose to judge them otherwise because God will not let them be otherwise than the way one judges them.[36]

What we have as the source of objective truth in Descartes, then, is a will determined by divine inspiration, not an intellect determined by the being of sensible things. Clearly such a source of truth can never be a philosophical one. The so-called *philosophy* of Descartes, therefore, is, more precisely, a *mythology*, or, as Maritain has rightly labeled it, *secularized theology*. For Descartes begins his reasoning not from principles derived from sensation, but from personal revelation based upon the authority of God as a perfectly good being. From this he proceeds to speak about the sense world the way Homer and Hesiod would speak to the ancient Greeks about the gods.

What Descartes gave the modern world was not a new philosophy; it was a new theology--a theology of the subjective spirit (what I call "psychotheology"[37]); and what he gave to the modern world along with this theology was a new mythological poetry, a mythology about the world. The "philosophers of subjectivity" who inhabit the Philosophy departments of so many of our universities today, therefore, as historical descendants of Descartes, are actually mythological poets and secularized theologians.

If one wants to know why Catholic theology is in such a mess today, one needs to look no further than this fact. Catholic theologians, even if they apprehend the way theology and philosophy have to be related in a Christian soul, have a totally inadequate handmaiden at their disposal when they attempt to apply modern philosophical principles to their

---

[36]*Ibid.*, 138-43.

[37]For a further discussion of what I call "psychotheology," see my article "Romance of Wisdom: The Friendship between Jacques Maritain and Saint Thomas Aquinas," in *Understanding Maritain*, ed. Deal W. Hudson and Matthew Mancini (Atlanta: Mercer University Press, 1987), 91-113.

study of revelation. For they are actually studying God not through the eyes of the saints, but through the mythology of the subjective spirit. Is it any wonder that our Catholic schools are in disarray today?

Is it any wonder, in addition, that Western culture is also in disarray? All our cultural institutions, which in one way or another have their roots in Greek philosophy and Christian theology, are being restructured to fit an alien myth. Is it any wonder that we in the West have lost our sense of identity? For the medieval Christian philosophical objectivity was guaranteed by principles of natural knowledge derived from sensation interpreted against the background of divine revelation. Today philosophical objectivity is guaranteed by mythological principles derived from the human consciousness interpreted against the background of the revelation of mathematical physics. Physical science alone today is the measure of objectivity. Consequently, outside this domain, human beings, if they are to be truly modern, must only talk in myth. The result of this arbitrary subjectivism is relativization of all knowledge which is not of a positivistic and mathematical sort.

Such a world, as Jacques Maritain saw so well, is fertile ground for totalitarian domination. For if we eliminate natures from physical reality, and make mathematicized human consciousness to be our criterion of moral and political truth when judging the objectivity of freedom and morality, we wind up losing both our liberty and our morals. In this sort of world we have no rational way of settling moral and political disagreements among people; we have only brute force.

What gave to Greek philosophy its objectivity and its greatness was the connection it maintained between natures and the physical world. Because they grounded human knowledge upon the being of physical things, and derived their philosophy from principles rooted in sense realities--rather than in their own fantasy--the ancient Greeks were able to establish a legitimate science of philosophy. What robs modern philosophy of the same legitimacy is its failure to imitate the wisdom of the Greeks. The whole of modern scholarship owes Jacques Maritain a debt of gratitude for awakening the twentieth century to this truth.[38]

---

[38]For a good example of Maritain's critique of the modern approach to doing philosophy see, in particular, Jacques Maritain, *The Dream of Descartes*, trans. Mabelle L. Andison (New York: Philosophical Library, 1944).

Curtis L. Hancock

A Return to the Crossroads: A Maritainian View of the New Educational Reformers

In his tragicomic essay, "The Great Liberal Death-Wish," Malcolm Muggeridge, recounts the following experience:

> On radio and television panels, on which I have spent more time than I care to remember, to questions such as: What does the panel think should be done about the rising rate of juvenile delinquency? the answer invariably offered is: more education. I can hear the voices ringing out now, as I write these words; the male ones throaty and earnest, with a tinge of indignation, the female ones particularly resonant as they insist that, not only should there be more education, but more and better education. It gives us all a glow of righteousness and high purpose. More and better education—that's the way to get rid of juvenile delinquency, and adult delinquency, for that matter, all other delinquencies. If we try hard enough, and are prepared to pay enough, we can surely educate ourselves out of all our miseries and troubles, and into the happiness we seek and deserve. If some panel member—as it might be me—ventures to point out that we have been having more, and what purports to be better, education for years past, and that nonetheless juvenile delinquency is still year by year rising, and shows every sign of going on so doing, he gets cold, hostile looks. If he then adds that, in his opinion, education is a stupendous fraud perpetrated by the liberal mind on a bemused public, and calculated, not just not to reduce juvenile delinquency, but positively to increase it, being itself a source of this very thing; that if it goes on following its present course, it will infallibly end by destroying the possibility of anyone having any education at all, the end product of the long expensive course from kindergarten to post graduate studies being neo-Stone Age men—why, then, a percep-

tible shudder goes through the other panelists, and even the studio audience. It is blasphemy.[1]

Muggeridge here unabashedly declares that contemporary education is a failure; even worse, a deception, an institution needing, if possible, a new direction, a radical change of course. More specifically, he draws attention to the fact that so much of what passes for educational improvement is no reform at all, itself being just another consequence of the same errant educational philosophy--another instance of the status quo. What is needed, then, is a genuine reform, a wholesale change.

With this lament, Muggeridge echoes Maritain, whose own call for educational reform is recorded, among other places, in his 1943 volume, *Education at the Crossroads*.[2] There Maritain describes the nature of that errant philosophy which has modern education in its grip. It is a doctrine of mechanistic and social science built upon an inadequate account of human nature and born out of Enlightenment conceptions of human reason, conceptions which neglect the metaphysical and theological dimensions of the human person and which deny a tradition where they are central. Moreover, this philosophy fails from an axiological point of view because, in light of its limited understanding of human nature, it uncritically embraces pluralism, and ultimately devolves into historicism and moral relativism.

That such a philosophy still dominates education is evident in the numberless drafts of policies and strategies proposed by educators yearly. Their efforts to engineer education generally resist any attempt to understand the human being except in terms of historical, social, and cultural manifestations, cast against a background of mechanistic, empirical science generally; and this is to say nothing of the actual content of classroom instruction, where students are evangelized accord-

---

[1] Malcolm Muggeridge, "The Great Liberal Death-Wish," in *The Portable Conservative Reader*, ed. Russell Kirk (New York: Penguin Books, 1982).

[2] Jacques Maritain, *Education at the Crossroads* (New Haven: Yale University Press, 1943). A later work on education is *The Education of Man*, ed. Donald Gallagher (Garden City, NY: Doubleday, Anchor Books, 1962).

ing to the gospel of Enlightenment science (or its nihilistic consequences) from faculty generally unaware of their own assumptions. Since, according to this philosophy of education, the human condition points to nothing but itself, to nothing transcendent, the principal objective of learning readily reduces to the dogma of technique or instrumentalism, according to which knowledge has value only because it is useful for individual or social advantage. Hence, the technical training and careerism rampant in today's curricula.

Instead of such a skeptical and narrow philosophy, Maritain proposes an education that retrieves the timeless principles of a Christian culture, and that also recovers the Jewish and Greek conceptions of the human condition. These elements are the constituents of a *theocentric humanism*, which provides a sure basis for education, since it understands comprehensively the nature and ends of human life. This is a humanism that honors the fact that the human person has both a secular and a trans-secular destiny, as well as a natural and a trans-natural end. To be human is to be a product of nature and of the human; but to be human is also to be a creature of God, to Whom the human person is supernaturally ordinated. Theocentric humanism is an alternative to an *anthropocentric humanism*, according to which human life is explained in purely secular and natural terms, that is to say, as though the human person were sufficient unto himself. Anthropocentric humanism is inadequate, since its explication of the human condition is too narrow, focusing only on two of its causes. Clearly, with its preoccupation with only the natural and secular dimensions of the human condition modern education is an edifice built on the rock of anthropocentric humanism.

In calling for a different foundation, however, one that recovers a different tradition, Maritain is neither a pathetic nostalgic nor an exclusivist. In the first instance, he aims to recover a tradition, not just because it is a tradition, but because it holds lessons and values for contemporary times. In the second, he has in mind a legacy that is inclusive, by virtue of its comprehensiveness and analogy, one that accommodates all peoples by not necessitating a commitment to formal institutions or canons but only to a world-view respecting the spiritual depth, dignity, and mystery of human personality.

In a Judeo-Greco-Christian civilization like ours, this community of analogy, which extends from the most orthodox religious forms of thought to the mere humanistic ones, makes it possible for a

Christian philosophy of education if it is well founded and rationally developed, to play an inspiring part in the concert, even for those who do not share in the creed of its supporters....

In answer to our question, then, 'What is man?' we may give the Greek, Jewish, and Christian idea of man: man as an animal endowed with reason, whose supreme dignity is in the intellect; and man as a free individual in personal relation with God, whose supreme righteousness consists in voluntarily obeying the law of God; and man as a sinful and wounded creature called to divine life and to the freedom of grace, whose supreme perfection consists of love.[3]

With this statement of his philosophical anthropology, Maritain is calling for educators to change direction and to journey along another, less worn path, a road more soundly constructed and with a more definite direction. The Frenchman's call is still timely, for the same crisis that educators faced in his day is still before us. Modern education has returned to or double-crossed, so to speak, the crossroads. The intersection that defines this crossroads presents educators with one of two alternatives: (1) to continue educating according to the assumptions of a positivistic social science, pressing on with a so-called *reform* that is, in fact, no reform; or (2) to provide a different foundation for education, one which is committed to a philosophical anthropology grounded in a tradition antedating the Enlightenment and rooted in more ultimate metaphysical and theological principles, while at the same time doing justice to the fact that the human condition is also situated socially, historically, and culturally.

Now, the question that compels my interest is how Maritain, or one committed to his philosophical principles, might judge certain recent critics of education, who, like him, have challenged education to change its course. Such an inquiry has value in illumining the thought of Maritain and the current reformers alike, since it specifies where the latter succeed and fail to make contact with the former's philosophy. In making this assessment, I must, of course, be selective; for I simply do not have the space here to examine all of those thinkers who might neverthe-

---

[3]Jacques Maritain, *Education at the Crossroads*, 7.

less deserve attention. Accordingly, for the sake of brevity, I will comment on the most conspicuous, or dare I say, most notorious, representatives of the new reform, whom I identify as E. D. Hirsch, Jr., Ernest L. Boyer, Allan Bloom, and Mortimer J. Adler.[4]

That these representatives have been read by a wide audience is no good reason in itself to discount them, so long as they are responsible scholars otherwise. In fact, given my purpose here there is good reason to select them precisely because of their celebrity, for I am of the conviction that what Maritain would find most remarkable about the new reformers is that they have so effectively captured the attention of the public; and this, by no means, is a trivial matter, since, in a democratic society, after all, it is ultimately the public that will benefit or suffer from educational change.

I. Hirsch

E. D. Hirsch contests the prevailing assumption that the American educational system has succeeded at reducing illiteracy. Of course, his point turns on the question, what is meant by "literacy." If the term signifies skill in the mechanics of reading, then Hirsch grants that Americans are relatively a literate people. However, if "literacy" refers to the ability to comprehend and to communicate cultural knowledge, then Hirsch charges that Americans are becoming woefully ignorant. Paradoxically, illiteracy in this second sense is occurring precisely because of literacy in the first. For he attributes American cultural illiteracy to an exaggerated emphasis on the teaching of developmental techniques at the neglect of content-laden curricula.

Hirsch discovers the source of this corrosive education of technique in the educational philosophies of Rousseau and Dewey, whom he labels

---

[4]E. D. Hirsch, Jr., *Cultural Literacy* (New York: Vintage Books, 1987); Ernest Boyer, *College* (New York: Harper and Row, 1987); Allan Bloom, *The Closing of the American Mind* (New York: Simon and Schuster, 1987); Mortimer J. Adler, *Reforming Education* (New York: Macmillan, 1988); see also Dr. Adler's article, "Great Books, Democracy, and Truth," in *Freedom and the Modern World*, ed. Michael D. Torre (Notre Dame: American Maritain Association, 1989), 33-45.

Romantic Formalists, committed to the view that education should be relatively indifferent to content. Confident in the native wit of the young, Rousseau and Dewey believe that, once equipped with basic skills, the student will be able to shape his life and knowledge by and for himself. This naive commitment to instrumentalism, Hirsch declares, has eviscerated academic curricula and has inevitably weakened our society itself, since citizens can no longer presume that the so-called *educated* have learned a body, however superficial, of cultural symbols enabling them to communicate with others who are likewise supposedly educated. The path to reform, then, is to restore content to curricula, so that our schools *educate* and do not merely *train*. Students need to be held accountable for knowing the chief symbols of present and past culture necessary to maintain our identity as a united and educated nation. In more specific terms, this accountability can be insured by restoring curricula that are, at once, *extensively* and *intensively* sound.

One can think of the school curriculum as consisting of two complementary parts, which might be called the extensive and the intensive curriculum. The content of the extensive curriculum is traditional literate knowledge, the information, attitudes, and assumptions that literate Americans share—cultural literacy....The extensive curriculum would be designed to ensure that all our high school graduates are given the traditional information shared by other literate Americans. This extensive network of associations constitutes the part of the curriculum that has to be known by every child and must be common to all the schools of the nation.

But the extensive curriculum is not a sufficient basis for the education by itself....The intensive curriculum, though different, is equally essential. Intensive study encourages a fully developed understanding of a subject, making one's knowledge of it integrated and coherent. It coincides with [the] recommendation that children should be deeply engaged with a small number of typical concrete instances. It is also that part of the total curriculum in which great flexibility in contents and methods can prevail. The intensive curriculum is the more pluralistic element of my proposal, because it ensures that individual students, teachers, and schools can work in tensively with materials that are appropriate for their diverse temperaments and aims.[5]

With this two-dimensional curriculum, Hirsch hopes to make possible an education that both informs students and teaches them to think. Students thereby become familiar with shared symbols in the context of the culture in which they live. They learn not only the symbols, but their rationale. If such a curriculum were put in place, then educators could graduate students who can live as responsible and informed citizens in a democratic society.

Assessment. Hirsch has written a worthwhile volume. It is to be commended for its bold criticism of the legacies of Rousseau and Dewey in education, a legacy in which skills and *content-neutral* curricula are ultimately favored. Hirsch is also subtle-minded enough to know that cultural literacy is not just an accumulation of facts. His demand for both an extensive and an intensive curriculum is rightly acknowledged.

Yet I think that Maritain would have me criticize Hirsch nonetheless. In the first place, Hirsch is naive about what cultural literacy can accomplish. He seems to think that the beginning and end of education is cultural literacy. He fails to see that literacy is only a symptom of a sound education, rather than its cause. This error is evident in his brazen remark that "the achievement of high universal literacy is the key to all other fundamental improvements in American education."[6] To his mind, the condition for a sound education is committed teachers who value cultural literacy; but this is not enough. What is required are committed teachers armed with a sensible vision of education, a vision that is provided only by grappling with foundational questions about human nature and its *telos*. Unfortunately, Hirsch sorely neglects these considerations. This neglect is especially apparent when he talks about the nature of the intensive curriculum. The extensive curriculum, he grants, can accomplish little without the intensive one; but the intensive curricu-

---

[5]E.D. Hirsch, *Cultural Literacy*, 127-128.
[6]*Ibid.*, 2.

lum itself has to be grounded in a sound philosophy of education, which, in turn, depends on a philosophy of the human person. Unless these deeper foundations are supplied, cultural literacy will be no significant or lasting solution to the ills of American education. He does not recognize that a sound intensive program must address concerns about an adequate metaphysics of knowledge. Indeed, his remarks on the intensive curriculum seem to suggest that any philosophy of education which reaches a judgment about such ultimate concerns is arbitrary. Hirsch, then, is content to abandon students to the pluralistic beliefs of a diverse faculty, as if diversity, without any self-conscious direction, can provide the unity and coherence of instruction necessary for a genuine education. An education that succeeds must embrace plurality only for the sake of unity. One must distinguish in order to unite, else knowledge becomes merely data, atomized and unconnected. As a result, the merit of Hirsch's book, which is to point out that American schools simply do not educate, is compromised by his failure to provide a genuine prescription for the problem, which would consist in proposing that there are very specific ends for education because education aims to perfect human nature. A long tabulation of items constituting "what every American needs to know" is no standard for educational improvement. Given the bankruptcy of his nostrums for reform, we are left only with a *Book of Lists*, Part III.

II. Boyer

Under the auspices of the Carnegie Foundation for the Advancement of Teaching, Ernest Boyer has put together a highly readable study, under the title *College: The Undergraduate Experience in America*. It supplies a wealth of information, and it also furnishes some interesting historical narrative about the way American pluralism and social values have influenced and shaped higher education over the centuries. Concerning the current state of higher education, his findings are paradoxical. On the one hand, the American university enjoys a certain vitality, making it "the envy of the world." On the other, "it is a deeply troubled institution." Its vitality is, of course, due to a democratic pluralism, which inspires the university to make a place for any and every point of view. However, this cause of vitality is also the same condition of divisiveness and fragmentation. This fragmentation is far-reaching and, in various forms, it is behind most of the afflictions of academe, but especially behind the failure of the academic community to agree on common goals and curricula. Boyer's study is a contribution to the debate on higher education precisely because it appreciates the problem of disunity in the academic community.

Boyer understands the embarrassment that comes with this fragmentation, since the very words "college" and "university" derive from Latin roots signifying "unity." It is a problem, he notes, that has not been un-noticed by students. Each of the sixteen researchers he sent forth with the mission to collect data so as to diagnose the ills of the American university (a *diaspora* which itself might create the impression of fragmentation, even if there were none) reports that students commonly express a dissatisfaction with curricula that need integration. In other words, students long for coherence.[7] The present generation of college professors does not seem to supply it. Boyer's prescription: design curricula in such a way so that students have an opportunity to integrate their knowledge before graduating, while also benefitting from a diversity of course offerings and majors. This is the problem of educational reform as he sees it: to bring unity out of the richness of diversity.

Assessment. Boyer's comments on the current state of higher education contain a number of explanations and recommendations which merit a response from Maritain's point of view. First, Boyer is right to recognize in America's democratic pluralism a valuable feature of our educational experience. It is delightful to read how Boyer describes the way in which this diversity helped change the nature of universities in America's history. Secondly, he is to be commended for recognizing that, as de Tocqueville prophesied, this diversity could become problematic for institutions of higher learning. Without coherence and synthesis, knowledge cannot be wisdom; and if educational institutions fail to lay, at least, the foundations of wisdom, they simply fail to educate.

---

[7]Ernest Boyer, *College*, 85.

It is on this point, however, that Boyer can give us little, if any, direction. Just as Hirsch, Boyer is a tinkerer who does not really understand the deeper problems. Again, educational reform is empty talk unless it addresses the problem of the foundations of knowledge and does not ignore the ends of the human person. Re-engineering of curricula is not enough to achieve coherence; the curricula must themselves reflect a coherent philosophy of education. If that is not provided in the first place, then curricula and the classroom experience itself, for that matter, are structures built on shifting sand.

In fairness to Boyer, it may be that, given the current state of American education, neither faculty nor administrators may be inclined or capable of wrestling with such ultimate issues. Indeed, it may be that the hope for educational reform is no longer realistic. It may be that, at last, the radical pluralism of American education has become an insuperable barrier to integral education according to an integral humanism. If that is so, then bad education may be the price we pay for living in the kind of democratic society we have (a question I will take up again at the conclusion of this article); but resignation is not the same as reform--and Boyer claims to be a reformer rather than an advocate of surrender. If Boyer will not have us surrender, what can he prescribe to transcend the fragmentation that he identifies and laments? He can prescribe nothing sensible unless it is rooted in the deeper considerations regarding metaphysics and philosophical anthropology. By neglecting these foundations, Boyer is a *reformer* in name only.

III. Bloom

Few writers among the current generation of scholars have been so successful at inciting outrage as Allan Bloom. His efforts at polemic have been so dramatic that they may create the impression that his indignation expresses profound truths; but, alas, an expression of moral indignation does not an argument make, and I fear that Bloom, except for an episodic chapter here and there, has written more of a Jeremiad than an argument; but there can be no doubt about one contribution Bloom (or his editor) has bequeathed us: a title. His title is a lasting achievement, one of those gradiose and gutsy *rouse-the-crusaders-and-impale-the-infidels* kinds of titles. It reads *The Closing of the American Mind: How Higher*

Education Has Failed Democracy and Impoverished the Souls of Today's Students.[8] Now this is a title that, on the face of it, would accord with Maritain's own judgment about the limitations of American education. For a moment, let me savor its three parts from a Maritainian perspective, keeping in mind that what Maritain might argue to justify Bloom's title might not at all accord with what Bloom himself argues.

First, it is all too apparent that the minds of modern educators and their students are closed. This is the inevitable consequence of embracing a narrow, positivistic account of knowledge, which carries with it other allied skepticisms, leading ultimately to the dismissal of axiology and metaphysics as genuine knowledge, since such disciplines are beyond empirical verification. In spite of the decline of logical positivism as a school of philosophy, its skeptical assumptions still generally flourish in academe; or, at least, its various by-products, emotivism, relativism, and historicism, may be said to still thrive. The result is ironic in that the closedness of the American mind is related to its supposed openness. Since openness means that any and every idea that is not "verified" by empirical science is not genuine knowledge, and since this is true of all metaphysical and axiological discussions, then such ideas are reduced to sheer opinion. Thus, nobody can argue that one moral or political or metaphysical judgment is, in the last analysis, any more sensible than any other. Accordingly, the standards of these disciplines undergo a kind of democratic leveling according to which everyone has as much intellectual right to speculate about such matters as anybody else, regardless of background or expertise. For expertise has to do with knowledge, not mere opinion. Hence, education on morality, metaphysics, and religion becomes no more instructive than a casual hour with Phil, Oprah, or Geraldo, where every audience member for a moment can be an authority, using up a slice of that fifteen minutes allotted each of us by Andy Warhol.

Another serious problem with this skepticism, of course, is that convictions regarding the value of education itself are compromised,

---

[8]Bloom originally preferred the title "Souls Without Longing." For an interesting comment on this, see Eva Brann's review in *St. John's Review*, 71 (1988), 38.

since they are axiological in nature. Indeed, the relationship of education to the civic good is also no longer a pressing issue, since the question of the social good has dissolved into the vortex of sheer opinion. The only time such a question becomes salient is when Americans begin to worry about their ability to compete economically with other nations. Except for this utilitarian interest, our own educational system actually undermines the belief in the structures and values necessary for the maintenance of our democratic way of life. Hence, Maritain would have us approve of the second expression in Bloom's title: American education has failed democracy, specifically in that it has failed to address those abiding concerns of philosophical anthropology and ethics necessary to make sense of our social lives.[9] Since such concerns are dismissed as unscientific, they are simply no longer a part of education, except as the objects of opinionated free-for-alls.

Maritain would also commend the title's third part, regarding the impoverishment of the souls of today's students. If education is sound only because it is responsive to the multi-dimensional ends of human nature, and if modern education is unable to contribute to these ends because it no longer makes sense out of the metaphysical and axiological principles necessary for understanding human existence, then education can no longer even begin to teach the human being what it is to be a human being. If so, the student ends his education as he began it, with no wisdom about himself. Hence, his soul is indeed impoverished, for, *even in general outline*, he cannot answer the question, what is it to live a human life? His education has failed to teach him how to understand himself and how to relate to his world.

---

[9]As I speculate at the conclusion of this article, it is difficult for education to serve democracy, since the latter manifests so many tendencies contrary to the aims of authentic education. Here is a paradox: democracy is vitalized by education, and yet democracy threatens to resist and undermine education. Education, then, is of incalculable value in that it can enhance democracy's finest features, while at the same time resisting its leveling influences. The best educational institutions, I suggest below, are religious-sponsored schools, because they can manifest a self-conscious and effective resistance to these leveling effects.

This failure to cultivate in students a due regard for their human nature sufficient to inspire them to believe that to live the human life is to live a life according to reason accounts, in my judgment, for the exaggerated careerism and bourgeois individualism among the youth today. Because education no longer assists students even in those first faltering steps toward wisdom—which, at minimum, is to exercise confidence in the conviction that reason, to a significant degree, equips one to deal with life effectively—students have come to fear the world and human life as an absurd, dangerous, and wholly mystifying place. Since they have not been taught to value or to depend on reason, they suppose that the world is, in fact, irrational. Since this condition makes for an insecure existence, they turn delusionally to the mystique of *job* and *technological expertise* to provide them security. For them a job is the only security possible in a world beyond the reach of reason.

Assessment. While these comments might express how Maritain would approve of Bloom's title, I am not so sure that, as I cautioned above, Bloom's rationale for the title would accord with Maritain's. I fear that, except for a few priceless passages and insights, the substance of Bloom's book is at loggerheads with Maritain's philosophy. In the first place, Bloom's prescription for reopening the American mind is unacceptable. His call is to recover reason, but his conception of reason is so narrow that what Bloom would have us in fact recover is only another version of a closed mind. For it is evident that when Bloom talks of reason, he has in mind a reason shaped and constricted by Enlightenment assumptions of human understanding.[10] According to these as-

---

[10]In point of fact, Bloom is ambivalent about his Enlightenment allegiances. While Bloom has affinities with the Enlightenment in that his philosophy promotes an alienated reason, a reason separated from revelation and cultural tradition, he does not represent the Enlightenment in that he condemns instrumentalism, which is an important theme in his provocative chapter "From Socrates' *Apology* to Heidegger's *Rektoratsrede*." By "instrumentalism," Bloom has in mind a view of knowledge which perceives learning as only a means to utilitarian or egoistic ends. This view of knowledge was engendered by Baconian science but

sumptions, human reason can be relatively indifferent to its cultural situation, since, in the last analysis, it is the only significant factor in culture. Genuine education cultivates pure reason, becoming somehow counter-cultural precisely to the extent it is isolated from culture; and the way, as it turns out, to nurture this transcendent reason—a reason that can perfectly assess culture because it is the only standard of value for culture—is to teach the student the Great Books, preferably after the fashions of Straussian interpretations.[11] The Great Books will acquaint students with pure philosophical personalities, such as Socrates, whom Bloom names as the paradigm mind that students should emulate. Socrates is presumably a precursor of Bloom's life of reason because he regards education as an instrument to criticize culture rather than as a means to rationalize it, but Bloom has set up a false dichotomy. It is true that reason should not be the blind thrall of culture, but reason itself demands the acknowledgement of other dimensions of human life besides the development of sophisticated, academic reason. A healthy reason knows that intellectual virtue is ordinated to the full complexities of culture. Socrates himself understood this only too well, and, for this reason, Bloom has misrepresented the ancient Athenian in making him

---

acquired influence through the advocacy of the Enlightenment *philosophes*. By the nineteenth century, this epistemology began to transform universities into institutions of technical training, pandering ultimately to individualist or utilitarian interests. The deformation of the contemporary university is the result of this legacy. For a clear treatment of how Enlightenment sources influenced modern education see Thomas A. Michaud, "An Indictment of Enlightenment Technique," *Proceedings of the Thirteenth Annual European Studies Conference*, K. Odwarka, ed. (Cedar Rapids IA: University of Northern Iowa, 1988), 193-202.

[11] For a critical review of such an educational use of the Great Books see Mortimer J. Adler, "Great Books, Democracy, and Truth." For a helpful reminder of Strauss's influence on Bloom, see George Anastaplo, "In Regard to Allan Bloom: A Respectful Dissent," in *The Great Ideas Today* (1988, 252-273). Reprinted in *Essays On The Closing Of The American Mind*, Robert L. Stone, ed. (Chicago: Chicago Review Press, 1987), 267-284.

the standard of Bloomian education. Socrates believed that his culture could benefit from the criticism of reason, but only because reason was not disconnected from or contemptuous of culture in the first place. While Socrates criticized the Athenian community, he did so as a political conservative, deeply committed to the Athenian way of life and ready to take up dialectical combat with the sophists to defend it.

In the main, Bloom's reason is only an abstraction, an anemic, rarefied reason that misrepresents the philosophical life as incompatible with the rest of human experience, especially religious faith. As a product of the Enlightenment, Bloom dismisses the religious life as something beneath the life of the truly educated, the life of the *philosophe*; but if philosophy, while a valid science, is nonetheless a limited one, the philosopher himself may have to look to revelation to explicate the drama of human history and to make sense of elements of his experience still mysterious to reason. As Russell Hittinger has pointed out, this false dichotomy between the life of reason and the life of faith has only recently become axiomatic among academics, and only among those of Bloom's ilk. History would remind us that the very education Bloom values so much was first made possible by medieval intellectuals working within a religious milieu. Indeed, Bloom's entire enterprise is shot through with irony, for the chaos of modern academe, which disturbs him so deeply, seems itself to be rooted in the irreligious Enlightenment deformations of reason which he so enthusiastically advocates.[12]

Since Bloom invests no value in religious faith, and thus would not connect the decline of education with the waning of religious values (not directly, at least), what, or rather, who for Bloom can be the cause of the erosion of education? It must be philosophers themselves who, somehow, have lost their way. Who else but nineteenth and twentieth century German thinkers could be the culprits? Of course, Maritain might argue

---

[12]Russell Hittinger, "Reason and Anti-Reason in the Academy," *The Intercollegiate Review* (Fall, 1987), 63-64. For a fine discussion of Bloom's commitment to Enlightenment presuppositions regarding the nature of reason, see Marion Montgomery, "Wanted: A Better Reason as Guide, " *Modern Age*, 32, 1, 1988, 39-44.

that a more convincing case can be made that educational decline is the result of the ultimate effects of thinkers like Descartes, Rousseau, and Luther. German philosophers are comparatively only marginal players; but even if one looks for more recent villains, German philosophers still may be an implausible choice. In fact, as Mortimer Adler has been quick to point out, more likely agents of decay hail from Britain rather than from Germany. He has in mind thinkers such as Stevenson, Russell, and Ayer, champions of ethical non-cognitivism. Non-cognitivism, rather than Nietzschean nihilism, is a more plausible source of moral, cultural, and educational decline.

Yet it might be that Bloom and Adler have arrogated too much to the influences of philosophers in the first place, a professional hazard I think that Maritain would warn us against. This excess is natural enough for Bloom, however, who does not seem to allow for other forces in culture besides the intellectual. Robert Paul Wolff has eloquently captured this intellectual *hubris* when commenting on the odd insularities of the University of Chicago, where Bloom resides.

> [the] virtue of a Chicago education was a certain intoxication with ideas, especially philosophical ideas, that sets off graduates of the Hutchins era from everyone else in the American intellectual scene ... [But] the vice of that same system is a mad hermetic conviction that larger world events are actually caused or shaped by the obscurest sub-quibbles of the Great Conversation. By a fallacy of misplaced concreteness...Chicago types are prone to suppose that it is the ideas that are real, and the people in this world are mere epiphenomena.[13]

III. Adler

As a philosopher himself, Mortimer J. Adler has proposed some remedies for education; and there is no doubt that Maritain would approve of the general outline of Adler's philosophy of education, includ-

---

[13]Robert Paul Wolff, Book Review: "*The Closing of the American Mind*," *Academe*, Sept.-Oct., 1987, 64-65.

ing his specific recommendations in the paideia proposal.[14] Maritain would commend Adler's proposal as a genuine effort at reform, since it does not supply band-aids but instead addresses the roots and causes of success and failure in education. As a fellow Thomist, Maritain was acquainted with Adler's reflections on learning. In *Education at the Crossroads* he lauds Adler's efforts. What merits Maritain's approval is that Adler, unlike so many other reformers, realizes that education can take place only when an understanding of human nature and its ends are vigorously evident and operative in the mission, curriculum, and instruction of a learning institution. Since this understanding is generally ignored by systems of education today, one must regrettably conclude that only nominal education is taking place. Universities may still impart knowledge, but this has only to do with data and technique. There is little effort to connect knowledge with those principles of coherence sufficient to make knowledge relate to human life and its ends. Hence learning in today's school system is about more or less discrete knowledge, but not really about education. Taking to heart the Latin root of education (from *ducere*), there is simply little, if any, leading out of ignorance to an enlightened reckoning of what it is to realize the potentialities of human life. Adler, however, understands that, without these ultimate foundations, there is no education. His *paideia proposal*, which accords with his earliest recommendations for educational reform, dating back to his association with Robert Maynard Hutchins in the thirties, is a program aiming to supply these foundations and, thereby, to bring about lasting educational improvements. His recommendation, like Bloom's, is to return to the Great Books; but whereas Bloom would have the Great Books be read authoritatively, according to the supervision of an autocratic, preferably Straussian, steward of the text, Adler proposes that these classic works be taught dialectically. In this way, instructors can better cultivate in students those intellectual virtues, such as independence of mind, which made possible the production of great books originally.

---

[14]See Adler's *The Paideia Proposal* (New York: Macmillan, 1982); *Paideia Problems and Possibilities* (New York: Macmillan, 1983); and *The Paideia Program* (New York: Macmillan, 1984).

This also sets up the conditions so that education can contribute to the moral and political reflections necessary for the formation of citizens in a democratic society.

Assessment. I have always admired Mortimer J. Adler as a thinker and a teacher. I even own a set of the Great Books. I especially marvel at his unfailing optimism. In spite of so much evidence to the contrary, he heroically maintains that Americans can be educated and labors tirelessly to support the conditions necessary fo that education. His *paideia proposal* is undoubtedly a noble effort. Unfortunately, I cannot share his optimism. Why? Because I have come to doubt whether education and modern democracy can ever be happily joined.

I do not want to be misunderstood here. I am by no means arguing that democracy is an undesirable form of government. I agree heartily with Maritain that, given the dignity and spiritual significance of every human personality, democratic social and political life is the most appropriate life for the human being; but at the same time a modern liberal democracy is a very challenging social order, and that challenge applies especially to education. It seems that democratic life, perhaps because its modern character has been too much influenced by seventeenth and eighteenth century ideologies, is committed to assumptions that dynamically resist education. These assumptions may have become lasting impediments, making the attainment of a genuine education virtually impossible today, at least with reference to our institutions. One such assumption is the suspicion against intellectual virtue. In a democratic society, such virtues suggest the resurrection and maintenance of aristocracy, in the form of an intellectual elite. Accordingly, citizens are as suspicious about high educational standards as they are about more obvious conspiracies; but if a society cannot prize intellectual virtue, it cannot educate, for, in the last analysis, education is about perfecting a human being--that is, about making him or her virtuous. In fact, this neglect of virtue is the source of many of our social ills, if we are to believe the likes of Bellah, Lasch, and, before them, de Tocqueville.[15]

---

[15]See Robert Bellah, et al., *Habits of the Heart* (New York: Harper and

There also appears to be a second suspicion militating against education. This is the tendency in democracy to doubt the validity of tradition, through which standards having to do with intellectual and moral virtues are transmitted. This suspicion, no doubt, in large measure results from the Enlightenment genesis of modern democracies, during which time ideologies contemptuous of tradition (especially, revealed tradition) championed human freedom. This suspicion, likewise, undermines education. For it is difficult to imagine how education can occur in a society which treasures no legacy. One cannot educate *ab ovo*. The student cannot be like Adam on the day of creation, connected with no authority from the past and with no inherited perspective on life. Education requires a starting point, and democracy may be unable to give him one.

If there is some substance to these reflections, they may intimate a vindication of religious sponsored education. Such schools may be of incalculable value in a democratic society, because they still make possible a system of learning where intellectual virtue and tradition are premiums. In light of this, religious sponsored institutions can be like oases in the desert, a desert created by democratic leveling. These oases can water and nourish that desert. Unfortunately, it appears that the sands of the desert are rapidly encroaching on these oases, and their future as distinctive, alternative systems of learning may also be in doubt.

Yet even if one can, on point of principle, reasonably protest my reservations about the compatibility of education and democracy generally, one will be surely challenged to muster a plausible objection with specific reference to American democracy. While, perhaps, ideally democracy and education may be able to wed, it seems, at this point in our history, counter-intuitive to suppose that *American* democracy and education can marry happily. Why? Because the cultural temperament of America, which inclines toward bourgeoisie individualism, an ideology that fos-

Row, 1985); Christopher Lasch, *The Culture of Narcissism* (New York: Norton, 1978); Alexis de Tocqueville, *Democracy in America*, trans. George Lawrence, ed., J.P. Mayer (New York: Doubleday, Anchor Books, 1969).

ters the tyranny of the majority as does nothing else, has been and seems destined to remain anti-intellectual. As a result, education, in spite of periodic spasms of indignation (recall Hutchins, Lasch, Barzun, Adler, and Bloom), will remain a low priority. It will only be seriously addressed to the extent that other priorities (for example, consumerism, international economic competition, private and public technical competence) seem for a time dependent on education; but our ideological soil will probably remain barren, meaning that learning will never be valued as a sacred thing; and if that never happens, education will not be truly reformed, not even by educators of Adler's stature. It may be that we must at last wake up to the possibility that institutions of American education are sick and destined to remain so. *Reformers* will come and go, continuing to overlook that the patient is terminally comatose, or worse.

Where does this leave us committed teachers? Am I prescribing that we abandon our vocations? No. As someone once put it, even if the world ends tomorrow, it still may be our Christian duty to plant our apple tree today. In other words, I am not advocating surrender, but realism. We must now appreciate the irony of our circumstances: that we may be called to educate with more devotion than ever precisely at a time when the institutions that employ us have abandoned, perhaps unwittingly, their mission. Institutions of learning have now been so compromised by the leveling effects of American democracy that they are beyond reform. It is a condition that we must simply live with. Reform can now only meaningfully apply to individual educators, or their *little flocks*, not to their institutions, which have meant so much to education in the past.

I realize that this is a rather mournful note, but it has its consolation. For now the vocation of teaching has signal significance for history. We must become that *diaspora* of enlightened educators about whom Maritain prophesied, a *diaspora* laboring in *the twilight of civilization*. It is a labor, I am confident, that Providence can put to a purpose.

Part VII
A New Dawn:
Transfiguring Integration

Deal W. Hudson

Maritain and Happiness in Modern Thomism

In the context of the thirteenth century, Aquinas's concern for earthly happiness--the *imperfect* version of the perfect beatitude bestowed by the vision of God--is unusual. Taken at face value, the account itself is not remarkable. The reference to *beatitudo imperfecta* in the five questions on happiness introducing the *Prima secundae* largely reiterates Aristotle on the possession of internal goods, external goods, and the goods of fortune in support of a life devoted to contemplation; but that St. Thomas provides any account at all is surprising, given the longstanding Augustinian suspicion of any claim to happiness on earth. This attention to human happiness *in via*, piecemeal as it is, places Aquinas closer to the brink of modernity than most of his medieval contemporaries and predecessors.[1]

Note: The author wishes to acknowledge the Earhart Foundation for their kind support of this research.

[1]For the Augustinian tensions underlying Aquinas's politics, see Thomas Gilby, *The Political Thought of Thomas Aquinas* (Chicago: The University of Chicago Press, 1958), 237-64, and his *Between Community and Society: A Philosophy and Theology of the State* (New York: Longmans, Green and Co., 1953), 124-48. The context of medieval views of happiness is discussed by George Weiland in "Happiness: The Perfection of Man," *The Cambridge History of Later Medieval Philosophy*, eds. Norman Kretzmann, Anthony Kenny, and Jan Pinborg (New York: Cambridge University Press, 1982), 673-86. A recent treatment of the controversy over natural beatitude prompted by Henri de Lubac's *Surnaturel* (1946) is found in Kevin Staley, "Happiness: The Natural End of Man?," *The Thomist* 53 (April, 1989): 215-34.

St. Thomas did not envisage that the happiness he helped to resurrect would take on a finality of its own, eventually evolving into the immanent and psychological conception first found in Hobbes and the later ideologues who employed it for the political ends. It has been left to later Thomists to provide a coherent and persuasive account of imperfect happiness to a society that no longer waits upon eternity for perfection. Obviously such projects are necessary if modern Thomism can make good on its claim as a *perennial philosophy*. The idea of happiness has no doubt fallen on hard times; however, in becoming the favorite come-on in the commerce of self-help, happiness continues to provide evidence of its force in our thoughts and our language to *recommend a way of life*.[2] As the *Prima secundae* itself demonstrates, the obstacle confronting any serious investigation of happiness is one of scope. A comprehensive study of happiness will encompass the foundations of morality and politics, the constitution and destiny of the human person, as well as the ordinate relation of all human goods. Nonetheless, there are signs of a renewed attention to happiness, but from philosophers outside the Thomistic tradition.[3]

This was not true a generation ago. Among twentieth-century Thomists, Gilson, Simon, Pieper, and Maritain made significant attempts to wrestle with the issues arising from the contemporary concern for earthly happiness. Central to their reflections were these two questions: 1) How are the *two happinesses* related so as to respect the integrity of earthly happiness and the ultimate finality of eternal happiness? 2) How

---

[2] This point, along with a general critique of happiness in the present age, is explored in my essay, "Can Happiness Be Saved?" in *Jacques Maritain: The Man and His Metaphysics*, ed. John F.X. Knasas (Notre Dame: American Maritain Association, 1988), 257-63.

[3] Elizabeth Telfer, *Happiness* (New York: St. Martins Press, 1980); Richard Warner, *Freedom, Enjoyment, and Happiness: An Essay on Moral Psychology* (Ithaca: Cornell University Press, 1987); James Griffin, *Well-Being: Its Meaning, Measurement, and Moral Importance* (Oxford: Clarendon Press, 1986); and, notable for its defense of *eudaimonism*, John Kekes, *Moral Tradition and Individuality* (Princeton: Princeton University Press, 1989). For an argument along Thomistic lines for the importance of identifying God as the object of happiness see Stephen Theron, "Happiness and Transcendent Happiness," *Religious Studies* 21 (Spring 1985): 349-67.

adequate is Aquinas's Aristotelian picture of imperfect happiness, particularly in reference to his intellectualist emphasis upon the virtue of contemplation? In other words, how is it possible to conceive of two happinesses without logical contradiction and without sacrificing one to the other; and do the resources of the *Nichomachean Ethics* as employed by St. Thomas remain suitable to our conception of earthly happiness? Their answers, as shall be seen, are remarkably diverse.

I.

Etienne Gilson offers the most conventional account of happiness among these Thomists. His interpretation of St. Thomas never deviates from a straightforward insistence on the primacy of contemplation in reaching toward God. More interesting is his explanation of how St. Thomas's teaching on beatitude was rejected by Dante only a generation after his death. Although the affinities between Dante's epic poem and the *Summa theologiae* are often explored, Gilson claims that Dante's view of happiness posed "one of the gravest dangers that have ever threatened" Thomism.[4] Basing his argument on Dante's philosophical works, *De monarchia* and *Il convivio*, Gilson locates the decisive move away from Thomism in Dante's positing of two final ends, *in duo ultima*, one belonging to the order of nature and the mortal body, the other to the order of grace and the soul. This distinction divorces the two orders of beatitude which St. Thomas had subordinated one to the other. As Gilson says of St. Thomas's imperfect happiness: "If there is a natural felicity in this life, far from constituting a goal distinct from the final goal, it is merely a stepping-stone to it."[5] For Dante the planes of nature and grace run along parallel lines which meet only at God. The natural order of earthly happiness, *beatitudo terrestris*, is governed by reason through the natural virtues, exemplified by the wisdom of the philosophers, and administered by the Emperor whose main responsibility it is to guide his people to their temporal happiness.[6] The order of nature, although admitted by Dante to lead toward an inferior end, is not strictly answer-

---

[4] Etienne Gilson, *Dante and Philosophy*, trans. L.K. Shook, C.S.B. (New York: Random House, Inc., 1956), 353.

[5] *Ibid.*, 194, n.2.

[6] *Ibid.*, 197.

able to the dictates of grace and its administrator the Pope, who oversees only the road leading to heavenly happiness, *beatitudo coelestis*, a journey requiring those supernatural virtues and wisdom bestowed by the sacraments and revelation.

Gilson attributes this separation of nature and grace to the direct influence of Aristotle rather that the Latin Averroists, whose influence he discounts as minimal. He argues Dante's reading of the *Nichomachean Ethics* fastened on Aristotle's notion that the happines of the *polis* is the primary concern for its ruler as directed by the virtue of justice. As Gilson shows, Dante bestows upon political happiness the significance of a final end and directly contradicts the teaching of Aquinas in *De regimine principium*.[7] Dante also subsumes the contemplative's happiness of *Ethics* X to the happiness of the state, in spite of his acknowledgement of its superiority over the happiness of the active life.[8] Suggesting that this interpretation of Aristotle, gleaned at least in part from Aquinas, is authentic,[9] in retrospect, Gilson proceeds to find greater historical innovation in Aquinas's emphasis than is generally acknowledged.[10]

Although Gilson could be challanged on this point, given Dante's version of Aristotle, the contemplative of St. Thomas does appear subversive because of his desire to transcend merely political ends. Seeking cognitive possession of an object outside the world, the contemplative has different grounds for happiness both in this world and the next. It is surprising, then, that Gilson's treatment of happiness in the *Prima secundae* focuses on Aquinas's dynamics of the intellect and the will, specifically on the ability of the will to apprehend and to possess ends without the intellect. Securing the inherent superiority of the contemplative to the active life becomes central to Thomistic accounts of happiness such as Gilson's. The argument for this position rests on the meaning of a rational human nature and the sole ability of an intellectual act to satisfy human desire. Paraphrasing St. Thomas, Gilson writes, "only the intellect is able

---

[7]St. Thomas Aquinas, *De regimine principium*, I, 13.

[8]Etienne Gilson, *Dante and Philosophy*, 134, n. 3.

[9]*Ibid.*, 218.

[10]For example, V.J. McGill discusses Aquinas's indebtedness to both Augustine and Plotinus in "The Concept of Transcendent Happiness," *The Idea of Happiness* (New York: Frederick A. Praeger, 1967), 58-90.

to grasp immediately the object of beatitude and our last end."[11]

Thus, according to Gilson, Dante's mistake is twofold: on the one hand, he has mistakenly conceived of a natural order which exists separately from grace; on the other, he has forgotten that the shape of both happinesses is determined by the intellectual matrix of human nature. Dante, who was nine when Aquinas died, just as Marsilio Ficino and Lorenzo Valla after him, resisted a paradigm of earthly happiness controlled by an educated and spiritual elite. Seeing no such problem, Gilson comments, "so far as St. Thomas Aquinas is concerned, the intellectual virtues are no less the prerogative of man than are the moral virtues."[12] What Gilson affirms as Thomas's undoubted intellectualism on the subject of beatitude, at least eternal beatitude, did not hold out very long against the mainstream of Renaissance thinkers, who preferring to bring happiness to bear on a broader arena of human endeavor, came down in favor of the will and its dynamism toward pleasure and satisfaction.[13] Gilson's own interpretative sympathy to the primacy of contemplation is indicative of both the tenor and limitation of many treatments in contemporary Thomism. Scant attention has been paid to the possibilities presented by Thomas's discussion of imperfect happiness in the context of the life of grace, the beatitudes, and the gifts of the Holy Spirit.

---

[11]Etienne Gilson, *The Christian Philosophy of St. Thomas Aquinas*, trans. L.K. Shook, C.S.B. (New York: Random House Inc., 1956), 353. See also *Moral Values and the Moral Life*, trans. Leo Richard Ward (St. Louis: B. Herder Book Co., 1931), chs. 1-2.

[12]Etienne Gilson, *Dante and Philosophy*, 135.

[13]See Agnes Heller, *Renaissance Man*, trans. Richard E. Allen (Boston: Routledge & Keegan Paul, 1978), 282-89; and Charles E. Trinkhaus, Jr. *Adversity's Nobleman: The Italian Humanists on Happiness* (New York: Columbia University Press, 1940).

II.

St. Thomas's insistence on the role of contemplation in happiness has a more eloquent defender than Gilson. In his *Happiness and Contemplation*, Josef Pieper persuasively advocates a position that could not be more at odds with the modern ethos. Pieper reminds us that it is Thomas's own unusual insistence on the act of contemplation that requires interpreters to pay him strict attention on this point: "What is under discussion here is nothing less than the inner structure of human nature, indeed of the spirit in general and of reality as a whole."[14]

His explanation of Thomas on the relation of the will and intellect in happiness is a masterpiece of apologetics. Pieper begins with the now familiar assertion that happiness cannot possibly exist in an act of the will because it can neither apprehend ends by itself nor possess those ends: both apprehension and possession are acts of the intellect. Happiness is a "having" and a "possession" that fully satisfies the motion of the will toward its whole good--*bonum univerale*.[15] Pieper's description of this distinction shows him to be more sensitive than Gilson to the problem of elitism. By arguing that love itself is dependent upon a cognitive act which makes the *beloved* actually present to the lover, Pieper takes the edge off his intellectualism. He writes, "Only the presence of what is loved makes us happy, and that presence is actualized by the power of cognition."[16] Pieper succeeds in linking contemplation to the "indispensible premise" of love and makes contemplation itself an integral possibility of daily life; his examples range from contemplation of creation, to the mystery of a child's face, to the experience of Gerard Manley Hopkins's poetic *inscape*.

Yet, just as Gilson, Pieper pays little attention to Thomas's own admission that there is an *active felicity* in this life.[17] In fact, his whole discussion is marked by a reluctance to speak of degrees of happiness.

---

[14]Josef Pieper, *Happiness and Contemplation*, trans. Richard and Clara Winston (New York: Pantheon Books, Inc., 1958), 61.

[15]*Ibid.*, 32 and 40.

[16]*Ibid.*, 71.

[17]St. Thomas Aquinas, *Summa theologiae*, I-II, q.5, a.4 resp.).

Pieper's analysis of the active life repeats the well-known thesis of his *Leisure: The Basis of Culture* that the realm of practical action, particularly work, points beyond itself, "that it makes arrangements for something else"[18]--namely, the leisurely contemplation of reality itself. Thus the eternal and uninterrupted happiness of the beatific vision can only be presaged by a cognitive act of the mind. Nevertheless, his three points of stress each add significant qualifications to three basic principles of beatitude in St. Thomas: not only intellectualism but also the insistence that happiness is an active state[19] (*operatio*) that excludes all *miseria*.[20]

Pieper describes the activity of earthly contemplation, even as it rises to the intuition of God himself, as a *dark night* which conjoins *repose* and *unrest*.[21] Pieper could have paid more attention to the implications of these remarks since our expectation of immediacy in contemplation can rule out in advance any expectation of suffering. His earlier allusions to the passive facet of contemplaation would help him account for the *unrest in repose* along with other affective aspects of his portrayal. The theme of passivity represents a challenge to both the classical and Thomistic views of happiness, both of which go to great lengths in maintaining that happiness consists in activity rather than passion. However, Pieper offers a much-needed nuance to this view in his discussion of the *gift-quality* of happiness, not as a consequence of Aristotelian good fortune, but as the gift of sight to the seer.

In Pieper's language, the act of contemplation becomes "an activity which we receive."[22] *Theoria*, a purely receptive approach to reality,"[23] arises from the capacity of the human intellect "to have something outside as an object" of our gaze.[24] Therefore, for Pieper, activity alone cannot raise a person to either perfect or imperfect happiness. Perhaps, even within Thomism, passion and passivity, along with the whole range

---

[18]Josef Pieper, *Happiness and Contemplation*, 92.
[19]St. Thomas Aquinas, *Summa theologiae*, I-II, q.3, a.2.
[20]Ibid., I-II, q.5, a.4, sed contra.
[21]Josef Pieper, *Happiness and Contemplation*, 108.
[22]*Ibid.*, 57.
[23]*Ibid.*, 73.
[24]*Ibid.*, 42.

of consequent affections, have their place in the process of human perfecting.[25] Pieper begins to offer *pathos* a place within his account by his discussion of love, but it is thwarted by the intellectualism he so deftly underscores in everyday life.

However, a distinction fundamental to love in St. Thomas goes unmentioned in this book--the principle that through an act of the will in loving we draw closer to God than in an act of the intellect or knowledge.[26] Although intellect is essentially superior to the will, it is not superior *in relation* to God, particularly in this life since we lack the *lumen gloriae* through which we are lifted to the vision of God. Aquinas acknowledged that intellectual apprehension of God in this life necessarily scales him down, while love working outwardly from our intellectual appetite preserves His Being. It seems that many of the stresses noted in Pieper could be more richly served if they were developed in the light of this distinction, allowing him greater flexibility to include the happiness of an active life.

III.

Yves R. Simon disagrees with Pieper's emphasis on leisure and contemplation. In his chapter "Happiness and the Last End" from *Freedom of Choice*, Simon manifests almost no interest in happiness as a contemplative activity; rather, he is more concerned with the overall rationality of the happy life. Happiness, for Simon, is the *end of voluntary action*, and true happiness involves the *real achievement* in satisfying without interruption the tendencies, desires, and inclinations of the whole person for the good.[27] Since all human desires (not solely those of the intellect) extend "in unlimited manner to the whole universe of being and its perfections," any happiness on earth can only be *strongly qualified*.[28] Indeed, Simon's approach is reminiscent of Augustine's restless heart, to which he explicitly alludes, rather than Thomas's intellectual desire to see the vision of God.

---

[25] *Ibid.*, 44.

[26] St. Thomas Aquinas, *Summa theologiae*, I, q.82, a.3, resp.

[27] Yves R. Simon, *Freedom of Choice*, ed. Peter Wolff (New York: Fordham University Press, 1987), 48.

[28] *Ibid.*, 53.

Simon, however, is not a voluntarist, as his discussion of practical reasoning makes clear. Means, or what he calls intermediate ends, are necessarily chosen in a teleological process culminating in the final good.[29] If Gilson can claim Book V of the *Ethics* as the key to the Aristotelian account of happiness, and Pieper lays claim to Book X, then Book VI on *phronesis* belongs to Simon. Just as Aristotle, he qualifies his discussion of teleology in a way that accounts for the diversity of claims to what makes a life happy. Concepts such as happiness and goodness each have the character of form in judgment which explains the fact that "Within the same day and of the same man the last end may be placed first in God, then in some good--say, pleasure--then in another created good --say, honor--and in God again."[30] In other words, the final end, which the will necessarily intends, bears both formal and final causality with the implication that the choice of means will eventually shape a person's entire life. Simon's analysis of moral action offers valuable support for the claim that ideas of happiness recommend a way of life.

The happiness of this world, however, is complicated by considerations that do not effect the happiness of heaven. Imperfect happiness is imperfect for the simple reason that in this world we cannot give ourselves totally to God. There always remain the demands of real goods other than God which are necessary to maintenance of our well-being-- health, pleasure, knowledge, citizenship, and so on. The temptation for Thomists in offering an intellectualist acount of happiness based upon contemplation is to extrapolate from the perfect happiness of the beatific vision to life in this world. In the final chapter of the French edition, only recently published in English, Simon comes as close as any in putting a finger on the difficulty of providing a neat and simple picture of imperfect happiness:

> In the present life, God, the last end, is loved in the manner of an intermediate end capable of bringing the soul to the only end which could be, here below, the object of unconditional volition, namely, the bare form of the universal good. In the present life, attachment to God is the result of deliberation and choice....In the present life, the last concrete end shares in the nature of a means, and

---

[29]*Ibid.*, 57.
[30]*Ibid.*, 59.

because it is the object of deliberation and choice, it is treated as a means by our intelligence and will.[31]

In other words, God has to compete for our attention in this life; and even the ordinate choice of God does not resolve life's difficulties. The juggling of different intermediate ends, as a means to a final end, goes on until death; but, as Simon shows, God becomes a formal cause of our choosing those intermediary goods, including Himself, while remaining the final cause determining the motion of the will itself. Simon's appeal to the rational teleology of human action is more persuasive, in my opinion, than Pieper's portrayal of earthly contemplation. In Simon's account the life of contemplation is only one option in the ordering of one's whole life toward what is truly final.

Aware of the problems besetting St. Thomas's intellectualist account of happiness, Simon, just as Pieper, turns to the contrast between love and knowledge in order to resolve it. He does not describe knowledge as receptive vision, as in Pieper, but calls it analytical and essential in contrast with love and desire which are concerned with *wholes*.[32] "The formal character attributed to the good, to happiness, and to the last end seems to conflict with the concreteness of whatever is loved or desired."[33] Love has to do with *that which* is loved, and knowledge has to do with *that on account of which* is loved. In our present life the reason that a thing is loved is always an aspect of the thing; thus love, rather than knowledge, offers the greatest possibility of earthly happiness.

Simon fills out the picture of imperfect happiness, along the lines suggested by St. Thomas, by attending to what is implied for the active life by the relation of love and knowledge to God. Thomists need not be condemned to a dark limbo about the happiness of this life, unless they picture it in strict analogy with the happiness of heaven. Simon's brief remarks can prompt one to ask whether or not Thomists are taking full advantage of St. Thomas on this point. Certainly Thomas's unquestioned distinction between the reach of love and the reach of knowledge in this life suggests more that can be said than has been said.

---

[31]Yves R. Simon "Law and Liberty," trans. Peter Wolff, *The Review of Politics* (Winter 1990), 115.

[32]Yves R. Simon, *Freedom of Choice*, 66.

[33]*Ibid.*, 67.

IV.

Against the background of this discussion, Maritain's evocative genius can emerge. Maritain never treated this question at length in the manner of Pieper or even Gilson; but he shares with his student, Yves R. Simon, the desire to broaden the domain of imperfect happiness to include heroic efforts at practical and political living. However, Maritain distinguishes himself even further for a willingness to pay philosophical attention to the role of the affections. His concern for emotional experience is evident in many of the central themes in his thought--connatural knowledge, creative intuitoin, poetry, spiritual experience, natural mysticism, and sanctity, among others.[34]

What Aristotelians and Thomists call the *passions* may seem strange at first for a man whose chief project in his early career was the "liberation of the intelligence" and the "restoration of the intellect"; yet, in all aspects of his work, from epistemology to aesthetics, Maritain demonstrates how crucial to the reaffirmation of human reason is the simultaneous affirmation of its connection to the body, its sensitive appetite, and the realm of what Freud wrongly labeled "the unconscious." The job of restoring the intellect, Maritain insists, calls for reconnecting it to the wholeness of the human person, rather than isolating the intellect from the body in the manner of a Cartesian angel.

Along with Simon, Maritain admits that our embodied existence makes happiness in this world difficult to describe. His attempt can be seen most prominently in *Integral Humanism* and associated works where he describes what he calls the "temporal task of the Gospel."[35] Maritain's desire to unify culture once again by allowing the spiritual to

---

[34]Maritain's interest in the way the *mind is taught by the heart* is apparent as early as 1914 in his first book, *Bergsonian Philosophy and Thomism*, trans. Mabelle L. Andison (New York: Philosophical Library, 1955), 166. Here he also shows his fondness for citing the remark of Pseudo-Dionysius from the *Divine Names* (2.9) to support his theory of connatural knowledge in the spiritual life--*non solum discens, sed et patiens divina* (167). Maritain will continue to refer to this text, especially throughout *The Degrees of Knowledge*, in spite of St. Thomas's own expressed discomfort with it (*De veritate*, q.26, a.3, ad 18).

[35]Jacques Maritain, *Integral Humanism: Temporal and Spiritual Problems of a New Christendom*, trans. Joseph W. Evans (New York: Charles Scribner's Sons, 1968), 42.

vivify the temporal[36] is well known and often criticized, especially for its overtones of political and economic radicalism. While certainly advocating the primacy of the contemplative life, Maritain could not reduce the pursuit of earthly happiness to such a fine point. Just as Simon, he insisted that the meaning of happiness must include the life of the city as well as of the individual, his work as well as his wisdom.

Similar to other Thomists, Maritain carefully preserves the hierarchy of the two happinesses. The happiness that St. Thomas calls "imperfect" and "intermediate," Maritain terms "infravalent."[37] Thus true humanism subordinates the happiness of man's temporal condition to his eternal origin and destiny. In his lectures on *Moral Philosophy* Maritain goes to some length in describing Aristotle's basic error of limiting the end of happinesss to a human ideal. As a consequence, Aristotle was unable to distinguish between the object of happiness as a final end and the subject's possession of happiness itself. Christianity, on the other hand, demands that the windows of human subjectivity be opened to an object of happiness outside the human. By implication, the earthly route to happiness must encompass the experience of self-giving and the suffering necessary to achieve it. A parallel can be drawn between Maritain's discussion of the wound that Beatrice inflicts on Dante which releases him from the prison of his self,[38] and the wound that Christianity, according to Maritain, inflicted on Aristotelian philosophy. Aristotle's moral teaching "leaves us enclosed in love of ourselves. It is my good that I love and will in willing and loving Happiness as the supreme Good supremely loved....It is the good which I will *propter me*, for my own sake, for love of myself"; and Maritain concludes, "It is impossible for Aristotelian ethics to escape from the embrace of the self....And yet in the end it is just such a deliverance that we long for."[39]

To describe this earthly happiness in Christian terms is not only more

---

[36]*Ibid.*, 112.

[37]*Ibid.*, 179.

[38]Jacques Maritain, *Creative Intuition in Art and Poetry* (New York: Pantheon Books, Inc., 1953), 371.

[39]Jacques Maritain, *Moral Philosophy* (London: Geoffrey Bles, 1964), 49. For an elaboration of this argument see Jacques Maritain, *An Introduction to the Basic Problems of Moral Philosophy*, trans. Cornelia N. Borgerhoff (Albany: Magi Books, 1990).

cumbersome than eternal happiness, it is also more difficult to attain.[40] The same "anguish of beatitude" which outstrips the ability of discursive reason to explain makes the happy life in this world a great deal more than the cultivation of contentment.[41] While Maritain associates the experience of anguish with earthly beatitude, he elsewhere chastises Kierkegaard for importing "anguish" into the philosophical vocabulary from the language of religion. "As a philosophical category," explains Maritain, "anguish is worthless....It is in the philosopher, not in his philosophy."[42] Maritain's inconsistency reveals the challenge facing Thomistic accounts of earthly happiness, at least those that would conceive of it as an activity and passion of love. The suffering and the passion of love appear to violate the Thomistic canons of activity, contemplation, pleasure, and possession in happiness. Nonetheless, Maritain can be admired for breaking his own rules, so to speak, by discussing the progress and "law of creative conflict" that he sees within suffering a movement toward "higher forms of peace and transfiguring integration."[43]

The perfecting of the human person in this life is not achieved without its agony, nor should it be. Who, it may be asked, is Maritain warning when he tells the Christian not "to take for his pillow the very love which he has received"?[44] Does Maritain have in mind the bourgeois in his repose, or the contemplative in his? The reason his view of earthly happiness embraces the active as well as the contemplative lives is that the happy are the sanctified, and neither is satisfied with anything less than the transformation of the temporal order. Of course, such a transformation can only be partial, but the saints suffer the difference. Their suffering transformed into a "closed secret" of a superior good is the good uniting them to God in this life.[45]

---

[40]*Ibid.*, 85.

[41]Jacques Maritain, *Integral Humanism*, 56.

[42]Jacques Maritain, *Existence and the Existent*, trans. Lewis Galantiere and Gerald B. Phelan (New York: Pantheon Books, Inc., 1948), 145.

[43]Jacques Maritain, *Integral Humanism*, 56. For an important development of this theme in both Augustine and Aquinas, see Nicholas Wolterstorff, "Suffering Love," in *Philosophy and the Christian Faith*, ed. Thomas V. Morris (Notre Dame: University of Notre Dame Press, 1988), 196-237.

[44]Jacques Maritain, *Integral Humanism*, 55.

[45]Jacques Maritain, *Moral Philosophy*, 461.

In the classical world some philosophers taught that misery destroys happiness; others taught that a man could be happy while roasting in the *Bull of Phalaris*. Maritain stretches the limits of philosophical discourse by imagining the relation of happiness and pain in a different way. Pain neither cancels happiness as it does pleasure, nor remains dissociated from the tranquil *apatheia* of the mind girded by virtue. It belongs to the inherent grammar of a life at once fully engaged in pursuit of the two happinesses rather than one.

Donald A. Gallagher

The Philosophy of Culture in Jacques Maritain

Throughout the writings of Jacques Maritain, particularly those works dealing with social and political philosophy, there runs like a *leit-motiv* the theme of cultural philosophy. For this reason I call him an outstanding and original philosopher of culture. I do not overlook the fact that I have hailed him, as distinct from a pure philosopher (who perhaps does not exist), the great Prophet-philosopher. I assimilate his cultural philosophy to his *prophetic philosophy* as an integral part thereof.

A rapid glance at the works of Maritain substantiates this view. In *The Twilight of Civilization* (along with other references to culture) he says that "in the dialectics of culture Communism is the final state of anthropocentric rationalism.[1] In *Integral Humanism*, in eloquent passages on *heroic humanism*, he calls for a cultural and temporal force of Christian inspiration able to act in history and come to the aid of men." In the same work, he opposes this heroic humanism (I call it his heroic humanistic culture) to the "zoological humanism of blood and race."[2] In *Science and Wisdom*, he refers to the studies contained in the volume, particularly those on "Science and Wisdom" and "The Philosophy of Faith" as touch-

---

[1]Jacques Maritain,*The Twilight of Civilization* (New York: Sheed and Ward, 1943), 23. This book appeared first in French in 1939.

[2]Jacques Maritain, *Integral Humanism and Spiritual Problems of a New Christendom*, trans. Joseph W. Evans (New York: Charles Scribner's Sons, 1968), "Heroism and Humanism, Introduction." See also Chapter VII. In *Religion and Culture*, (London: Sheed and Ward, 1931), I, "Nature and Cul-

ing "on questions whose importance for the philosophy of culture is, in my opinion, vital."[3]

In *Saint Thomas Aquinas* and even in the early work, *Anti-Moderne*, there are overtones or perhaps anticipations of the philosophy of culture. In the philosophical work on St. Thomas, Common Doctor of the Church, Maritain emphasizes the truth that this philosophy aims to enlighten human beings in every walk of life and not simply the learned scholars. This I look upon as one of Jacques Maritain's great texts showing forth his all-embracing philosophy of culture.[4]

Jacques Maritain's book, *On the Use of Philosophy*, brief as it is, is a valuable contribution to his philosophy of culture. The essay "The Philosopher and Society" is especially pertinent here. Maritain brings out a theme dear to him in insisting that the philosopher should not dwell in an ivory tower but should be concerned with the role of sound moral philosophy for all of human society. Such a philosophy has to restore intellectual faith to society in the value of its ideals. Where there is so much emphasis on the *phenomenal*, there should be a recall to "the ontological mystery of personality and freedom."[5]

It is above all, as the very titles indicate, in *Religion and Culture* and in the short essay *Some Reflections on Culture and Liberty*, that Jacques Maritain develops at length his own thought on philosophy of culture. Again as the titles indicate, Maritain does not take *culture* as an isolated phenomenon; it is essential to see it in its dynamic relation to religion and liberty.

Although a short work, *Some Reflections on Culture and Liberty* is important for more than one reason. For one thing, this publication was issued by the University of Chicago and signalized his first voyage to the United States in 1933. For another, it bears directly on our topic.

---

ture," Maritain says that culture and civilization are interchangeable for him, although he recognizes a subtle nuance in the meaning of these two terms.

[3]Jacques Maritain, *Science and Wisdom* (New York: Charles Scribner's Sons, 1940), "Preface."

[4]Jacques Maritain, *Saint Thomas Aquinas*, trans. Joseph W. Evans and Peter O'Reilly (New York: Meridian Books, 1958), Ch. I.

[5]Jacques Maritain, *On the Use of Philosophy* (Princeton, New Jersey: Princeton University Press, 1961), IX and 35.

The dialectic of modern culture displays three aspects or moments. These are: (1) an inversion of the order of ends; culture seeks its last end in itself and its end is domination over matter; (2) an almost demiurgic imperialism in regard to the forces of matter; culture proposes to change the conditions of nature so as to dominate it by a technical or artificial process; (3) the progressive driving back of the human by matter. All these *moments* involve matter and they show that the conditions of human life are becoming more and more inhuman.[6] In my view *Integral Humanism* is the very opposite of these aspects of the dialectic of modern culture and presents the positive program of humanity over matter.

Religion and Culture is a short work of not quite one hundred pages. It is replete with quotations suitable for our purpose; one could indeed quote the entire book. Such procedure is otiose; I know *les amateurs de Maritain* are familiar with the contents. However, some quotation is unavoidable, given our objective.[7] These are ordered so as to show the significance of philosophy of culture in our philosopher's thought.

For Jacques Maritain, true religion transcends every civilization or culture and is the *supreme beneficent* of *all* civilizations and cultures. At the present time, we are faced with an anthropocentric culture, which is dissociated from the Incarnation. This modern conception of culture displays three degrees or moments (note that these differ from the three moments presented in *Some Reflections on Culture and Liberty*, but they bear upon the same theme). These are: (1) the classical moment of our culture, marked by *Christian naturalism*; (2) the bourgeois moment, marked by rationalist optimism; (3) the revolutionary moment of our culture, marked by materialistic pessimism. These *moments* or conceptions misinterpret human nature. Radically opposed to this outlook, is the Christian conception, one truly human and humanist, ultimately the humanism of the Incarnation. Nevertheless, while the Christian view is opposed to the modern world (materialistic capitalism as well as Marxism), it recognizes that this culture involves historic growth and aims to incorporate this richness into itself.

---

[6]Jacques Maritain, *Some Reflections on Culture and Liberty* (Chicago: The University of Chicago Press, 1933), Part I.

[7]Jacques Maritain, *Religion and Culture*. In these writings as well as others, there are references to culture too numerous to quote. I have selected ones bearing on my immediate theme.

Maritain's program for overthrowing the modern culture (a gigantic task!) and for installing in its place *integral humanism* is twofold and is staggering in its implications: the first point is that Catholicism vivify all aspects of culture, and the second point is that Catholics form sound cultural, philosophical, historical, social, political, economic, and artistic conceptions, and with them as guiding ideas enter history and make them real. For too many years, Catholics have been asleep. A Catholic should have written *Das Kapital* from the Christian standpoint. Maritain seems to cry out in his anguish at the sleepiness of Christians.

The consideration (brief as it is) of these two major texts leads us to an evaluation of the significance of the philosophy of culture in the total work of Jacques Maritain. To understand the importance of this cultural philosophy, it should be seen in relation to other vital elements in the philosopher's thought. I consider here three important examples, (1) his advocacy of appealing to those inexpert as well as those expert in philosophy, (2) his advocacy of *integral humanism*, and (3) the relationship of this philosophy to his *strict but open* Thomism.

(1) Maritain sees culture as something no longer gathered as in the Middle Ages in a homogeneous body of civilization but as a reality scattered over the whole network of the globe. It is a living network of hearts of the Christian life disseminated among the nations within the great supra-cultural unity of the Church. Here we have Maritain's pervasive thought that the Church is not bound to any one culture but aims to vivify each and every one. Bound up with this idea is the guiding principle that the appeal should go forth not only to the philosophical scholar but to persons in every activity, from scientists and poets to those working with their hands; in short, to all human beings. Otherwise, the concrete ideal will never be attained.

(2) Again and again, Maritain relates his philosophy of culture to one of his most profound and original conceptions, that of *integral humanism*. As he views it, integral humanism has as its goal the restoration of the temporal order as a community of persons, but to be *efficacious* it needs supernatural aid. Hence it is rightly called the *Humanism of the Incarnation*. In this context, culture, as Maritain habitually regards it, is not something prized in itself or treated like a hot-house flower, but something in vital contact with the humanism of which it is a part.

Jacques Maritain does not hesitate to call himself a Thomistic philosopher. He rejects the appellation "Neo-Thomist." In his carefully elaborated structure of the *divisions* of philosophy (above all in *The Degrees of Knowledqe*), philosophy of culture as we understand it belongs to what he calls "speculative-practical" philosophy; it belongs with moral and political philosophy.

It is Thomistic philosophy which has the scope and the depth needed if we are to recover "the conditions of a truly human culture which assimilates the things of man to the things of the spirit." The Thomist renaissance, as he calls it, faces formidable obstacles. It irks whoever hates Christian culture. Maritain proclaims the necessity of two tasks which may seem inconsistent or at least are difficult to conjoin. He insists that the utmost speculative power is needed to provide the basis for the philosophy of integral humanism and of culture. At the same time, he envisions the wisdom of St. Thomas as "running along the highways of the world before the footsteps of God."[8]

In this twofold task, the insistence upon vigorous technical thought and the insistence upon the appeal to all human beings "on the highways of the world," I see the program of Jacques Maritain, the program to which he dedicated his life; I dare to discern Maritain's inmost self. The whole problem of culture and humanism presents itself to him; his answer is sanctity, the humanism of the Incarnation (and this in one of his early philosophical works!).[9]

Maritain invokes the role of Thomism (and its part, the philosophy of culture) in this great task of restoration. However, while Thomism is in the service of human aspirations and needs, he does not subordinate it to them. Thomism as a form of wisdom is above every particularization. There must be vital exchanges with any particular form of culture, but in essence it is vigorously independent of any and all forms.[10] It forms civilization; it is not formed by it. (In a religious dimension, Jesus Christ is immanent in a given sound and flourishing culture and is yet absolutely transcendent in regard to it.)[11]

The originality of Jacques Maritain consists in the according to the philosophy of culture a definite place in the structure of speculative-practical philosophy. In his thinking, philosophy of culture becomes aware of itself in the order of thought. In the order of action, as an integral

---

[8]Jacques Mariatin, *Saint Thomas Aquinas*, "Preface."
[9]*Ibid.*, Ch. I.
[10]*Ibid.*, Preface.
[11]See *Religion and Culture* (emphasis mine).

part of speculative-practical philosophy, it does not descend to the field of action itself but orientates those working in that field.[12]

We proceed to an important topic, namely the great obstacles facing Jacques Maritain's *philosophy of integral humanism and culture*. In Maritain's outlook, as we have indicated, culture is never alone. It is part of a total world-view; in the Middle Ages it was (in that "unselfconscious time") subordinated to religion and its values. In the modern age, culture is part and parcel of a society characterized by anthropocentric humanism, a society which either theoretically or practically excludes God or considers Him irrelevant. Modern culture glorifies or accepts as part of itself "the consumer crowned with science."[13] Maritain's remarks (expressed in the 1930s) remind one of Pope John Paul II's severe excoriations of *consumerism* as the sad but typical note of modern times, particularly in the *advanced* countries. Is such a culture authentic or is it a sham?

In his day, Jacques Maritain considered that the modern age was passing away before our very eyes (perhaps he was speaking as a philosopher who dwells in the centuries). This modern age glorifies hate; it is the reign of absolute totalitarianism. Against this stands an age glorying in its dependence on God and the true independence of persons. The *modern age* has lasted perhaps longer than Maritain thought; it persists and appears even stronger than ever. The values Maritain championed and called for preserving or restoring are to a large extent deemed irrelevant (perhaps *irrelevance* is an even deadlier weapon than a direct onslaught on God, Truth, and Goodness).

Maritain says that in the realm of culture, science now holds sway over human civilization (he does not belittle or condemn science; he is thinking of the *use* to which it is put).[14]

---

[12]The philosophy of culture reflects a philosophical awareness of culture itself as well as the recognition of it as a vital part of human socio-cultural being.

[13]*Some Reflections on Culture and Liberty*, 9.

[14] *On the Use of Philosophy*, 49. Jacques Maritain lays stress on the fact that generations may pass before the New Christendom (a temporal society imbued with religious values) comes about. He also stresses that the reign of Christ, already present in the hearts of little flocks here and there, will grow in spite of the obstacles confronting it (see *Integral Humanism*, especially Ch. VI).

CONCLUSION

Let me now summarize rapidly the results of this study on the philosophy of culture of Jacques Maritain.

The *great idol of our time*, he affirms, is the titanism of human effort.[15] This titanism makes use of rich temporal means. Against this formidable adversary, the integral humanist should use poor temporal means. Poor as they are, they should (believes Jacques Maritain) in the end prevail, as did David over Goliath.

Is it not appropriate to call *The Twilight of Civilization* the twilight of culture? For Maritain, as we have seen, the terms are interchangeable. Culture connotes to me the pervasiveness of ideas, the dynamism more than the structures. *The Twilight of Civilization* dwells on the evils menacing our culture. There is an unsound culture (I dare call it a *sham culture*) which glorifies *twilight* as though it were *dawn*, which glorifies hatred of *the enemy* over love of our fellow human beings, and which glorifies a murky hell as though it were heavenly (this language is not unlike Maritain's own use of strong figurative expressions).

More precisely, we are faced by a political totalitarianism which reduces the person to mere individuals marching-in-step and which ultimately obliterates every vestige of personality. In the economic order (more on the side of extreme or unmitigated capitalism), the productive person is reduced to a mere consumer of goods, goods often unneeded, which are, therefore, *sham goods*.

Against these powerful trends (in Maritain's time, *totalitarianism* was a fearful menace), integral humanism arises. Though like David against Goliath, it is fearless. This humanism is at one and the same time a true philosophy of the human person in the temporal order and a religious vivification called the Humanism of the Incarnation (Maritain holds that the *full* philosophical conception of integral humanism is realizable

---

[15]Jacques Maritain, *The Peasant of the Garonne*, 234. This work, written in Maritain's last period, is ostensibly one composed by an "old and inveterate" layman and not by a philosopher. It still bears the marks of philosophy. The *habitus* of sixty years is not easy to shed. I consider the work as important in the philosophy of culture as written for the educated person not well versed in philosophy.

when the philosopher, even as philosopher, is in vital union with the supernatural).

In opposition to the formidable trends of which we have spoken, involving as they do the insidious power of matter, Maritain's philosophy of culture brings out forcibly the idea that not only the political but every element of society is infected with "the dialectic of modern culture." To oppose such a dialectic, a comprehensive and integral humanism is demanded.

It is relevant to recall Maritain's observation that "in the realm of culture, science now holds sway over human civilization."[16] The resultant is, to repeat, "consumerism crowned with science." When appetites are rendered unruly and are tempted by a multitude of *goods*, it is difficult from the natural point of view to lead them back to the one thing essential, to the asceticism which leads to The Good.

One of the appeals of Marxism (at least in its pristine phase) is its emphasis on the *basic productivity* of the worker. Maritain (and we may add, Pope John Paul II) stresses that productivity is part of the dignity of man the worker.

On the more philosophical or intellectual plane, Maritain argues that the crucial question for our age of culture is whether reality can be known not only *phenomenally* by science but also *ontologically* by philosophers.[17] Here again he holds that an arduous task awaits him and his colleagues, for many philosophers (he calls them "ideosophers") as well as scientists (he calls them "exclusive scientists") are immersed in the phenomenal.

On the level of action, or on the level of the so-called "average person," the danger is that he or she suffers the loss of the sense of being and of the sense of truth. Truth is understood as mere verification, being is merely the passing scene. While the *average* individual does not put the matter in philosophic terms, his or her brain is steeped in these ideas. Against this basic attitude there must be an heroic effort to restore the sense of being and truth, not to mention goodness. This is ultimately a

---

[16]Jacques Maritain, *On the Use of Philosophy*, 49. This theme is developed *ex professo* in *Science and Wisdom*. Maritain is at pains to show that he is not opposed to science. Far from it! He is showing that what he calls "exclusive scientists" often succumb to placing their science at the service of demiurgic imperialism

[17]*Ibid.*, 56.

philosophic task but it involves *protophilosophic* appeals to the *average* educated person. This is the task of philosophy of culture, a task not only aimed at philosophers but at people "along the highways of the world."

To understand the full dimensions of the philosophy of culture of Jacques Maritain, it is necessary, as we have attempted to show, to see it in its many relationships. It should be seen in its relation to all cultures and not merely our own Western one. It should be seen in its relation to the prevalent though deficient culture (the *modern age*) in which we live and have our being. It should be seen in its relation (a dynamic organic connection) with *integral humanism*. It should be seen in its relation to the basic dignity of the human person (this is really his integral humanism, but deserves emphasis here). It should be seen in its relation to the *freedom of fulfillment* to which persons aspire and which fulfill their personality. Above all, it should be seen in its relation to the Humanism of the Incarnation, which comprehends everything included in this passage.[18]

---

[18]I am aware that others have written on Maritain and his philosophy of culture, notably Charles O'Donnell, R. Falconer, and H. Robbins. However, I have drawn these reflections from my own meditation on the texts of Jacques Maritain.

Ralph McInerny
Evening Knowledge: Reflections on *La Crépuscule de la Civilisation*

There is an interchange of metaphors between heavenly bodies and living ones: the rising sun is day aborning and the sun setting is the death of day; but we also speak of morning and evening of a life. There is inevitability is such metaphors, I think. They do not strike us as the intervention of any particular poetic genius but seem to have dawned, so to say, on all of us. When Shakespeare, in *Cymballine*, speaks of golden lads and golden lasses, then too we seem in the presence of another fundamental way in which men speak of youth by way of contrast with age. The critic William Arrowsmith learned to his delight that the Shakespearean metaphor is actually much more specific. He found that around Stratford, dandelions are called golden lads, and thus Shakespeare must have had in mind the brief flourishing of those flowers, followed by their going to seed. Hugh Kenner, in *The Pound Era*, makes much of this, astonishingly concluding that our response to poetic metaphors is independent of understanding the meaning of the constituent words; but surely we have here an exchange of metaphors of a quite natural kind--the bloom of flowers being seen on an analogy with youth and their going to seed with aging. The reference to dandelions, which you and I might not have known apart from Arrowsmith's discovery, is a metaphor for what we would in any case have understood--namely, the transition from the ripeness of youth to a later stage in life.

All this is by way of preface to some reflections on the fact that Jacques Maritain called the essay he wrote at the dawn of a dark decade half a century ago *The Twilight of Civilization*. This is an employment of a metaphor so fundamental it seems inescapable, so much so that it can lose its metaphorical quality. When Oswald Spengler wrote *The Decline of the West*, the German word he used for the West etymologically means

287

the twilight lands--*abendsland*. Geography--the Orient and Occident--refers to astronomy, the solar passage, as if one man's east were not another man's west, and the round earth's imagined corners could be definitely dubbed dawn and twilight. "The Land of the Rising Sun" may sound metaphorical while "orient" sounds literal, suggesting that, as Aristotle recognized, the foreignness or unfamiliarity of a word may lend it metaphorical force.

Maritain himself comments on his title, the suggested pessimism of which he characterizes as relative only.

> Si le crépuscule annonce le nuit, la nuit elle-même précède le jour. Et même, dans l'histoire humaine, il arrive souvent qu' au crépuscule du soir se mêlent déjà les premières lueurs d'un crépuscule du matin.[1]

I will be returning to the sequel of these words; for now it can be said that Maritain acknowledges the familiarity of the simile.

It would thus be possible to pass over the title of his essay, to see in it a powerful but otherwise uninteresting use of a basic metaphor, transferring to the presumed demise of an historical era the term used to signify the end of a single day; but the Thomist will find in this choice of the title the possibility of deeper significance.

When St. Augustine commented on *Genesis* and confronted the hexameron--the work of the six days--he faced a problem that has always faced exegetes of that book. The first day of creation precedes the creation of the sun, but what then can a "day" mean if day is precisely measured by the passage of the sun across the earth? Augustine ingeniously suggested that the stages of creation could be read from the knowledge of the angels. The six days of creation would then correspond to the six genera of created things presented to the angels. In terms of this, Augustine and Aquinas after him, spoke of the morning and evening knowledge of the angels.

Sicut autem in die consueto mane est principium diei, vespere au-	In the usual sense of 'day,' morning is the beginning of day and

---

[1] Jacques Maritain, *Le Crépuscule de la Civilisation* (Montréal: Editions de l'Arbre, 1941), 9.

tem terminus, ita cognitio ipsius primordialis esse rerum, dicitur cognitio matutina: et haec est secundum quod res sunt in Verbo. Cognitio autem ipsius esse rei creatae secundum quod in propria natura consistit, dicitur cognitio vespertina: nam esse rerum fluit a Verbo sicut a quodam primordiali principio, et hic efflexus terminatur ad esse rerum quod in propria natura habent (*Summa theologiae*, Ia, q.58, a.6, c.).

evening its end; so knowledge of the primordial being of things is called morning knowledge--that is, insofar as things are in the Word. Knowledge of the being of a created thing which consists in its proper nature is called evening knowledge, for the being of things flows from the Word as from a primordial principle, and this outflow terminates in the existence things have in their proper natures.

Something can be illumined with reference to one thing and dark with respect to another, needless to say, and the metaphor progresses through the comparison of earthly life and the life of glory—the former being as morning to the latter as evening. So the lives of the faithful here below are morning as compared to the night of the impious and wicked. That is why the evening knowledge the angels have of created things in their own natures is, nonetheless, as morning knowledge compared with ignorance and error.

I find it difficult to believe that a Thomist such as Maritain, his head and heart full of texts of the Master, was not himself at least unconsciously aware of such discussions as these when he wrote the little book that is the subject of these reflections. Indeed, the sequel of the works quoted earlier echo those of Thomas.

Dans ma pensée l'idée des épreuves actuellement soufferts par la civilisation était inséparable de celle d'un nouvel humanisme, qui se prépare dans la présente agonie du monde, et prépare en même temps le renouveau de la civilisation, fût-ce seulement pour ce temps que saint Paul nous annonce comme une résurrection 'entre les morts.'

The dark times into which the world had fallen were seen by Maritain as the result of a humanism gone mad. The humanism we find among the Greeks is open because Greek wisdom sought to attain "that which, being the principle of reason, is better than reason." Things started to go wrong when humanism became anthropocentric, closed upon itself, excluding the transcendental. Rejecting his status as creature, man saw himself as coming into control of nature. Enormous promises have been made, from Descartes on: the Enlightenment would automatically produce happiness and leisure--an earthly paradise.

It did not happen. The reign of reason ushered in a period of profound unreason and absurdity, or irrationality. Anthropocentric humanism produced an anti-humanist irrationalism. Dark as this all is, Maritain's point is that it is the corruption of a good thing. It is not humanism that is wrong, but anthropocentric humanism. What is needed, what will bring the dawn of a new day, is a Christian humanism. The false idea that each of us is, as it were, an individual God must give way to the true conception of the person as the image of God.

Cast in the stages of angelic knowledge that St. Thomas borrowed from St. Augustine, Maritain's point could be put as follows. We will emerge from the twilight in which we find ourselves today only if we recapture something like the evening knowledge of the angels. Angelic morning knowledge sees things in the Divine Word as their source, whereas their evening knowledge sees creatures in their own natures. *Creatures*. Not human artifacts, not mere stuff to be bent to the whim and the will of man, but things made by God. Christian humanism is not merely the periodic pious lifting of the eyes beyond; it is a way--the true way--of seeing ourselves and the world in which we are, as creation.

It is interesting to compare George Steiner's *In Bluebeard's Castle* with this little book of Maritain. Steiner is speaking later, looking back on the dreadful times in which Maritain wrote *Le Crépuscule de la Civilisation*, though without referring to him. How could the bloody totalitarianisms of the Twentieth Century have emerged from the Enlightenment? It astounds Steiner that an era which put such a premium on universal education, the lifting of the masses, on culture, on political freedoms, should have come to this. Just as Maritain, Steiner sees our times as the failure of the Enlightenment. This is the theme that has been struck by many others, of course--notably by Alasdair MacIntyre. By now it has become almost received opinion that we live in the collapse of all those bumptious Enlightenment promises and assumptions; but Steiner, unlike Maritain, has only more of the same to offer as a solution. It was not the Enlightenment that is wrong, Steiner suggests, but the perversion of it; but unless one sees the failure as part and parcel of an anthropocentric humanism--one closed on itself, excluding the transcendent--no future worth considering can be envisaged.

It could be asked whether Maritain was wise to retain the note of humanism and to speak of good and bad versions of it. What he calls Christian Humanism would be rejected on historical grounds. Oh, one can find, as in Renaissance humanists, the tendency to use the language of religion, to speak of man as the priveleged creature of God, but this should not be understood to mean that the term "humanist" as used by Maritain signifies identically the same concept as it does when used by a contemporary, modern, or, even, Renaissance humanist. Pico della Mirandola did not think he was simply repeating standard Christian lore. *A fortiori*, when Kant and Hegel used the language of Christianity, it was clear that what was going on was a replacement of meanings, not an interpretation. If this be so, the very use of the term "humanism," however qualified, invites misunderstanding. We should not have even a terminology with the Gentiles, St. Thomas suggested about the word "fate," even though he could give an acceptable meaning of the term. To use it ran the risk of being understood to say exactly what one did not want to say.

Well, we know that Maritain's use of "humanism" and of "personalism" was taken to imply what he did not intend. I have no suggestion on the matter. There is a limit to one's responsibility for hasty and distorted readings of what one writes. In favor of "humanism" is that it corrects an impression a reader might get from "*l'evangile et l'empire paien*"--namely, that the only weapon against the twilight of civilization is Christianity. Maritain's citation of Cardinal Cerejeira's praise of Pius XI is more than justified by the stirring tone of the text. "Ceux qui se scandalisent de la suprême condamnation par le Pape des régimes persécuteurs qui se vantent d'avoir sauvé l'Europe du communisme ne savent pas (comme dit l'Evangile) de quel esprit ils sont."[2] The modern reader, living during the collapse of both socialisms, National and Communist, may have been scandalized by those who professed to find the Soviet Union benign because it played a role in the defeat of Fascism and Nazism. The victims from the East will have been more than scandalized, but it is not the Church that must answer to their accusation.

We remember that Maritain was a great interpreter and champion of natural law, that he saw the possibility of agreement between men whose disagreements seem to go all the way down. This little book should not be taken to mean that the only bulwark against the evils it condemns is

---

[2]Jacques Maritain, *Le Crépuscule de la Civilisation*, 70.

Christianity. That Greek style wisdom to which he alluded could also provide a standpoint for the task. Nonetheless, the Christian answer is the complete one, comprising and including the natural one. Perhaps Maritain is reminding us it is often that Christian ambience which enables the consciousness of natural law to survive in times when it seems wholly forgotten.

Contributors

D.T. Asselin, an Assistant Professor of Philosophy at Hillsdale College in Michigan, has written several reviews and scholarly articles on Maritain. He is also the author of the book *Human Nature and Eudaimonia in Aristotle* .

William J. Boyle is a graduate of the Center for Medieval Studies at the University of Toronto, where he wrote his dissertation on the "Weakness of the Will and Self-Control According to St. Thomas Aquinas" under Fr. Joseph Owens, C.Ss.R. He is currently Associate Professor of Philosophy at St. John's University (Jamaica, NY).

William Bush, Professor of French Literature at the University of Western Ontario, is, perhaps, North America's leading authority on Maritain's friend, the novelist Georges Bernanos, of whose *Monsieur Ouine* he has done a definitive translation.

Joseph J. Califano is Professor of Philosophy at Saint John's University (Jamaica, NY). He has published articles in *The Thomist*, the *Divus Thomas*, and several articles in volumes published by the American Maritain Association. He has presented papers in Tokyo, Berlin, the United States, and Canada which were sponsored by several governments and published by The International Association of Energy Use Management and the International Association of Hydrogen Energy.

Bernard Doering is a Professor of French literature at the University of Notre Dame. He is author of *Jacques Maritain and the French Catholic Intellectuals* and has published an annotated English translation of the correspondence between Jacques Maritain and Julien Green, *A Story of Two Souls*. At present he is preparing for publication the correspondence between Maritain and Saul Alinsky.

John M. Dunaway is Professor of French and Great Books at Mercer University in Macon, Georgia. He is author of books on Julien Green, Jacques Maritain, and Simone Weil; his work in progress includes "Christian Presence in Twentieth Century French Fiction," as well as editing the Maritain-Tate correspondence. He is currently serving his second term on the Executive Committee of the American Maritain Association.

Donald A. Gallagher is President of the De Rance Foundation, President Emeritus of the American Maritain Association, and co-author, with his wife Idella, of the definitive Maritain bibliography, *The Achievement of Jacques and Raïssa Maritain*.

Curtis L. Hancock is currently Associate Professor of Philosophy at Rockhurst College (Kansas City, MO). A former Schmitt Fellow at Loyola University, he is co-author of *How Should I Live? Introduction to the Moral Life Through Conversations*. His many reviews and articles have appeared in publications such as *The Modern Schoolman*, *The Journal of the History of Philosophy*, and *Contemporary Philosophy*.

John Hellman, a Professor of History at McGill University, Montreal, is the author of books and articles on Simone Weil, Emmanuel Mounier, the French-Catholic culture in the interwar years, and the Introduction to the revised edition of Yves R. Simon's *The Road to Vichy 1918-1938*.

Deal W. Hudson is Associate Professor of Philosophy at Fordham University (Bronx, NY). He is co-author of *Understanding Maritain: Philosopher and Friend*. In addition, he has published articles and reviews in the *International Philosophical Quarterly*, *Notes et Documents*, *Homiletic and Pastoral Review*, *Cross Currents*, the *International Journal of the Philosophy of Religion*, and is Vice President of the American Maritain Association and a member of the Scientific Council of the *Instituto Internazionale Jacques Maritain*.

Robert E. Lauder, a Roman Catholic priest of the Diocese of Brooklyn, and an Associate Professor of Philosophy at St. John's University (Jamaica, NY), is the author of seven books--the most recent of which is *God, Death, Art and Love: The Philosophical Vision of Ingmar Bergman* (Prologue by Liv Ullmann [Mahwah, NJ: Paulist Press, 1990]). Author of a weekly column for the *Brooklyn Tablet* and the *Long Island Catholic*,

Father Lauder has had several articles about film appear in the *New York Times*.

Matthew J. Mancini, currently Visiting Associate Professor of History at Rice University in Houston, Texas, has published articles and reviews in *The Journal of Negro History*, *The Journal of Southern History*, *Notes et Documents*, and is the co-author of *Understanding Maritain: Philosopher and Friend*. Presently he is preparing a book on Alexis de Tocqueville as part of the Twayne World Author Series.

Ralph McInerny has taught at the University of Notre Dame since 1955 where he is Michael P. Grace Professor of Medieval Studies and Director of the Jacques Maritain Center. His most recent books are *Art and Prudence* and *A First Glance at Thomas Aquinas: A Handbook for Peeping Thomists* (University of Notre Dame Press) and *Boethius and Aquinas* (Catholic University of America Press). He is also the author of many novels, among them the Father Dowling mysteries.

Ralph Nelson is Professor of Political Science at the University of Windsor. He is currently co-translating Jacques Maritain's *Neuf Leçons sur les Notions Premières de la Philosophie Morale*.

Charles P. O'Donnell received his Ph.D. from Harvard University, writing as his doctoral thesis "The Political Philosophy of Jacques Maritain" (1940). He taught Political Science at De Paul University, and has been Associate Dean of the School of Foreign Service at Georgetown University as well as a Fullbright Professor (Zaire). In addition, he has served in the United States Department of State and the United States Foreign Service for two decades. He has, also, edited *Symposium on the Church in the Modern World* and Yves R. Simon's *Freedom and Community*.

Peter A. Redpath, Associate Professor of Philosophy, St. John's University (Staten Island, NY), is the author of two books on the thought of St. Thomas Aquinas, plus numerous articles and reviews in scholarly journals, including *The New Scholasticism*, *The Thomist*, and *Speculum*. He is a member of the Executive Committee of the American Maritain Association and the Board of Directors of the Yves R. Simon Institute. He is, also, a member of the Board of Trustees and is Co-Moderator of the Institute for Advanced Philosophic Research (Boulder, Colorado), and has lectured extensively both nationally and internationally.

Robert Royal is Director of Catholic Studies and Vice President for Research at the Ethics and Public Policy Center (Washington, DC). His articles and reviews have appeared in numerous publications, among them *The National Review* and *The Spectator*.

James V. Schall, S.J. is currently a Professor of Government at Georgetown University. Formerly he taught at the Gregorian University in Rome, Italy, and at the Department of Government at the University of San Francisco. He is a member of the National Council on the Humanities of the National Endowment for the Humanities, has written numerous books, articles, and reviews for scholarly journals, and writes a monthly column entitled "Sense and Nonsense" for *Crisis*.

Judith D. Suther is Professor of French at the University of North Carolina at Charlotte. Her book *Raïssa Maritain, Pilgrim, Poet, Exile* appeared in 1990 from Fordham University Press. She is now at work on *Kay Sage, The Art of Exile*, on the American surrealist painter and poet, to appear in 1992 from Rutgers University Press.

John G. Trapani, Jr., an Associate Professor of Philosophy at Walsh College in Canton, Ohio, has written several articles on Maritain for books and scholarly journals, in particular in the area of aesthetics. Recipient of the 1990 Outstanding Educator of the Year at Walsh College, he is also a professional musician conducting a seventeen-piece Big Band.

Select Bibliography

Abrams, M.H. *Doing Things With Texts: Essays on Literary Theory*. New York: Columbia University Press, 1989.

Adler, Mortimer J. *Reforming Education: The Opening of the American Mind*. New York: Macmillan Publishing Co., Inc, 1988.

_____. *The Paideia Proposal*. New York: Macmillan Publishing Co., Inc., 1982.

_____. *Paideia Problems and Possibilities*. New York: Macmillan Publishing Co., Inc., 1983.

_____. *The Paideia Program*. New York: Macmillan Publishing Co., Inc., 1984.

Aglion, Raoul. *Roosevelt and De Gaulle: Allies in Conflict*. New York, 1988.

Anastaplo, George. "In Regard to Allan Bloom: A Respectful Dissent." *The Great Ideas Today*. Chicago: Encyclopaedia Brittanica, 1988. Reprinted in *Essays On The Closing Of The American Mind*. Ed. Robert L. Stone. Chicago: Chicago Review Press, 1987.

Aron, Raymond, *La Sociologie Allemande Contemporaine*. Paris: Presses Universitaires de France, 1966).

Asselin, D.T. *Human Nature and Eudaimonia in Aristotle*. New York: Lang, Publishing Co., Inc., 1989.

Barrett, William. *Death of the Soul: From Descartes to the Computer*. New York: Doubleday and Co., Inc., 1986.

Bars, Henry. *La Politique selon Jacques Maritain*. Paris: Les Editions Ouvrières, 1961.

Bazin, André. *What Is Cinema*, Vol. 1. Trans. Hugh Gray. Berkeley: University of California Press, 1967.

Bellah, Robert, et al. *Habits of the Heart*. New York: Harper and Row, 1965.

Bergman, Ingmar. *Four Screenplays of Ingmar Bergman*. Trans. Lars Melmstrom and David Kushner. New York: Simon and Schuster, 1960.

Bernanos, Georges. *Le Chemin de la Croix-des-Ames*. Paris: Gallimard, 1948.

————————. *La France Contre les Robots, Suivi de Textes Inédits.* *Présentation et Notes de Jean-Loup Bernanos.* Paris: Plon, 1970.

————————. "Nous Autres Français." *Essais et Ecrits de Combat.* Paris: Bibliothèque de la Pléiade, Gallimard, 1971.

————————. *Oeuvres Romanesques. Dialogues des Carmélites.* Paris: Bibliothèque de la Pléiade, Gallimard,1961.

————————. "Scandal de la Vérité." *Essais et Ecrits de Combat.* Paris: Bibliothèque de la Pléiade, Gallimard,1971.

————————. *Sous le Soleil de Satan. Premère Edition Conformé au Manuscrit Original. Texte Etabli et Annoté par William Bush. Avant-propos par William Bush.* Paris: Plon, 1982.

Blake, Richard. "When out of the Past." *America* (March 21, 1987).

Bloom, Allan. *The Closing of the American Mind.* New York: Simon and Schuster, 1987.

Bowra, C.M. *The Greek Experience.* New York: New American Library, Mentor Book, 1957.

Boyer, Ernest. *College.* New York: Harper and Row, 1987.

Brann, Eva. "Review of *The Closing of the American Mind.*" *St. John's Review.* 71, 1988.

Brown, Ashley. "The Novel as Christian Comedy." *Reality and Myth: Essays in American Literature in Honor of Rickard Croom Beatty.* Eds. William E. Walker and Robert L. Welker. Nashville: Vanderbilt University Press, 1964.

Bush, William. *Genèse et Structures de Sous le Soleil de Satan d'Après le Manuscrit Bodmer: Scrupules de Maritain et Autocensure de Bernanos.* Paris: Archives des Lettres Modernes,1988.

Califano, Joseph, J."Maritain's Democracy of the Human Person or Man as a Moral Agent." *Jacques Maritain: A Philosopher in the World,* Ed. Jean-Louis Allard. University of Ottawa Press, 1985.

————————. "Technology and Violence." *Divus Thomae,* Collegio Alberoni, Piacenza, Italy, Vol. 78, 1975.

————————."Modernization and Human Values." *Jacques Maritain: The Man and His Metaphyics,* Ed. John F.X. Knasas. Notre Dame: American Maritain Association, 1988.

————————."Modernization and the Law of the *Prise de Conscience.*" *Freedom in the Modern World.* Ed. Micheal D. Torre. Notre Dame: American Maritain Association, 1989.

————————."Maritain's Philosophy of the Person and the Individual," *Notes et Documents,* Rome, Italy, vol. 8 (August 1977).

Caputo, John. *Radical Hermeneutics*. Bloomington: Indiana University Press, 1987.

Connolly, F.G. *Science versus Philosophy*. New York: Philosophical Library, 1957).

Gouhier, Henri. "Le Bergsonisme dans l'Histoire de la Philosophie Française." *Revue des Travaux de l'Academie des Sciences Morales et Politiques,.*" Fourth Series, 1959, FirstSemester.

The Crisis of Liberal Democracy. Eds. Kenneth L. Deutsch and Walter Soffer. Albany: State University of New York Press, 1987.

Dennehy, Raymond. "The Ontological Basis of Human Rights." *The Thomist* 42 (July 1978).

Derrida, Jacques. *The Ear of the Other*. Trans. Peggy Kamuf and Avital Ronnell. New York: Schocken, 1985.

_____.*Of Grammatology*. Trans. Gayatri Chakravorty Spivak. Baltimore: Johns Hopkins University Press, 1976.

_____. *The Margins of Philosophy*. Trans. Alan Bass. Chicago: University of Chicago Press, 1982.

_____. *Writing and Différance*. Trans. Alan Bass. Chicago: University of Chicago Press, 1978.

Doering, Bernard. *Jacques Maritain and the French Catholic Intellectuals*. Notre Dame: University of Notre Dame Press, 1983.

Dunaway, John M. *Jacques Maritain*. Boston: Twayne Publishers, 1978.

Eguin, Albert. *Bernanos par Lui-Même*. Paris: Seuil, 1954.

Feldman, Robert. *Understanding Psychology*. New York: McGraw Hill, Inc., 1987.

Fergusson, Francis. *Dante's Drama of the Mind: A Modern Reading of the Purgatorio*. Princeton: Princeton University Press, 1953.

Farias, Victor. *Heidegger and Nazism*. Philadelphia: Temple University Press, 1989.

Ferry, Luc.and Alain Renaut. *French Philosophy of the Sixties: An Essay on Antihumanism*. Trans. Mary Schnackenberg Cattani. Boston: University of Massachusetts Press, 1990.

Fowlie, Wallace. "Remembering Jacques Maritain." *The American Scholar* (Summer 1987).

For the President. Personal and Secret: Correspondence Between Franklin D. Roosevelt and William C. Bullitt. Ed. O.H. Bullitt. Boston, 1972.

Freedom in the Modern World. Ed. Michael D. Torre. Notre Dame: American Maritain Association, 1989.

Fukuyama, Francis. "The End of History." *The National Interest* (Summer 1989).

Gide, André. *Journal d'André Gide*. Paris: Gallimard, 1951.

Gilby, Thomas. *Between Community and Society: A Philosophy and Theology of the State*. New York: Longmans, Green and Co., 1953.

_____.*The Political Thought of Thomas Aquinas*. Chicago: The University of Chicago Press, 1958.

Gisan, Gilbert. *C.F. Ramuz, ses Amis et son Temps. Vol. VI, 1919-1939: Les Oeuvres Majeures*. Lausanne - Paris: La Bibliothèque des Arts, 1970.

Gordon, Caroline. *The Malefactors*. New York: Harcourt, Brace, 1956.

_____. *"Old Red" and Other Stories*. New York: Scribner, 1954.

_____. *The Southern Mandarins: Letters of Caroline Gordon to Sally Wood, 1924-37*. Sally Wood, ed. Baton Rouge: Louisiana State University Press, 1984.

Gourevitch, Victor. "On Natural Right," in *The Crisis of Liberal Democracy*. Ed. Kenneth L. Deutsch and Walter Soffer. Albany: State University of New York Press: 1987.

Griesbach, Marc. "Restoring Philosophical Realism in Today's Intellectual World." *1983 Proceedings of the American Catholic Philosophical Association*.

Guggenheim, Peggy. *Out of this Century: Confessions of an Art Addict*. New York: Universe Books, 1987.

Guthrie, W.K.C. *A History of Greek Philosophy. Plato: The Man and His Earlier Period*. Cambridge: Cambridge University Press, 1975.

Heidegger, Martin. *Basic Writings*. Ed. David Farrell Krell. New York: Harper and Row, 1977.

Hellman, John. *Simone Weil. An Introduction to her Thought*. Philadelphia, 1984.

Higgins, George. "Reformers Should Emphasize Hope." *The New World*. Chicago (June 30, 1989).

Hirsch, E. D., Jr. *Cultural Literacy*. New York: Vintage Books, 1987.

Hittinger, F. Russell. "Reason and Anti-Reason in the Academy."*The Intercollegiate Review*. (Fall 1987).

Hudson, Deal W. "Can Happiness be Saved?."*Jacques Maritain: The Man and His Metaphysics*. Ed. John F.X. Knasas. Notre Dame: American Maritain Association, 1988.

Hurstfield, Julian G. *America and the French Nation, 1939- 1945*. Chapel Hill, North Carolina, 1986.

Jacques Maritain: The Man and His Metaphysics. Ed. John F.X. Knasas. Notre Dame: American Maritain Association, 1988.

Jaeger, Werner. *Paideia: The Ideals of Greek Culture*. Second ed. Oxford: Oxford University Press, 1965.

_____.*The Theology of the Early Greek Philosophers*. Oxford: The Clarendon Press, 1947.

Kaufmann, Walter. *Existentialism from Dostoyevsky to Sartre*. New York: Meridian Books, 1967.

Lalande, André, *Vocabulaire Technique et Critique de la Philosophie*. Paris: Presses Universitaires de France, 1962).

Langer, William. *Our Vichy Gamble*. Hampden, Connecticut, 1965.

Lasch, Christopher. *The Culture of Narcissism*. New York: Norton, 1978.

Leitch, Vincent. *Deconstructive Criticism: An Advanced Introduction*. New York: Columbia University Press, 1986.

Lonergan, Bernard. *Insight: A Study of Human Understanding*. New York: Philosophical Library, 1957.

Mabille, Pierre. *Thérèse de Lisieux*. Paris: Corti, 1936.

MacIntyre, Alasdair. *After Virtue*. Second ed. Notre Dame: University of Notre Dame Press, 1984.

_____.*Whose Justice? Which Rationality?* Notre Dame: University of Notre Dame Press, 1988.

Maritain, Jacques. *Antisemitism*. Geoffrey Bles: The Centenary Press, London: 1939.

_____. *Art and Scholasticism and Other Essays*. Trans. V. F. Scanlon. New York: Charles Scribner's Sons, 1935.

_____. *Carnet de Notes*. Paris: Desclée de Brouwer, 1965.

_____. *A Christian Looks at the Jewish Question*. Arno Press, New York: 1973.

_____. *On the Church of Christ*. Notre Dame: University of Notre Dame Press, 1983.

_____. *Le Crépuscule de la Civilisation*. Montréal: Editions de l'Arbre, 1941.

_____. *Creative Intuition in Art and Poetry*. Princeton, New Jersey: Princeton University Press, 1953.

_____. "Démocratie et Autorité." *Annales de Philosophie Politique: Le Pouvoir*. Vol. 2. Paris: Presses Universitaires de France, 1957.

_____. *The Dream of Descartes*. Trans. Mabelle Andison. New York: Philosophical Library, 1944.

_____. *Distinguish to Unite: Or, the Degrees of Knowledge*. Trans. under the supervision of Gerald B. Phelan. New York: Charles Scribner's Sons, 1959).

_____. *Education at the Crossroads*. New Haven: Yale University Press, 1943.

_____. "Education for the Good Life." *The Education of Man*. Ed. Donald and Idella Gallagher. Garden City, New York: Doubleday and Co., Inc., 1962.

_____. *Existence and the Existent*. Trans. Lewis Galantiere and Gerald B. Phelan. Westport, Connecticut: Greenwood Press, Publishers, 1975.

_____. *Freedom in the Modern World*. Trans. Richard O'Sullivan. New York: Charles Scribner's Sons, 1936.

_____. *An Introduction to the Basic Problems of Moral Philosophy*. Trans. Cornelia N. Borgerhoff. Albany: Magi Books, 1990.

_____. *Man and the State*. Chicago: University of Chicago Press, 1951.

_____. *Moral Philosophy*. New York: Charles Scribner's Sons, 1964.

_____. *Oeuvres Complètes*. Fribourg: Editions Universitaires,1987.

_____. *Le Paysan de la Garonne*. Paris: Desclée de Brouwer, 1967.

_____. *On the Philosophy of History*. New York: Charles Scribner's Sons, 1957.

_____. *Philosophy of Nature*. New York: Philosophical Library, 1951.

_____. *A Preface to Metaphysics: Seven Lectures on Being*. London: Sheed and Ward, 1939.

_____. *Principes d'une Politique Humaniste*. Paris: Hartmann, 1945.

_____. *Raison et Raisons*. Paris: Egloff, 1947.

_____. *The Range of Reason*. New York: Charles Scribner's Sons, 1958.

_____. *Ransoming the Time*. Trans. Harry Lorin Binsse. New York: Charles Scribner's Sons, 1941.

_____. *Du Regime Temporel et de la Liberté*. Paris: Desclée de Brouwer, 1933.

_____. *Reflections on America*. New York: Charles Scribner's, Sons, 1958.

_____. *Religion and Culture*. London: Sheed and Ward, 1931.

_____. *Réponse à Jean Cocteau*. Paris: Stock, 1926.

_____. *The Responsibility of the Artist*. New York: Gordian, 1972 (reprint of original edition, Charles Scribners Sons, 1960).

_____. *Saint Thomas Aquinas*. Trans. Joseph W. Evans and Peter O'Reilly. New York: Meridian Books, Inc., 1958.

_____. *Scholasticism and Politics* . Garden City: Doubleday and Company, 1960.

_____.*Science and Wisdom*. London: Geoffrey Bles, 1954.

_____.*The Twilight of Civilization*. New York: Sheed and Ward, 1944.

_____. *On the Use of Philosophy*. Princeton: Princeton University Press, 1961.

Maritain, Raïssa. *Les Grandes Amitiés*. New York: Maison Française, 1941.

_____. *Journal de Raïssa*. Ed. Jacques Maritain. Paris: Desclée de Brouwer, 1949.

_____. *Poèmes et Essais*. Ed. Jacques Maritain. Paris: Desclée de Brouwer, 1968.

McCool. "Maritain's Defense of Democracy." *Thought*, 54 (June 1979).

Michaud, Thomas, A. "An Indictment of Enlightenment Technique." *Proceedings of the Thirteenth Annual European Studies Conference*. Ed. K. Odwarka.Cedar Rapids IA: University of Northern Iowa, 1988.

Montgomery, Marion. "Wanted: A Better Reason as Guide." *Modern Age*. 32, 1, 1988.

Muggeridge, Malcolm. "The Great Liberal Death-Wish." *The Portable Conservative Reader*. Ed. Russell Kirk, New York:Penguin Books, 1982.

Murray, John Courtney. *We Hold These Truths*. New York: Sheed and Ward, 1960.

Nearing, Scott. *Living the Good Life*. New York: Schocken, 1970.

Novak, Michael. *Free Persons and the Common Good*. Lanham, Maryland: Madison Books, 1989.

O'Connor, Flannery.*The Habit of Being: Letters of Flannery O'Connor*. Ed. Sally Fitzgerald. New York: Farrar, Strauss, and Giroux, 1979.

"Pain." *The Journal of the International Association for the Study of Pain* , "Classification of Chronic Pain," Supplement 3, 1986.

Percy, Walker. *Lost in the Cosmos*. New York; Farrar, Strauss, and Giroux, 1983.

Popper Karl.*The Open Society and Its Enemies. The Spell of Plato*. Fifth, rev. ed. Princeton: Princeton University Press, 1966.

Rifkin, Jeremy. *Declaration of a Heretic*. New York: Routledge and Kegan Paul, 1985.

Roosevelt and Churchill: Their Secret Wartime Correspondence. Ed. Francis Lowenheim et al., New York, 1975.

Rorty, Richard. *Philosophy and the Mirror of Nature*. Princeton: Princeton UniversityPress, 1979.

Rosenberg, Harold. *The Profession of Poetry or, Trials Through the Night for M. Maritain*. Partisan Review 9 (September-October, 1942).

Ryan, Michael. *Marxism and Deconstruction: A Critical Articulation*. Baltimore: Johns Hopkins University Press, 1982.

Scarry, Elaine. *The Body in Pain* New York: Oxford University Press, 1985.

Sheehan, Thomas. "Heidegger and the Nazis." *The New York Review of Books*. (June 16, 1988).

Simon, Yves R., *"Connaissance de l'Ame."* *Gants du Ciel*. Montreal: Fides, 1944).

_____. *The Community of the Free*. Trans. Willard R. Trask. Revised ed. Lanham, Maryland: University Press of America, 1984.

_____. *Freedom and Community*. Ed. Charles P. O'Donnell. New York: Fordham University Press, 1968.

_____. *Freedom of Choice*. Ed. Peter Wolff. Foreword by Mortimer J. Adler. New York: Fordham University Press, 1987.

_____. *A General Theory of Authority*. Revised ed. Intro. by Vukan Kuic. Notre Dame: University of Notre Dame Press, 1980.

_____. *The Definition of Moral Virtue*. Ed. Vukan Kuic. New York: Fordham University Press, 1989.

_____. *Nature and Functions of Authority*. Milwaukee: Marquette University Press, 1940.

_____. "Knowledge of the Soul." *The Thomist* 54 (April, 1990).

_____. "Trois Leçons sur le Travail." Collection *Cours et Documents de Philosophie*. Paris: Pierre Tequi, 1938.

_____. *Work, Society and Culture*. Ed. Vukan Kuic. New York: Fordham University Press, 1971.

Staley, Kevin. "Happiness: The Natural End of Man?" *The Thomist* 53 (April 1989).

Steiner, George. *Real Presences*. Chicago: University of Chicago Press, 1989.

Strauss, Leo. "An Epilogue." Ed. Herbert J. Storing. *Essays on the Scientific Study of Politics*. New York: Holt, Rinehart, and Winston, 1962.

_____. *Liberalism Ancient and Modern*. New York: Basic Books, 1968.

_____. *Natural Right and History*. Chicago: University of Chicago Press, 1953.

_____. *On Tyranny*. Ithaca: Cornell University Press, 1968 [Glencoe: Free Press, repr.].

_____. *What is Political Philosophy?* New York: Free Press, 1959; repr. Westport: GreenwoodPress, 1973.

Sullivan, Walter. *Allen Tate: A Recollection.* Baton Rouge: Louisiana State University Press, 1988.

Suther, Judith D. *Raïssa Maritain, Pilgrim, Poet, Exile.* New York: Fordham University Press, 1990.

Tate, Allen. *The Fathers.* Baton Rouge: Louisiana State University Press, 1977 (revised from original edition, New York: G. P. Putnam's Sons, 1938).

Tocqueville, Alexis de. *Democracy in America.* Ed. Phillips Bradley. New York: Vintage, 1945.

Understanding Maritain. Ed. Deal W. Hudson and Matthew J. Mancini. Atlanta: Mercer University Press, 1987.

Weil, Simone. *La Condition Ouvrière.* Paris: Gallimard, 1951.

_____. *Réflexions sur les Causes de la Liberté et de l'Oppression Sociale.* Paris: Gallimard, 1955.

Weiland, George. "Happiness: The Perfection of Man." *The Cambridge History of Later Medieval Philosophy.* Eds. Norman Kretzmann, Anthony Kenny, and Jan Pinborg. New York: Cambridge University Press, 1982.

Wolff, Robert Paul. "Book Review: *The Closing of the American Mind."* *Academe.* (Sept.-Oct. 1987). Reprinted in *Essays On* The Closing of The American Mind. Ed. Robert L. Stone. Chicago: Chicago Review Press, 1987: 18-21.

Wolterstorff, Nicholas. "Suffering Love." *Philosophy and the Christian Faith.* Ed. Thomas V. Morris. Notre Dame: University of Notre Dame Press, 1988.

Zeldin, Theodore. *Intellect, Taste, and Anxiety.* Vol. 2 of *France 1848-1945.* Oxford: The Clarendon Press, 1977.

Index of Names